Library of
Davidson College

Between Two Worlds

The Political Thought of Graham Wallas

Between Two Worlds

The Political Thought of Graham Wallas

MARTIN J. WIENER

CLARENDON PRESS · OXFORD

1971

Oxford University Press, Ely House, London W.1

GLASGOW NEW YORK TORONTO MELBOURNE WELLINGTON
CAPE TOWN SALISBURY IBADAN NAIROBI DAR ES SALAAM LUSAKA ADDIS ABABA
BOMBAY CALCUTTA MADRAS KARACHI LAHORE DACCA
KUALA LUMPUR SINGAPORE HONG KONG TOKYO

© OXFORD UNIVERSITY PRESS 1971

PRINTED IN GREAT BRITAIN
BY
WILLIAM CLOWES AND SONS LIMITED
LONDON, BECCLES AND COLCHESTER

FOR CAROL

PREFACE

No serious study has ever been made of Graham Wallas's life or thought. Yet he was a prominent figure in British public and intellectual life in his day. One of the original group of Fabian Socialists, an important member of London government, a leading teacher at the London School of Economics from the day it opened, and author of several influential books ranging over history, politics, sociology, and psychology, Wallas played many roles. Moreover, through his teaching and writing, most notably in his pioneering work *Human Nature in Politics*, he made lasting contributions to political and social thought. This present volume is not a full biography but rather an intellectual study, for it was chiefly through his ideas that Wallas affected his time and ours.

ACKNOWLEDGEMENTS

I SHOULD like to thank John L. Clive of Harvard University for his advice and guidance during the writing of an earlier version of this work, and Miss May Wallas for bringing order to her father's papers and for supplying information about his family background and personal life. However, the opinions expressed here are of course my own, with which Miss Wallas has not always agreed.

I am grateful for discussions with Eugene C. Black and Heinz M. Lubasz of Brandeis University, H. Stuart Hughes and the late David Owen of Harvard University, and Edwin Harwood of Rice University. I am especially indebted to Samuel H. Beer of Harvard and Ira D. Gruber of Rice, both of whom read early chapters of the book and offered helpful criticism. Most of all, my wife Carol gave continual, thoughtful encouragement and criticism.

For permission to publish materials in their charge, I wish to thank Miss May Wallas; Mr. C. G. Allen, Keeper of Manuscripts of the British Library of Political and Economic Science; the Fabian Society, London; Mr. Walter Lippmann.

For quotations from copyrighted material, I have been given permission by: the Society of Authors, London, for a letter of August 24, 1899 from Bernard Shaw to Wallas (in the Wallas Papers); Constable and Company and Appleton-Century-Crofts Educational Division, Meredith Corporation, for Graham Wallas, *Human Nature in Politics*; George Allen and Unwin for Graham Wallas, *The Life of Francis Place*.

I would like to express my appreciation, finally, to the Woodrow Wilson National Foundation and Rice University for grants that enabled this work to be brought to completion, and Mrs. Sylvia Ross, who typed the manuscript.

Houston, Texas
October 1970

CONTENTS

	Abbreviations	x
	Introduction	1
I.	Victorian Origins	3
II.	'Evangelical' Fabianism	14
III.	From Socialism to Social Psychology	30
IV.	A New View of Politics	61
V.	Human Nature in Modern Society	98
VI.	Towards a 'Great Community'	127
VII.	From the Old World to the New	161
VIII.	Reconstruction (1919–1932)	175
IX.	Wallas in His Time—and in Ours	203
	Bibliography of the Writings of Graham Wallas	217
	Index	223

PLATES

Wallas as a Fabian	*facing page*	3
Wallas in later years	"	203

ABBREVIATIONS

The following abbreviations have been used:

WP   Wallas Papers, British Library of Political and Economic Science, London School of Economics.

PP   Passfield Papers, British Library of Political and Economic Science, London School of Economics.

Wells H. G. Wells Collection, University of Illinois, Urbana.

BM   G. B. Shaw Papers, British Museum Additional Manuscripts.

INTRODUCTION

RECENT studies of the Edwardian period have stressed its transitional character,[1] but it remains obscure precisely what this transition was, and how it was made. What intellectual content was embodied in the shift from 'Victorianism' to 'modernity', and what were the mental dynamics of this shift? We could begin to answer these questions if we knew more about the intellectual development of individuals who themselves bridged the two worlds. Graham Wallas was such a figure, an eminent and a representative Edwardian. His work helped lay the foundations of twentieth-century political and social thought, yet it was rooted in an earlier outlook.

Wallas's career, like that of his friend and exact contemporary Beatrice Webb, illustrates the survival of Victorian characteristics into the twentieth century, and their application to the problems of a new era. Wallas thought of himself as a 'modern' man, who in his youth had rebelled against Victorianism in religion, society, and politics. Certainly he and his generation, reaching maturity in the 1880s, had rebelled against much. But there was also much in his inheritance that neither Wallas nor most of his contemporaries really discarded or escaped. This transmitted inheritance was 'evangelicalism', not in its original strictly religious form, but in the diffused, 'latitudinarian' form through which it pervaded mid- and late-Victorian life.

For many, the emotional dynamic and the moral preoccupation of Evangelicalism survived the shedding of the creed itself.[2] Firm moral values, a sense of life as a struggle of will, a dedication to service and to duty, a fervent drive to seek and to preach ethical and spiritual uplift—all these survived the loss of the religious faith out of which they had sprung. Again and again, underneath the numerous '-isms' of the later nineteenth century—Idealism, Rationalism, Positivism, Atheistic Humanism—lay the same evangelical ethos. 'The impulse of self-subordinating service',

[1] Samuel Hynes, for example, has argued that the Edwardian period 'stands in an odd pivotal position between the nineteenth century and the twentieth: it was not quite Victorian, though conservatives tried to make it so, nor was it altogether modern, though it contained the beginnings of many ideas that we recognize as our own'. *The Edwardian Turn of Mind* (Princeton, N. J., 1968), vii.

[2] Two especially useful studies of this survival and 'secularization' of Evangelical traits are Melvin Richter, *The Politics of Conscience: T. H. Green and His Age* (Cambridge, Mass., 1964) and Noel Annan, *Leslie Stephen: His Thought and Character in Relation to His Age* (Cambridge, Mass., 1952).

noted Beatrice Webb (herself an outstanding example) was transferred, logically or not, 'from God to man'.[3] Indeed, it is possible, as Gertrude Himmelfarb has argued, that 'the loss of religious zeal resulted in an intensification of moral zeal'.[4]

Evangelicalism, however, was not the only intellectual inheritance Wallas drew upon; the nineteenth century also bequeathed him utilitarianism or 'Benthamism'. In many ways these two traditions were opposed, even direct opposites: the tone of Benthamism was rationalist, that of Evangelicalism emotional; the thrust of the former was outward, towards institutional and legal change, that of the latter was inward, towards psychic change. Their coexistence always implied an element of tension and lack of clarity. Yet in many practical ways they were similar—both fed the Victorian drive to activity and to self-sacrificing service, for example—and as the dogmatic founding generation of each passed from the scene, the sharpness of their differences began to blur and the two came closer together both in outlook and in social aims.[5] Wallas was at least as much Benthamite as Evangelical, and both to a consummate degree. This combination, though a source of intellectual confusion, was not peculiar to Wallas and marked him as a 'Victorian' to the end of his life, three decades after the Queen's death.

This fusion of intellectual traditions does not merely place Wallas as a Victorian, but is the key to understanding the intellectual advances made in his important works—*Human Nature in Politics* and *The Great Society*. Both traditions were broad and rich enough to provide the seeds for a new outlook going beyond their limitations. Wallas's career is the result of the interaction of these nineteenth-century traditions with the new circumstances and concerns of the twentieth century.

[3] *My Apprenticeship* (London, 1926), 139.
[4] *Victorian Minds* (New York, 1960), 303.
[5] See ibid., 287.

Wallas as a Fabian

[*To face p. 3*

CHAPTER I

VICTORIAN ORIGINS

THE eldest son of an Anglican priest, Graham Wallas was born 31 May 1858 in Monkwearmouth, Sunderland, in the north-east of England. Before he was three his father, Gilbert Wallas, was appointed to the vicarage of Barnstaple, an old market-town in North Devon, at the opposite corner of the country. Here he grew up, fifth of nine children. North Devon was then, as it is largely now, rural and agricultural. Passed over, for the most part, by the industrial revolution, the region was becoming a backwater of English society, poor and stagnant. Wages were among the lowest in England, and even that great Victorian instrument of change, the railway, had reached Barnstaple only in 1854; a direct line east was not completed until 1873, after Wallas had gone off to school.[1] The world in which he spent his childhood was placid, self-contained, and traditional, its way of life far removed from that of the industrial and urban world he attempted to study and reform throughout his adult life.

His father, intended for the Bar, had abandoned legal studies to follow an inner call to holy orders.[2] He was one of the 'new model' clergymen—earnest, energetic, and Evangelical—who remade the sleepy eighteenth-century Church into an ever-active and omnipresent institution. Theology did not interest him; his concern was for living a Christian life of piety and good works. Urging his new parishioners to 'show what they believe by what they do', the Reverend Gilbert Wallas took from the very beginning of his stay in Barnstaple a prominent part in public activities.[3] A leading member of the Board of Guardians, which administered municipal charities, a vigorous proponent of education and chairman of the School Board from its founding in 1871, he was an important figure in Barnstaple

---

[1] See Francis G. Heath, *The English Peasantry* (London, 1874), 2, 25, 99–100, 124–5, 138–58, 231, and W. G. Hoskins, *Devon* (London, 1954), 67, 99–100, 158–63.

[2] The following paragraph draws upon private information from Miss May Wallas and from *Barnstaple and North Devon Times*, 3 May 1861, *Barnstaple Times*, 16 September 1890 (obituary), and *North Devon Herald*, 11 September 1890 (obituary).

[3] Nor were his interests confined to Barnstaple; within a few weeks of his arrival, he was urging townsfolk to contribute generously to Indian famine relief (*Barnstaple and North Devon Times*, 3 May 1861).

life. His life was similar to that of many another mid-Victorian cleric in town and village, 'always on the go', a contemporary observed, 'with his penny readings, harvest home festivals, church services, lectures, entertainments.' The 'modern' clergyman, this observer continued,

> strives earnestly and laboriously to identify himself with the amusements of his people, as well as in serious things. He is anxious to show that the Church is everywhere and that his sympathy is with everybody. His life is one long effort. He is always to be seen in a long single-breasted coat, and slouched billycock hat, hurrying at a half run from one end of the village to the other, intent upon some new scheme for what is called interesting the people.[4]

'Progressive' in his energetic activity, Gilbert Wallas was yet conservative, as a good Evangelical should be, where doctrine and liturgy were concerned. Like his parishioners, he stoutly resisted the High Church innovations that began to spread in the 1860s and 1870s. Upon leaving Barnstaple in 1877, he was praised at a testimonial dinner for the 'purity and simplicity' of his doctrine, a Protestant in 'perfect harmony with the feelings and wishes of his congregation'.[5] He was what the Low Church townsfolk of Barnstaple wanted in a clergyman—a preacher, not a priest.

Though his son soon lost his faith, the boy's character bore the father's stamp. From the first Graham Wallas showed the moral seriousness and sensitivity to the call of duty of a true Evangelical. Even his eventual rejection of religion stemmed from the early training he received from his father to look for his beliefs only within, to his conscience, and not to any external authority. The most fervent recruits to rationalism, as Noel Annan has remarked, came from Evangelical homes.[6]

At Shrewsbury, Wallas was hardly the model of a carefree schoolboy. Already grappling with theological and moral issues, he was considered something of a prig by his classmates. H. W. Nevinson, a fellow student, later recalled how Wallas had 'represented his chance thoughts as communications from the Holy Ghost'.[7] As a monitor in the sixth form, he read the lessons at Chapel services, and was dismayed by the profound lack of interest shown by his fellow pupils.[8]

---

[4] Quoted by A. Tindal Hart and E. Carpenter, *The Nineteenth Century Parson* (Shrewsbury, 1954), 32.
[5] *North Devon Advertiser*, 25 May 1877.
[6] Leslie Stephen, op. cit., 110.
[7] To Harold Laski. *Holmes-Laski Letters*, ed. Mark de Wolfe Howe (Cambridge, Mass., 1953), 1058 (28 May 1928).
[8] Fragment on 'Education', intended for his uncompleted last book, *Social Judgment* (WP). It contains a brief account of his own education.

Shrewsbury, the 'Roughborough' of Samuel Butler's *Way of All Flesh*, was the epitome of conservatism, educational, social, and religious.[9] The school strove to produce 'God-fearing earnest Christian(s)',[10] yet in his six years there, Wallas's faith began to dissolve and a naturalistic and critical habit of mind began to take its place. Among that minority who, like himself, took religious questions seriously, doubt was spreading rapidly. More than theological or ethical objections, Wallas remembered, it was the dissolvent effect of historical knowledge upon biblical fundamentalism that precipitated loss of faith. Rumours of the 'Higher Criticism' caused inner struggles for the more thoughtful schoolboys. 'We all fought against our doubts', Wallas recalled; 'those who succeeded in the fight mostly became clergymen; those who failed became agnostics.'[11]

Fighting back these new doubts, Wallas held to his religious faith at Shrewsbury. However, the rationalist outlook that was shortly to make orthodoxy intolerable for him was already making its appearance. He had the good fortune to receive the special attention of an exceptional sixth-form master, A. H. Gilkes—'the nearest approach to Socrates I have known', as another pupil described him.[12] Gilkes encouraged Wallas to think about the classics, instead of merely learning them by rote as was usual.[13] Discussing Aristotle's *Politics*, they came one day to his anthropological analysis of society's origins. 'Wallas', Gilkes burst out, 'what a sceptic you will be in a year or two's time.' When Wallas objected that he was an orthodox Christian, Gilkes added, 'I see the way your mind works', and left it at that.[14]

Soon after this, in 1877, Wallas went up to Corpus Christi College, Oxford, on a classical scholarship, and was not there long before Gilkes's forecast was fulfilled. By the end of his first year Wallas had abandoned his religious faith. Indeed he rejected not only orthodox religion but all metaphysical philosophy, including the Idealist philosophy just then coming into fashion. This latter rejection was not an inevitable consequence of his crisis of faith, for many of similar background and mental develop-

---

[9] H. W. Nevinson, *Changes and Chances* (London, 1923), 30. Wallas found Nevinson's autobiographical account of the intellectual atmosphere of Shrewsbury in the 1870s 'extraordinarily accurate'. *The Art of Thought* (London, 1926), 289. The headmaster in Wallas's time was a fervent Imperialist and a keen advocate of national military training. See J. Basil Oldham, *A History of Shrewsbury School, 1552–1952* (Oxford, 1952), 150.
[10] *The Way of All Flesh* (New York, 1960), 104. See also Oldham, op. cit., 155–6.
[11] 'The Future of Cowper-Templeism', *Nation* v (24 July 1909), 597.
[12] Nevinson, op. cit., 29. Gilkes's ability to stimulate young minds was further testified to by the medieval historian G. G. Coulton, in *Fourscore Years* (Cambridge, 1943), 218–20. See also M. Leake, *Gilkes and Dulwich* (n.d.).
[13] Fragment on 'Education' (WP). [14] Ibid.

ment were strongly attracted to the Idealism exemplified by T. H. Green. Indeed, Idealism was one possible solution to the psychological and moral vacuum left by the decay of religious belief. Green's philosophy was essentially a secularized Evangelicalism, appealing to displaced religiosity and moralism. Green himself was, like Wallas, the son of an Evangelical priest in the Church of England.[15]

Why then did Wallas take the 'scientific 'rather than the 'idealist' turn in the Victorian road? His family background provides some clues. Gilbert Wallas had been politically liberal, and enthusiastically welcomed the extension of primary education to all brought about by the Education Act of 1870.[16] His earnestness had been directed more at good works than salvation, at doing good in this world rather than agonizing about the next. Far from being hostile to science, the elder Wallas regarded himself as a 'modern' man, subscribing to several popular science magazines which his son read avidly.[17] His religious dedication, genuine enough to have led him to abandon the Law for the Church, was not narrow-minded or intolerant; although deeply grieved when his son formally renounced the Church (by quitting his grammar-school post rather than take Communion),[18] Gilbert Wallas was never a Samuel Butler father. Open-minded and consciously 'modern', his outlook and also his character were continued in his son.

The formal education Graham Wallas received, however, was certainly not designed to lead him to a scientific orientation. A more traditional schooling than Shrewsbury and Oxford could hardly be imagined. Shrewsbury was outstanding for its production of classical scholars. It achieved this repute by almost total concentration on the subject; the classics, and especially Greek, 'permeated and coloured the whole school life'.[19] 'The school', H. W. Nevinson recalled, 'breathed Greek, and through its ancient buildings a Greek wind blew.'[20] Indeed, nothing else was really taught.[21] Although a Royal Commission studying the leading public schools had recommended years before that science should be introduced into the curriculum at Shrewsbury, Wallas remembered that 'we had no laboratory of any kind, and I never heard in my time of any Shrewsbury boy receiving a science lesson'.[22] When not being ignored, science was being castigated. Wallas recalled the visit of 'an earnest young Hegelian

[15] Richter, op. cit., 39.
[16] See *Barnstaple Messenger*, 4 April 1871.
[17] Fragment on 'Education' (WP).
[18] Private information from Miss May Wallas.
[19] Oldham, op. cit., 196.
[20] *Changes and Chances*, 27.
[21] See ibid., 25–30.
[22] Fragment on 'Education' (WP).

tutor from Christ Church (who was afterwards Bishop of Oxford)' to warn the boys 'against relying on the ever-shifting theories of Natural Science'.²³
At Oxford, even outside Christ Church, science was held in little higher esteem. The small number of 'Stinks' men (as the nickname itself indicates) lived largely outside the everyday life of the University, and were generally patronized, if not totally disregarded by those studying the combination of classics and philosophy known as *Literae Humaniores* or 'Greats'. To a 'Greats' man, Nevinson later noted,

always just on the point of having the Divine Mystery revealed by the process of philosophic or inspired thought, the salivary glands of a mad dog, the stomachs of Miller's Thumbs, or the circumvallate papillae of ox-tongues would have appeared a little irrelevant, a little minute compared to the glory of the universal soul.²⁴

Though a 'Greats' man himself, Wallas reacted sharply against the prevailing climate at Oxford. He was able to do this through the access Oxford afforded to a wider world beyond its own narrow curriculum and attitudes. The official curriculum for the first two years was nothing but a continuation of the classical translation and composition that had been drilled into him at Shrewsbury. Wallas's real education was carried on outside this, in discussions with new acquaintances, in visits to London, and in reading books on his own—Darwin, Butler's *Erewhon*, the essays of W. K. Clifford.²⁵ Clifford's rationalist essays were strikingly 'evangelical' in their demand for unsparing self-examination and intellectual honesty, and had a strong appeal to one of Wallas's upbringing.²⁶ Belief, Clifford preached, was not a private matter, but a social one, for belief and action were inseparable. Error must be exposed, not tolerated. 'It is wrong always, everywhere, and for anyone', he insisted, 'to believe anything upon insufficient evidence',²⁷ and Wallas now agreed enthusiastically.

²³ Fragment on 'Education' (WP).
²⁴ H. W. Nevinson, 'The Oxford Mood', (1911), in *Visions and Memories* (London, 1944), 119–20. Gillian Sutherland has pointed out that the case for more scientific education was almost always presented in narrowly vocational terms, as appropriate for managers, engineers, and technicians. Even most proponents of science deferred to the centrality of the classics. 'The Study of the History of Education', *History*, liv (1969), 49–59.
²⁵ See Fragment on 'Education', (WP), letter to H. G. Wells, 6 Oct. 1926 (Wells), and speech at annual meeting of the Rationalist Press Association, in *Literary Guide and Rationalist Review*, ccci (July, 1921).
²⁶ See Noel Annan, op. cit., 146.
²⁷ 'The Ethics of Belief' (1877), in *The Ethics of Belief and Other Essays* (London, 1947), 77.

Science seemed to be opening up a new approach to life, sweeping away the oppressive dogmas of religion and metaphysics. The 'warfare between science and religion' was for Wallas and his generation a fact of life. The religion of his day was authoritarian, literalist, and rigid; the science was aggressively secular. One could not belong to both camps with an easy conscience, as one might today. Then, acceptance of the new rational-empirical outlook entailed, as Wallas put it, 'a violent break with the past'.[28]

With his newly acquired faith in science, Wallas resisted the Idealism being preached with great success at Oxford by T. H. Green. In 1878 he was taken by a fellow under-graduate—Hastings Rashdall, in after years the historian of the medieval universities—to hear Green lecture at Balliol: Wallas recalled,

The lecture was an argument for human immortality, based on the statement that since we only knew of the existence of our bodies from the testimony of our conscious mind, there is no *a priori* reason for believing that the dissolution of the body affects the continued existence of the conscious mind. Green asked for questions; I, being fresh from reading Darwin, asked him whether his argument applied to the conscious mind of a dog, and Green answered that he was not interested in dogs.[29]

Darwin had convinced Wallas that a philosophy that 'was not interested in dogs', that dealt with man in isolation from the rest of his world, was no longer satisfactory. Science promised a new philosophy that would bring man and his environment into the same framework of explanation. The trial of a man for tuberculosis in *Erewhon*, a satiric thrust at mid-Victorian moralism, had an immediate effect on Wallas when he read it in 1878; it brought 'human conduct into a universe of cause and effect'.[30] Human behaviour was not a matter of incomprehensible dogma and rigid moral injunctions, but a natural phenomenon in an ordered and understandable world.

This budding rationalism was encouraged by his tutor for his last two years, Thomas Case. Case did not belong to the rising Idealist school, but thought of himself as a defender of the 'English' tradition of Locke and Mill. 'I hope you won't get led away', he warned Henry Newbolt, another tutee, 'by fellows like T. H. Green. I've not read a word of him myself, and of course I wouldn't condemn any man unheard, but I can assure you that

[28] 'The Future of Cowper-Templeism', op. cit. 597.
[29] Review of J. A. Hobson and M. Ginsberg, *L. T. Hobhouse*, in *New Statesman & Nation*, i (25 April 1931), 326.
[30] Letter to H. G. Wells, 8 Oct. 1926 (Wells).

his Philosophy is all rot.'³¹ Case kept Mill's *System of Logic*, being superseded elsewhere in the University by the works of Kant, Hegel, and Green, as the basis of his teaching.³² This sort of education, stressing the scientific approach and the prime importance of clear thinking, was more typical of Cambridge at that time than of Oxford. It formed, certainly, an excellent training for rationalists.³³ To some degree, then, Wallas's scientific rationalism was due to the timing of his stay in Oxford. By coming just before the temporary prestige of science in general English culture, deriving from the Darwinian controversy, had begun to fade, just before Philosophic Idealism extended its influence, Wallas joined the ranks of the 'last Utilitarians' at Oxford.

Yet his Millite tutor, however 'scientific' in logic and epistemology, was as traditional as any when it came to social or political philosophy. Mill's statement in the *Logic* that 'the backward state of the Moral Sciences can only be remedied by applying to them the methods of Physical Science' made a great impression on Wallas.³⁴ But Case (in this respect exactly like all Oxford tutors of the time) neither used nor urged him to use the methods or the temper of experimental science. Wallas recalled,

We wrote essays upon the State which, like our tutor's lectures, took no heed of political facts later then Aristotle's lost collection of Greek city constitutions. The Greats lecturers gave us psychological generalisations about human behaviour, they either made them up as they went along or took them from some author not later than the eighteenth century.³⁵

Economics was completely ignored. If any student inquired about it he would be referred to Mill's *Political Economy*, taken to be the last word on the not-very-interesting subject.³⁶

Wallas and his friend, Sydney Olivier, having abandoned religion and taken up Rationalism as undergraduates, began to chaff under this traditional approach to social and political questions. Their generation would not be content with replacing a theological world-view with a 'scientific' one, but would insist upon carrying this scientific outlook into every sphere of life. Coming to maturity after the *Origin of Species* and the theological crisis it had set off, Wallas, Olivier, and many of their generation accepted an historical, evolutionary outlook and discarded a static, fundamentalist

---
³¹ Henry Newbolt, *The World as in My Time* (London, 1932), 111.
³² Fragment on 'Education' (WP).
³³ See Noel Annan, op. cit., 141-4.
³⁴ Fragment on 'Education' (WP).
³⁵ Ibid.   ³⁶ Ibid.

one 'as a matter of course'.[37] As the future secretary of the Fabian Society recalled,

> Cut adrift as we were from the intellectual moorings of our upbringings, recognising, as we did, that the older men were useless as guides in religion, in science, in philosophy because they knew not evolution, we also felt instinctively that we could accept nothing on trust from those who still believed that the early chapters of Genesis accurately described the origin of the universe, and that we had to discover somewhere for ourselves what were the true principles of the then recently invented science of sociology.[38]

This intellectual movement became, almost inevitably, a reform movement as well, for the mid-Victorian world-view formed an integrated whole, one part of which could not be discarded without bringing the rest into doubt. Religion had provided justification for the existing social order; with that prop removed, doubt was bound to spread from theological to secular questions. Indeed, the very continuance and even intensification of moral zeal in the wake of the decline of religious zeal, contributed to the undermining of social as well as theological orthodoxy. No longer securely anchored to a conservative world-view, the 'free-floating' moralism of the later Victorian era began to be a critical force, placing heavier demands upon social and economic institutions. When, for example, in the late 1860s, Charles Booth lost his Evangelical faith, he gained a 'social conscience', a secular Evangelicalism, which led to a career of pioneering social investigation. No longer able to accept the explanation that poverty resulted from the working of the will of God, Booth found the only alternative was to attribute its existence to human causes. 'Slowly', his biographers relate, 'the implications of this conclusion became clear to him: it placed upon him a burden of personal responsibility for the welfare of his fellow-men which was at once so weighty and so unwelcome that he shrank from its acceptance.'[39]

In this process science and Evangelical dedication often fused into a new outlook on life. Science by itself was not a philosophy of life; there remained the question, as Beatrice Webb noted, 'to what end, for what purpose, and therefore *upon what subject-matter* was the new faculty of the intellect to be exercised?'[40] Here the process of 'Evangelical sublimation' played a crucial role: for many of Evangelical background science was to be employed in the 'self-subordinating service . . . of man'.[41]

[37] Edward Pease, *History of the Fabian Society* (London, 1916), 17-18.
[38] Ibid.
[39] T. S. and M. B. Simey, *Charles Booth: Social Scientist* (Oxford, 1960), 41-2.
[40] *My Apprenticeship*, 138-9. [41] Ibid., 139.

In Wallas's character, as in that of many others, the Evangelical impulse, joined with the new faith in science, was redirected to social service. His education, however, had provided a broader intellectual framework for the expression of this impulse than that possessed by most other Rationalists. Wallas became that rare hybrid—a secularist Radical with a Greek vocabulary.

Wallas's classical education, first at home and then at Shrewsbury, had been, according to the custom of the time, purely linguistic and grammatical. No interest was taken at Shrewsbury in the literary or even historical value of the works studied with minute care. 'Our sole duty', Nevinson observed, 'was to convert, with absolute precision, so much Greek into so much English.'[42] This was hardly a technique calculated to help a student find a new philosophy of life:

... we were daily reading (in order to win University scholarships by imitating their phrases in our 'baboo-Greek' compositions) the writings of those Athenian dramatists, historians, and philosophers who shattered in a single century the intellectual structure of the world into which they had been born, and formed a new mould into which Greco-Roman civilisation was to run ... In a Jesuit, or Bolshevik, or Fascist, or Sinn Fein school our minds would have been forced all day long into a particular application to life of the books which we read. At Shrewsbury we hardly ever heard a suggestion that any application at all was either desirable or possible.[43]

Though no application was suggested, the possibility of application was there. Encouraged by Gilkes, Wallas had begun to study Greek thought. He spent many hours discussing Aristotle's ideas with Gilkes, particularly those expounded in the *Politics*. This attachment to Aristotle was confirmed at Oxford, and remained with him for the rest of his life. From Aristotle, Wallas took what he could not accept from religion or from Green's Idealism—a social ethic. Aristotle's ideal of the 'good life', attainable only in a 'good society', and his ideal of this 'good society'—the *polis*— became Wallas's ideals.[44] The contrast between this Greek ideal and late Victorian society helped to push Wallas towards social criticism. In the *polis* Wallas saw a society sharing a common lofty purpose, where ethical values came before material ones—a moral community. England of the 1870s and 1880s, on the other hand, seemed to be dominated by the middle-class creed of self-help and material progress. This society, to one immersed

[42] *Changes and Chances*, 26.
[43] Fragment on 'Education' (WP).
[44] Wallas's debt to Aristotle is evident from his first work. See a lecture, probably given in 1887, to a Socialist audience on Aristotle's *Politics* (WP), and an article in the Socialist magazine, *Today*, July and Aug., 1888.

in Greek values, appeared to be a chaotic agglomeration of self-seeking individuals, neither moral nor a community.

The contrast was brought home to Wallas by one of the leading social philosophers of the time, John Ruskin. During Wallas's first year at Oxford, Ruskin lived in his college, Corpus Christi. Wallas heard his lectures, which were immensely popular, and for a short time saw him almost every day.[45] 'Everyone in Oxford then', Nevinson recalled, 'attended those lectures.'[46] Though his subject was art, Ruskin wandered far afield:

> His magical voice held the crowded audience spellbound far beyond the appointed hour. Upon me the humour, the irony, and keen flashes of satire made the deepest impression, but beyond these lay the depth of thought and the passion of indignation which raised his lectures far above the height of religious services. In the last lecture of the course he so overwhelmed us with solemn awe that when he closed his note-book no one moved or spoke. We no more thought of the usual applause than we should have thought of clapping an angel's song.[47]

Ruskin's message of social criticism and his gospel of spiritual reform were winning many converts in these years, among them Arnold Toynbee and Alfred Milner.[48] His preaching was especially appealing to one, like Wallas, brought up on Evangelicalism and immersed in the Greek classics, for he called for self-sacrifice and service to others while asserting the primacy of ethical and social values. 'There is no wealth but life', he insisted. That country is rich, not which accumulates the most money, but which 'nourishes the greatest number of noble and happy human beings'. Wallas's social credo could have been taken from Ruskin's *Unto This Last*: 'Government and Co-operation are in all things the Laws of Life; Anarchy and Competition the Laws of Death.'[49] The image of the *polis*, as seen through the idealization of Aristotle and the social gospel of Ruskin, was destined to shape Wallas's social thinking and social activity.

By the time he went down from Oxford in 1881, Wallas's outlook had set. Characteristic of his age in its components, it was yet unique in their combination. He was a partisan of scientific method, a rationalist agnostic,

---

[45] See Wallas's introduction to the first cheap edition of Ruskin's *The Two Paths* (1907), in *Men & Ideas*, ed. May Wallas (London, 1940), 80.
[46] *Changes and Chances*, 55.
[47] 'How I Knew Ruskin', (1936) in *Visions and Memories*, 126.
[48] For Ruskin's message and influence at Oxford at this time, see Nevinson, op. cit., 53-5, *Oxford: Its Life and Schools*, ed. A. M. M. Stedman (Oxford, 1887), 127, G. W. Kitchin, *Ruskin in Oxford and Other Studies* (New York, 1904), 39-40, and R. H. Murray, *Studies in the English Social and Political Thinkers of the Nineteenth Century* (Cambridge, 1928), 128.
[49] *Unto This Last* (London, 1862), 102.

VICTORIAN ORIGINS

an opponent of all metaphysics; yet he was equally firm in attachment to the ideals of Greek thought, grounded in one of the oldest metaphysics of all. This paradox gave Wallas no philosophical anxieties, for he was never a rigorous thinker, least of all at this early age. He was not yet a Socialist, but all the intellectual and emotional elements that were to lead him to that were present: Scientism and the hope of applying scientific method to society, a general rebelliousness against accepted beliefs, an ethical-social idealism taken from the Greeks, and an inner drive toward self-sacrificing service, implanted in his Evangelical childhood. The two greatest influences upon his thinking in these early years, Aristotle and Darwin, were to remain, with the important addition of Bentham, his chief mentors throughout life.[50] From these thinkers, and from his early self-examining Evangelicalism, Wallas developed a psychological approach from which were to come his important contributions to social and political thought.

[50] Wallas encountered Bentham at Oxford only as a figure of derision: '... many of us at Oxford were trained to despise Bentham. Some of our "Greats" tutors made, indeed, a considerable proportion of their income by jeering at those quotations from Bentham's writings which they met with in the manuals of philosophy.' 'Bentham as a Political Inventor', (1925), in *Men & Ideas*, 34.

CHAPTER II

'EVANGELICAL' FABIANISM

For Wallas the years immediately following Oxford were uneventful. In poor health during his last year at the University, he disappointed his tutor by only taking a second-class honours degree.[1] Perhaps with a first, he might have gone into the Civil Service, as did his close friend Sydney Olivier. Instead, he became a classical schoolmaster. Teaching young boys offered little mental challenge and only strengthened the disposition to preach Wallas had acquired from his father. He might have fallen into intellectual stagnation had it not been for his correspondence with Sydney Olivier, who went down from Oxford the year after Wallas and, from a post in the Colonial Office in London, kept Wallas in touch with the latest ideas in the capital.

Anxious to be in London himself, Wallas in the autumn of 1884 obtained an appointment as classics master at Highgate School, and took up residence in that suburb. By this time, however, his rejection of religion had become militant secularism, and he was dismissed from his position within a year: prodded by his Rationalist conscience, he had refused to take Communion as part of his duties.[2] After this crisis, Wallas fell into a period of uncertainty: what was to become of his life? Growing a beard, worrying over the grey hairs he began to find, he saw, as a more settled friend warned, his 'chances of getting on in life disappearing'.[3] He considered becoming an author, and was advised to try the Law.[4]

Wallas (though his family had money) was now in effect a member of that new class which George Gissing was to identify a few years later as 'a class of young men distinctive of our time—well educated, fairly bred, *but without money*'.[5] This new class provided many recruits for radical move-

[1] In a testimonial, his tutor claimed that with health he would have taken a first. In the last year of his life, Wallas took an inordinate pleasure in receiving an honorary degree from Oxford; perhaps this loss had never been forgotten.
[2] Miss May Wallas.
[3] Letter from H. Carey, a master at the first school Wallas had taught at, 9 Aug. 1886 (WP).
[4] Letters from Sidney Webb, 2 July 1885, 14 June 1887 (PP).
[5] Quoted by Herman Ausubel, *In Hard Times: Reformers Among the Late Victorians* (New York, 1960), 96.

'EVANGELICAL' FABIANISM

ments, and so it was with Wallas. He resolved his personal crisis by throwing himself whole-heartedly into the Socialist movement.[6] Though he taught in other schools, on and off, for the next few years, he no longer looked upon it as a career, but only as a way of supporting himself.

The 1880s were years of unusual intellectual and moral ferment; economic depression and the weakening of mid-Victorian self-satisfaction had opened the door to a new concern with 'the condition of England'. In the heady atmosphere of London Radicalism, which Wallas found immensely exciting,[7] one social gospel vied with another for adherents. While differing in every particular, Single Taxers, Positivists, the settlement movement led by Arnold Toynbee, the Marxists of the Social Democratic Federation, and others united in challenging existing society and orthodox political economy. Shortly after his arrival in London, Wallas became part of a group of young radicals that included Bernard Shaw and Sidney Webb, the latter of whom he had met two years before, during a visit to London. Webb remembered many years later,

Wallas called at the Colonial Office to see a college chum, Sidney Olivier, who was living in Downing Street with me, both of us being at the time Resident Clerks. Olivier was not in, and Wallas waited for his return. Almost instantly, with Wallas's characteristic gift of intellectual intimacy, I found myself engaged in a game of chess, and simultaneously discussing the state of the nation. For the ensuing couple of decades our intellectual intimacy was close and continuous.[8]

In the spring of 1885 Wallas's new friends joined an obscure group, the 'Fabian Society', and quickly dominated it.[9] Fabianism, as it took form under its new management, might seem a poor home for a secularized Evangelical such as Wallas. After all, it has usually been seen as the vehicle for that brand of narrow 'bureaucratic' socialism—the socialism of scientific order and efficiency—associated with the partnership of Sidney and Beatrice Webb. The Webbs, as H. G. Wells harshly portrayed them in his novel *The New Machiavelli*, 'loved a world' that was 'flat and metallic'. 'If they

[6] Unfortunately, Wallas left no account of precisely how he became a socialist.
[7] Letter from Geoffrey Faber, 24 May 1932, suggesting Wallas write his reminiscences for publication by Faber & Faber (WP).
[8] *Economica*, xxxviii (Nov., 1932), 403. See also the three letters from Webb, written in 1885, in PP. 'Taken all in all,' Webb concluded a memorial address for Wallas, 'I feel I have learned more, and gained more intellectually from Graham Wallas than from any other friend.' Ibid., 404.
[9] For the early history of Fabianism, see Edward Pease, op. cit., Anne Fremantle, *This Little Band of Prophets* (New York, 1959), Margaret Cole, *The Story of Fabian Socialism* (Stanford, California, 1961), and A. M. McBriar, *Fabian Socialism and English Politics 1884–1918* (Cambridge, 1962).

had the universe in hand', Wells remarked, 'they would take down all the trees and put up stamped tin green shades and sunlight accumulators.'[10]

Alternatively, the Fabian Society has been pictured as a group of irreverent and sceptical intellectuals, with 'the invaluable habit of freely laughing at ourselves which always distinguished us, and which saved us from becoming hampered by the gushing enthusiasts who mistake their emotions for public movements'. 'Such people', Bernard Shaw noted, 'fled after one glance at us, declaring that we were not serious.'[11]

However, both of these images of the Society are misleading. Wells's comment was made in Edwardian times, when the character of the Society had changed substantially, while Shaw's picture was that of one side only of early Fabianism. The original Fabian Society has to be seen in its time, as one of many radical and reforming organizations arising out of the ferment of the 1880s. As such, it was more earnest than Shaw would have us believe, more moralistic, and even emotional than when it later became dominated by the Webb partnership.

After the anarchists and utopians among the founders of the Society had been driven out, the remaining Fabians prided themselves on being scientific. The appeal to statistics and to empirical, quantitative 'facts' was indeed to be one of the distinguishing marks of Fabian Socialism, setting it apart from the numerous other radical groups and '-isms' of the late nineteenth century. But the Society was not only 'scientific'; it was also part of the general climate of 'neo-Evangelical' social conscience that characterized the 1880s. Science was not alien to this mental climate; in the Positivist movement, among the various branches of Secularism,[12] in the minds of such people as T. H. Huxley, Charles Booth, and the young social investigator Beatrice Potter (later Mrs. Sidney Webb) science was to be the means by which the aroused social conscience was to act.

Before joining the Fabian Society, Webb, Shaw, Olivier, and Wallas 'were already looking', as Olivier's wife recalled, 'for some form of social organization which would remedy the deplorable conditions of the time. They discussed Positivism. The Positivist system seemed then to be a

---

[10] *The New Machiavelli* (originally published 1911; New York, 1919), 201.
[11] *Essays in Fabian Socialism* (New York, 1932), 131.
[12] For a picture of the blend of moralism and science that pervaded late-Victorian Secular movements, see Frank Kent, *Radical London* (London, 1932), Gustav Spiller, *The Ethical Movement in Great Britian* (London, 1934), and Warren Sylvester Smith, *The London Heretics* (London, 1967). Wallas was very much part of the Secular movement, and lectured frequently at the South Place Ethical Society.

hopeful solution.'[13] 'Most of the free-thinking men of that period', noted Edward Pease, secretary of the Fabian Society, 'read the "Positive Polity" and the other writings of the founder, and spent some Sunday mornings at the little conventicle in Lamb's Conduit Street, or attended on Sunday evenings the Newton Hall lectures of Frederic Harrison.'[14] Olivier, for a while, became an enthusiastic advocate of Positivism, and even Webb was sympathetic.[15]

Positivism claimed to offer a way out of the 'anarchy' of existing society, through a new scientific religion to come. While giving an honoured place to science, the movement was essentially ethical and idealistic. Its remedy for social evils was neither structural nor political reform, but a growth of 'social feeling', a sense of responsibility to society on the part of both employers and workmen. The Positivists stressed neither economics nor politics as much as psychology; the real task for them was to change people's attitudes, motives, and values.[16]

In spite of its avowed 'scientism', Positivism had much in common with another reformist movement stirring the London of the 1880s—the 'Idealist' social gospel inspired by T. H. Green and spearheaded by the historian Arnold Toynbee. Resolutely ethical and anti-materialistic, Toynbee preached social co-operation and spiritual uplift. He favoured economic and political reforms, but only as a means to psychological change, to the ultimate 'moralization' of both employers and employed. Toynbee's programme rested on the faith that human nature is gradually 'modified by higher ideals and wider and deeper conceptions of justice'.[17] Toynbee cautioned:

High wages are not an end in themselves. No one wants high wages in order that working men may indulge in mere sensual gratification. We want higher wages in order that an improved material condition, with less of anxiety and less uncertainty as to the future, may enable the working man to enter on a purer and more worthy life.[18]

[13] Margaret Olivier (ed.), *Sydney Olivier: Letters and Selected Writings* (London, 1948), 60.
[14] Op. cit., 18.
[15] Webb's Fabian lecture on 'The Economics of a Positivist Community', delivered on 14 January 1886, was so favourable as to bring questions of whether he himself was a Positivist. *Practical Socialist*, i (Feb. 1886), 37–9.
[16] On English Positivism, see John E. McGee, *A Crusade for Humanity* (London, 1931), Walter M. Simon, *European Positivism in the Nineteenth Century* (Ithaca, New York, 1963), Royden Harrison, *Before the Socialists* (London, 1965), ch. 6, and W. S. Smith, op. cit., 84–104.
[17] Arnold Toynbee, 'Wages and the Natural Law' (1880), *Lectures on the Industrial Revolution* (London, 1890), 175.   [18] Ibid., 176.

In 1883, Olivier had attended Toynbee's London lectures.[19] Wallas took part in Toynbee Hall, the first settlement house, from its founding in 1885.[20] The influence of these ethical social gospels stayed with Wallas and Olivier. In the *Fabian Essays* of 1889, Olivier announced his faith in the evolving ethical consciousness of the age. He declared:

> The moral ideas appropriate to Socialism are permeating the whole of modern society. They are clearly recognisable not only in the proletariat, but also in the increasing philanthropic activity of members of the propertied class, who, while denouncing Socialism as a dangerous exaggeration of what is necessary for social health, work honestly enough for alleviatory reforms which converge irresistibly towards it.[21]

The importance of the Evangelical ethical tradition in the English radicalism of the 1880s accounts for the Fabian distaste for much of Continental radicalism. Marxism in particular offended the Evangelical sensibility by its aggressive materialism and 'debunking' attitude toward existing society. Though Webb, Shaw, Wallas, and Olivier saw themselves as more radical than Positivists or Idealists, they shared too much with them to feel comfortable with Marxism.

Reading *Capital* together during 1885, they found their initial expectant hopefulness turned into determined opposition.[22] Their attack upon Marx centred on economic theory—the labour theory of value[23]—but the dispute involved wider issues: the degree to which existing society was reformable, the best means of effecting change, and the validity of economic determinism and historical materialism. The confrontation with Marx forced Wallas and his friends to define what they meant when they called themselves Socialists, and the result of this re-examination was Fabian Socialism.

Against Marx's 'revolution' they put forward 'evolution'; 'constructive' Socialism against what they saw as his purely 'destructive', 'negativist' Socialism. They felt, as Wallas put it, that 'the Marxists had a formula for

---

[19] Margaret Olivier, op. cit., 55.
[20] See the testimonial to Wallas upon his marriage in 1897 (WP).
[21] *Fabian Essays in Socialism*, ed. G. B. Shaw (London, 1948), 119.
[22] Wallas recalled their state of mind in a lecture on 'Social Purpose in Education', *Morning Post*, 1 Jan. 1923. See also 'Socialism and the Fabian Society', (1916), *Men & Ideas*, 103; Wallas's letter to Pease, 10 Jan. 1916 (WP); Archibald Henderson, *George Bernard Shaw* (London, 1911), 96–8; M. Olivier, op. cit., 64; Margaret Cole (ed.), *The Webbs and Their Work* (London, 1949), 6.
[23] See Shaw, 'Bluffing the Value Theory', *Today*, xi (May 1889), and Wallas, 'An Economic Eirenicon', *Today*, xi (March 1889), 80–6. Also see 'Socialism and the Fabian Society', *Men & Ideas*, 103–4, and A. M. McBriar, op. cit., 31–4.

'EVANGELICAL' FABIANISM

a revolution, but no formula for afterwards'.[24] For the spreading of Socialist principles, Olivier argued,

it is ridiculous to rely upon a work of the nature of Marx's 'Capital'. I am not acquainted with any of the Socialist writings of Marx. 'Capital', as far as it goes, and the other fragments of his writings which are accessible to English readers are, in their practical application, merely anti-Capitalist polemics. They do not teach Socialism.[25]

To some degree, their rejection of Marx was based on misunderstanding. Marxist determinism, for example, seemed to deny their powerful faith in self-discipline and will-power. Wallas recalled,

We never believed in an inevitable, automatic, and 'scientific' process by which a social revolution would come of itself. That theory is apt to present itself to the young reformer as a reason why he should trust to his own automatic impulses, should read and think such eloquence as comes from the exaltation of the moment, and should attend committees as long as they interest him. During ten years of constant intimacy we learnt ... that one could only get things done in politics by a steady and severe effort of will.[26]

Wallas and his friends, moreover, had a natural practical bias against Marxism. With the exception of Shaw (who not surprisingly was the most sympathetic to Marxist ideas), they all came from respectable, comfortable backgrounds and held congenial jobs in the Civil Service or in teaching. They were not so alienated from the existing order as to relish giving up *all* respectability by embracing extreme revolutionary positions. Thus the new form of socialism they developed in the later 1880s was gradualist, laying great stress on being 'constructive' and 'practical'. Accepting the existing political framework, they set out to work within it, by 'the ordinary political methods'.[27]

Democracy had just arrived with the Franchise Acts of 1884 and 1885, and great things were expected of it. The young Fabians looked to the enfranchisement of the working class to force, democratically and gradually, the adoption of socialist measures. Whatever might be true on the Continent, England, they felt, with its constitutional tradition, democratic machinery, and strong radical movement, could have social progress without serious conflict. They renounced the doctrine of class conflict

---

[24] H. G. Wells, in *Literary Guide and Rationalist Review*, Sept. 1932.
[25] 'Perverse Socialism', *Today*, vi (Aug. 1886), 54.
[26] 'Socialism and the Fabian Society', *Men & Ideas*, 105. Marx, of course, would have thoroughly agreed with Wallas.
[27] Shaw, *Essays in Fabian Socialism*, 142.

and class consciousness, almost as sharply as had the Positivists and Idealists. Social co-operation and integration were to be the goals, both as a practical policy and as an ideal, and were to be attained by altering and directing public opinion.

In his writing and lecturing in the later eighties and early nineties, Wallas emphasized the Evangelical side of early Fabianism almost to the point of forging a distinct species of Fabian Socialism. Indeed, moral questions became his 'speciality' (all the more so as Sydney Olivier, another 'moralist', ceased, because of his trips abroad for the Colonial Office, to play a major role in the Society). As Beatrice Webb, in her inimitably condescending fashion, described in her diary the workings of the 'Fabian Junta' in the early nineties:

> Sidney is the organiser and gives most of the practical initiative, Graham Wallas represents morality and scrupulousness, Bernard Shaw gives the sparkle and flavour. Graham Wallas appeals to those of the upper and educated class who have good intentions; no one can doubt his candour, disinterestedness, enthusiasm and extreme moral refinement. Sidney insinuates ideas, arguments, programmes, and organises the organisers. Bernard Shaw leads off the men of straw, men with light heads—the would-be revolutionists, who are attracted by his wit, his daring onslaughts and amusing paradoxes.[28]

To Mrs. Webb, Wallas was 'six feet with a slouching figure—good features and genial, open smile—utterly unselfconscious and lacking in vanity or personal ambition'.[29] Too lacking, for her taste:

> In spite of his moral fervour, he seems incapable of directing his own life, and tends to drift into anything that other people decide. This tendency is accentuated by his benevolence and kindliness and selflessness—almost amounting to a weakness. Thus, while his intimate friends love him and impose upon him, superficial strangers of poor character often actually despise him. To some men and women he appears simply as a kindly, dull fellow—an impression which is fostered by a slovenliness of dress and general worn-out look. He preaches too, a habit carried over from his life as usher and teacher of boys.[30]

Her assessment of Wallas (she 'assessed' everyone she came into contact with) was that

> if enthusiasm, purity of motive, hard if somewhat mechanical work, will make a man a success, then GW has a great career before him. He has plenty of intellectual ability too; what he lacks is deliberate concentration and rapid decision what to do and how to do it. A loveable man.[31]

[28] *Our Partnership*, 38–9. [29] Ibid., 37 (17 Sept. 1893).
[30] Ibid., 37–8. [31] Ibid., 38.

'EVANGELICAL' FABIANISM

However, Wallas was not only a 'loveable' moralist, but a serious thinker. 'To his disciples', Beatrice Webb conceded, 'he appears a brilliant man, first-rate lecturer, a very genius for teaching, a great thinker and a conscientious writer.'[32] Herbert Samuel, one of these 'disciples', later recalled the appearances of the Fabian 'Junta' at Oxford when he was an undergraduate in the early nineties: 'Bernard Shaw was the brilliant propagandist, Sidney Webb the practical politician; but Graham Wallas was the careful builder of ideas, and he was the one who influenced us most.'[33] Samuel continued:

His personality was attractive—a tall figure, very good-looking, an intellectual head, a kindly expression, with an easy friendliness of manner. He had a powerful mind of wide range, and a style of speaking and writing, lucid and persuasive, that was at once restrained and dynamic.

During his Fabian years, Wallas was working out a social philosophy that was not abandoned when he later left the Society. Rather, it formed a necessary stage in his life-long intellectual journey.

Wallas was different from Webb and Shaw, not only in personality, but in his way of thinking. Reflecting those influences in his background that they did not share—the self-examining Evangelicalism of his childhood, the immersion in the Greek philosophers at school, and his years of teaching—he tended always to relate social questions to questions of individual psychology. Wallas arrived at Fabian 'realism' by way of a 'realistic' assessment of human nature. As Aristotle, his 'master', had pointed out,

a system which obliges men to live in constant close companionship with each other and which puts before them the public good as their chief motive instead of private advantage really ignores human nature as it is. As men now are, constant companionship means constant friction and few are capable of sustained work whose object is general and not individual good.[34]

Socialists aimed at the public ownership of the means of production, but, Wallas cautioned, 'public spirit' was at the time too low to sustain general socialization, even if by the municipality and not the national state.[35] Public ownership, he told his fellow Socialists, would probably only spread with the growth of public spirit. Their efforts, therefore,

---

[32] *Our Partnership*, 38.
[33] 'Master Builder of Ideas', *The Times*, 31 May 1958. See also Samuel's *Memoirs* (London, 1945). Upon taking a first, Samuel told Wallas of the influence he had had on him. Letter, 28 July 1893 (WP).
[34] Lecture on Aristotle's *Politics*, probably 1887 (WP).
[35] Lecture on 'The Morals of Interest', c. 1890 (?) (WP).

ought to be directed towards bringing about as much socialization as was practical in the existing situation, while at the same time working to alter that situation for the better.

'We should not strive', he warned, 'to bring in a constitution which the average man is not at present fit to work, without first or at the same time striving . . . by education and good laws to improve the average man.'[36] Parliamentary action and improved education were, from this point of view, necessary preliminaries to a Socialist society. Within Fabian circles, Wallas became one of the firmest 'parliamentarians', urging, against the 'revolutionary' left wing, taking a full part in politics at every level, especially that of the municipality, as the most readily accessible. During 1887 he became Secretary of the Fabian Parliamentary League, which had originally been set up as a compromise solution to the conflict between 'right' and 'left' within the Society. This League, which members could join or not, as they wished, was to engage in political activity without committing the parent body. In April 1888, the 'parliamentarians' at last in firm control, the League was turned into the Political Committee of the Fabian Society.

By then Wallas's gradualism had found a more specific outlet. To show Socialists the need to work within the existing political framework, and not to wait for 'the revolution' to solve all problems, he turned to the field he knew best—education. Socialists, he charged, were far too apt to suppose that if they could convert one generation or the majority of one generation to their ideas, their task would be done for ever. But, he pointed out, that had never been true. Previous revolutions had all failed to perpetuate themselves to the next generation, while 'Spartan laws made minute provision for the education of children and the Spartan constitution lasted till the Spartans themselves died out'.[37] Socialism was not something that could be bestowed upon men; rather, men had to be educated for it. Aristotle, 'the keenest observer that ever lived', had said 'that it is absurd to expect any constitution of society to be permanent which does not rest upon an education shared by all the citizens and deliberately intended to produce the kind of character required'.[38]

Wallas's own father had been an enthusiastic partisan of education, for, as he had put it,

God sent us into the world with minds and souls as well as bodies, and all our faculties, mental as well as physical, ought to be trained both for the benefit of

[36] Lecture on Aristotle's *Politics* (WP).
[37] Lecture on 'Education', 1886 (WP).
[38] Ibid.

our souls, and to enable us to carry out our duties towards our fellow creatures... Some persons had asked where was the use of education to the people who had to earn their livelihood by manual labour? What was the use of geography to the housemaid or arithmetic to the fisherman? When people talked in that way it was difficult to argue with them, but it might be fairly left to our consideration... the more men became intelligent the better members of society they would make, and this could only be by sending them to school.[39]

Wallas shared, with even greater enthusiasm, the faith of his father in education as a means of social betterment, and preached this faith to his fellow Socialists. This educational task, Wallas told them, could not await a political revolution, but had to precede it, if that revolution were to endure. A. M. McBriar's observation that the Fabians, in contradistinction to the Marxists, emphasized administrative and minimized political difficulties is especially true of Wallas.[40] He pointed out,

Suppose that the Social Revolution comes as soon and as successfully as every one of us hopes for in his most sanguine moments. You will have your provisional Minister of Education sitting in his Whitehall office writing for dear life with fingers still black from the gunpowder of the barricades. He will have to face the difficulties which I have suggested to you. Will he find it easy to provide all those new schools, all those new and better teachers? He will be lucky if in ten years he gets one quarter of his task done, while all the time the young generation will be growing up in ignorance and confusion of mind and the reaction will be at hand.[41]

Immediate action was imperative. Fortunately, he felt, it was not only imperative but quite possible. The existing system of public elementary education, 'slowly built up by the ordinary uninviting method of political action and compromise', though insufficient in its aims and results, formed a solid basis for improvement.[42] Little more than a decade and a half had passed since the first provision for a national educational system, and progress had been impeded by religious quarrels and a shortage of funds. Yet much of the psychological groundwork for improvement, he was convinced, had already been laid:

---

[39] Speaking at the opening of a parish school in a district of mainly poor people. *Barnstaple and North Devon Times*, 17 May 1861. One of Wallas's sisters, Katharine T. Wallas, shared this family zeal for education as an alderman for twenty-one years on the L.C.C.
[40] McBriar, op. cit., 70.
[41] Lecture on 'Education' (WP).
[42] Ibid.

the conception of education itself as a thing desirable, of the state as the only body powerful, earnest and impartial enough to provide it, and of direct contribution from the national income as the proper method of meeting the cost, has already spread into every country village, and every back street in every town.[43]

Right at home in London, Socialists had an unequalled opportunity to make their influence felt. In the School Board elections, Wallas observed, only an extraordinarily small fraction of the possible voters took the trouble to go to the poll. This, and the cumulative method of voting used, made it possible for any organized body of men who knew what they wanted, even though small, to get their candidate elected. 'If we had one or two good men on the London School Board', he pointed out, 'their presence there would be a constant encouragement to our party, a constant advertisement of our principles, and a constant criticism of our national backwardness in education.'[44]

Education became Wallas's speciality in the Fabian Society.[45] It was the key, he decided, to everything else:

If this generation were wise, it would spend on education not only more than any other generation has ever spent before, but more than any generation would ever need to spend again. . . . it would seriously propose to itself the ideal of Ibsen, that every child should be brought up as a nobleman. Unfortunately, this generation is not wise.[46]

In 1887 he received an appointment as one of the managers of an elementary school, beginning twenty years of official connection with London public education. In the following year he published an article in *Today*, again urging Socialists to take part in improving London education, either as teachers or as managers.[47] His interest in education led him to become one of the organizers of the Progressive campaign for the London School Board in 1894, and a successful candidate himself.

[43] Lecture on 'Education' (WP).
[44] Ibid.
[45] For an account of Fabian efforts in education, see Ernest Stabler, 'London Education, 1890-1910, with special reference to the work of Sidney and Beatrice Webb', Ed.D. thesis, Harvard, 1951. Stabler, however, over-emphasizes Webb's role in the formation of *early* Fabian educational policy. Webb made no reference to education in his writings, as Stabler admits, before 1889, while Wallas was lecturing the Fabians on educational policy as early as 1886, and co-authored *The Case Against Diggleism*, an important critique of London education, in 1894. By the late 1890s, Webb had come to dominate Fabian educational policy, but he was not its founder.
[46] Lecture on 'Education' (WP).
[47] 'Socialists and the School Board', *Today*, x (Nov. 1888), 126-32.

'EVANGELICAL' FABIANISM

The task of education, and particularly of public educational institutions, was to raise the ethical and spiritual level of a population 'saturated with immoral principles by our commercial system'.[48]

If we wish London to be a different city from Rome at the time when the 'sweepings of the nations' were supported by their daily dole of bread and amused by a constant succession of brutal spectacles, we must see that all understand what is the nature of the life to which we call them, and the way to do so lies clear before us.[49]

The elementary school class-room was to become the pulpit of the new social religion; the teacher the new preacher of higher ideals. Along with 'psychological realism', Wallas carried a deep idealism, implanted by his parents and nourished by Plato and Aristotle. He observed in the *Fabian Essays*,

Fifty years ago Socialists were tempted to exaggerate the influence of the ideal, to expect everything from a sudden impossible change of all men's hearts. Now-a-days we are tempted to under-value the ideal—to forget that even the Time Spirit itself is only the sum of individual strivings and aspirations, and that again and again in history changes which might have been delayed for centuries or might never have come at all, have been brought about by the persistent preaching of some new and higher life, the offspring not of circumstance but of hope.[50]

His first Fabian lecture dealt, characteristically, with ethics. In it he 'preached' to the middle classes on 'personal duty under the present system', taking pains to distinguish his Socialist message from the more conventional kind:

Remember that the feeling of duty, common as it is, is more than useless if misdirected, and therefore, realise clearly, what actions you now feel yourselves bound to do, and judge wisely whether you ought not to do something else. Remember, that whatever you spend beyond your just share of the produce of the world belongs not to yourself, but some other, and see that you spend it for him and not for yourself. Your intellectual advantages are the property of the community, see that you earn and pay the rent for them. Seek for comfort by simplifying, not by complicating, your surroundings. Remember when you plan your day's work that you are a man, not a machine. Do not refuse to share in the interests, and take part in the politics of today.[51]

Moral exhortation easily shaded, in Wallas's mind, into psychological analysis, for the point of his message concerning duty was that this common

---
[48] *Fabian Essays*, 136.   [49] Lecture on 'Education' (WP).
[50] *Fabian Essays*, 123-4.
[51] 'Personal Duty Under the Present System', *Practical Socialist*, i (July and Aug. 1886), 125.

Victorian sentiment, 'powerful, all-pervading and easily excited', was being 'almost entirely wasted under the present system'.[52] It was 'at present misdirected, partly owing to the enormous influence of habit, and partly owing to the narrowness of the ordinary human imagination'. Habit had to be overcome, and the ordinary imagination widened; how, other than by preaching and educating, he did not yet know.

With this psychological and ethical approach, Wallas saw Socialism as the 'good life' towards which the Greeks had aimed, translated into modern terms. Industrialism had changed the possibilities of life; Greek ideals could now be realized under conditions more hopeful than those of classical Greece. Before industrialism, most men were shut out from the very possibility of the 'good life'. As Aristotle had said, 'no man living the life of a common labourer has any opportunity to practise virtue'.[53] This was still true, but, Wallas contended, no longer necessary. The development of machinery had made possible the 'good life' for all. He argued,

If all take their part in necessary human production, the life we can offer each will not it is true be a perfectly easy one, but in it there will be room for leisure, for intellectual interest and for the arts which will humanise life—above all we shall be able to work under such conditions and with such motives [that] toil shall lose more than half its toilsomeness.[54]

Wallas's ultimate aims were similar to those of William Morris, despite their great differences over tactics. A frequent participant in Morris's weekly Hammersmith meetings, Wallas often joined in discussions, and was on good terms with Morris personally.[55] Morris wrote to Wallas in 1888 asking for articles for his magazine, *The Commonweal*, noting that 'the differences between us are not very great'.[56] For both the 'gradualist' and the 'revolutionist' psychological and spiritual reform was primary, and changes in 'machinery' alone would never achieve the better life towards which they worked. Both sought a new spirit, a new way of life, and not simply a more collectivized and efficient society. 'The system of property holding which we call Socialism', Wallas wrote, and Morris would not have disagreed, 'is not in itself such a life any more than a good system of draining is health, or the invention of printing is knowledge.'[57]

---

[52] 'Personal Duty Under the Present System', *Practical Socialist*, i (July and Aug. 1886), 118.
[53] Quoted in lecture on Aristotle's *Politics* (WP).
[54] Lecture on 'Education' (WP).
[55] See Walter Crane, *An Artist's Reminiscences* (New York, 1907), ch. 8, and H. G. Wells, *Experiment in Autobiography* (New York, 1934), 193.
[56] Letter, 14 June 1888 (WP).   [57] *Fabian Essays*, 139.

Without the machinery of collectivism, however, Wallas held, the 'good life' would be impossible for the large majority of people. For these,

the long hours of work done as in a convict prison, without interest and without hope; the dreary squalor of their homes; above all that grievous uncertainty, that constant apprehension of undeserved misfortune which is the peculiar result of capitalist production; all this would be gone; and education, refinement, leisure, the very thought of which now maddens them would be part of their daily life.[58]

The conception of the 'good life' and the 'good society' which Wallas derived from his classical studies was not difficult to harmonize with Fabian collectivism. Indeed it served to reinforce the collectivism he and the other Fabians drew from the Utilitarian tradition and from the 'Darwinism' that saw society as an organism. Society for Aristotle, and for Wallas, was first of all a moral community. Wallas began an article in *Today* by quoting Aristotle:

Every state is a community of some kind, and every community is established with a view to some good, for mankind always act in order to obtain what they think good. But if all communities aim at some good, the state, or political community, which is the highest of all, and which embraces all the rest, aims, and in a greater degree than any other, at the highest good.[59]

Perhaps it was this additional influence that made Wallas even more collectivist than his colleagues. The Fabian Society in the later 1880s was quite cool to 'interests' of any sort—trade unionism was ignored, and Co-operation was viewed as 'little more than a method of turning workingmen into petty capitalists'.[60] Any kind of 'workers' control' was lumped together with Anarchism. But Wallas stood out, even among this group, as 'a passionate opponent of "interests"'.[61] His lecture to the Society in July 1888, criticizing Co-operation provoked an animated discussion, and he continued his criticism in the *Fabian Essays*.[62] The state, Wallas believed, as the highest community, had to embrace all other subsidiary communities. Only the state, democratically constituted, could work for the highest

[58] *Fabian Essays*, 139. In his lecture on 'Art', given at Kelmscott House between 1886 and 1888, Wallas took up Morris's view that the quality of art depended on the quality of society; great art, he argued, could only come out of a healthy social life.
[59] 'Aristotle on Wealth and Property', *Today*, x (July 1888), 16–17.
[60] Margaret Cole, *The Story of Fabian Socialism*, 30.   [61] Ibid., 31.
[62] *Our Corner*, Aug. 1888. *Fabian Essays*, 128. However, while the book was being published, a series of conferences with Co-operators caused him to moderate his views. He intended to eliminate the critical reference to the movement in a later edition, but never did. See letter to Edward Pease, 10 Jan. 1916 (WP).

general good; all less inclusive groups necessarily worked for lower, less general goods.

In the Greek *polis*, the community had been bound together and given an ethos by a common education. Wallas sought this same end through the public educational system of his day. All citizens had to be fitted to play their proper role in the new *polis*. They had to receive the best possible training in science, technical skill, and culture. As with the Greeks, each was to be ready after childhood 'to take with understanding, with sympathy and with humbleness his or her place in the great organism of a state where each shares with full consciousness the common purpose and where each attains the common end'.[63]

'Socialism hangs above them', he believed, 'as the crown hung in Bunyan's story above the man raking the muck heap—ready for them if they will but lift their eyes.'[64] Education, guided by men like himself, would raise and open their eyes.

Wallas's Fabianism, while 'orthodox' in its gradualism, parliamentarism, and collectivism, contained the seeds of his later divergence from the Society. Feeling himself at one with his colleagues,[65] he was, unawares, moving along an independent path, for a time parallel to theirs, but for a time only. His psychological approach and ethical outlook increasingly tended to clash with the institutional approach of Webb that more and more came to dominate the Fabian Society. In addition, Wallas's mind was more reflective, more prone to ponder fundamental theoretical questions, while his colleagues concentrated on practical, immediate problems. Once his theoretical ideas had formed, Sidney Webb in particular lost interest in theory. Wallas, on the contrary, while he was happy to engage in practical politics, never stopped re-examining his theories, to the impatience of Webb.[66]

Certain 'Fabian' characteristics were to remain in his thought: a pluralism, critical of all monistic explanations, a historical and empirical outlook questioning abstractions and dogma, a commitment to gradualism, and a rejection of all 'easy answers', all quick and complete solutions. Society was never for Wallas, as for Marxists, a single system which was born,

---

[63] Lecture on 'Education' (WP). [64] *Fabian Essays*, 139

[65] In a letter to Webb, Shaw, and Olivier, suggesting that they jointly write what later became the *Fabian Essays*, Wallas remarked that only the four of them should write the essays, since 'we are the only four people in England who are agreed about anything' (probably May 1888 (WP)).

[66] Many entries in Beatrice Webb's diaries illustrate the gradual divergence of interest between the Webbs and Wallas. See especially the entry for 9 Aug. 1932, on Wallas's death (PP).

matured, and died, but an infinitely complex assortment of facts, too complicated and incoherent to deal with as a whole. The engineer, not the dogmatist, the inventor, not the revolutionist, were his models for a social reformer. From these Fabian years on, he was always seeking social and political 'invention', which would 'rationalize' the complexities of modern life, and for this Bentham was his model.[67] This Benthamism was more than a philosophy; it was part of his personality. Walking with his friend, G. Lowes Dickinson, years later on the Cambridge Backs, Wallas's tidy eye was caught by the time-honoured kink in Clare Bridge. 'Dickinson', he said, 'don't you think it would be possible to get the Cambridge Town Council to send out a crane and some workmen to repair that fault in Clare Bridge?'[68] This intolerance for the irrational in bridges and in institutions, which he shared with Sidney Webb, set Wallas apart from most of his contemporaries.

Fabianism was a decisive experience for Wallas. Though he later left the Society, he took with him its imprint. It was during his Fabian years that Wallas was trained in social analysis and developed his characteristic outlook of 'evangelical Benthamism'. Through Fabianism, too, he began to work out the psychological approach to social questions that was to lead to his major Edwardian works.

[67] 'Bentham', *Men & Ideas*, 19-32, and 'Bentham as Political Inventor', *ibid.*, 33-48.
[68] Kingsley Martin, *Harold Laski* (London, 1953), 50.

CHAPTER III

FROM SOCIALISM TO SOCIAL PSYCHOLOGY

A BEGINNING—SOCIO-POLITICAL INQUIRY

ALTHOUGH Wallas remained one of the leaders of the Fabian Society until 1895, and a member until 1904, after the publication of the *Fabian Essays* in 1889, he began moving in new directions. For the first few years it was not a deliberate movement. Wallas's restlessness grew, but he was not clearly aware that he was diverging from Fabianism. In retrospect, however, we can see a steady and cumulative development away from old interests and towards new ones. All of Wallas's new activities in the 1890s—lecturing for the University Extension and at the London School of Economics, standing for and winning election to the London School Board, and writing the *Life of Francis Place*—contributed to this mental journey. Wallas recalled that he emerged from the 1890s 'a different man'.[1] By the end of the decade his apprenticeship was over; the author of *Human Nature in Politics* and *The Great Society* had appeared.

One of the formulators of the Fabian policy of 'ordinary political methods', Wallas in the 1890s was drawn into a close involvement with, and study of, these methods. The early Fabians had moved in the mental climate of radicalism; to them, democracy was a faith, not a subject for argument. Consequently, they had never given much serious thought to the actual workings of democratic politics. In the 1880s, critical examination of democracy in England, and even more so on the Continent, had been largely confined to its opponents. Democracy, not yet firmly established, was too controversial an issue to allow much dispassionate thought. Books like Maine's *Popular Government* were openly hostile and thus not taken seriously by the partisans of democracy. Nor had the system yet been given a practical test.

However, the seeds of a critique of democracy were already present in the intellectual elitism of Fabianism, and only needed the proper stimulus

[1] 'Physical and Social Science' (1930) *Men & Ideas*, 208. Wallas was referring specifically to his years of research on Francis Place but the remark is even more applicable to those years as a whole.

to sprout. The Fabians envisaged progress coming through the reshaping of public opinion in a 'collectivist' mould. This reshaping, however, was to be accomplished by an intellectual *élite* possessing expertise and a scientific knowledge of society, not by a mass movement. Social and political progress was for them an intellectually demanding task.

This outlook was not far removed, at bottom, from that of many Liberals who, in the 1870s and 1880s, were turning against Liberalism as democracy was arriving on the scene. Beginning with John Stuart Mill's hesitations about the political capabilities of democracy, a drift of Liberal intellectuals towards Conservatism became increasingly pronounced. This drift was accelerated by the Reform Act of 1867 and the subsequent 'demagoguery' of Gladstone. Most mid-Victorian Liberals, coming predominantly from the upper middle class, had opposed aristocracy and tradition, but in the name of meritocracy and utility, not of democracy and natural rights.[2] After 1867 these intellectual elitists discovered that they had more in common with their Conservative antagonists than with the new advocates of 'the people'. Now on the defensive, they joined the anti-democratic chorus, but in their own 'scientific' fashion.[3]

For them, the great fault of democracy was its intellectual inadequacy, its inability to provide the expert, intelligent guidance that a modern state required. Their distinctive note was sounded by Robert Lowe in 1865. Claiming that he had been a Liberal all his life, and that he had full confidence in the further progress of society, he went on to caution that,

because I am a Liberal and know that by pure and clear intelligence alone can the cause of true progress be promoted, I regard as one of the greatest dangers with which this country can be threatened a proposal to subvert the existing order of things, and to transfer power from the hands of property and intelligence to the hands of men whose daily life is necessarily occupied in daily struggle for existence.[4]

Frequently, these 'old Liberals' were or had been Civil Servants, and reflected the natural predilection of professional administrators for a minimum of interference from the ignorant masses and from 'politics'. What

---

[2] Even their belief in meritocracy was more conservative than has usually been recognized. Underlying it lay 'deferential and corporate assumptions' which have recently been brought out by D. C. Moore in a series of articles. See particularly 'Political Morality in Mid-Nineteenth-Century England', *Victorian Studies*, xiii (Sept. 1969), 5–36.

[3] See John Roach, 'Liberalism and the Victorian Intelligentsia', *Cambridge Historical Journal* (1957), 58–81.

[4] A. Patchett Martin, *Life and Letters of Viscount Sherbrooke*, ii (London, 1893), 263–4.

was needed, they could see from their own experience, was more expertise, not less, more efficiency in national life rather than the 'anarchy' that resulted from treating the intelligent and informed on a plane with the unintelligent and uninformed. As J. F. Stephen remarked to a friend, it was from 'the educated and driving part of the country' that leadership ought to come, but to this concept he saw the new Liberalism of Gladstone as fatal, because it 'taught the public that there is no such thing anywhere as legitimate authority'.[5]

This rightward trend of Liberal thought in England reflected a general movement throughout Western Europe. Wherever democracy was becoming a reality, many Liberals saw *intellectual* as well as social and political authority challenged. In France it was the advent of the Third Republic that exposed the 'contradiction' within Liberalism. However much they had criticized the Empire, many Liberals had no liking for universal suffrage and fully representative government. Their Liberalism stood for liberty, but more exactly, liberty of those most fit to think and to preserve government from the whims and emotions of the 'unfit'.

Ernest Renan, as Roger Soltau pointed out, 'virtually divide[d] mankind into two classes: those called to knowledge, and thereby to leadership, and those who, while undoubtedly worthy of development, were essentially meant to be led'.[6] Democracy for Renan, at least for the present age, was a leveller of ability and intelligence as well as privilege. 'The opinion of the majority', he argued, 'has the right to prevail only when it represents reason and the most enlightened opinion. The only sovereign by divine right is reason.... For a long while yet mankind will need to have good done to it in spite of itself; here can be no blind obedience to mere opinion.'[7] However, Renan was a realist, and accepted democracy as a *fait accompli*, proposing only some electoral and institutional reforms to moderate its influence. Nor did he wish to abandon the idea of universal political rights— he still considered himself a Liberal and not a Conservative. 'One must admit that every citizen has a certain right in the direction of public affairs; but', he cautioned, 'this right must be regulated and used in an enlightened way.'[8]

The same 'intellectual' fear of democracy was expressed by Hippolyte Taine. He too accepted universal suffrage both as inevitable and as

---

[5] Quoted by Roach, op. cit., 72.
[6] *French Political Thought in the Nineteenth Century* (New Haven, Conn., 1931), 216.
[7] Quoted by Soltau, op. cit., 225.
[8] Quoted by J. P. Mayer, *Political Thought in France* (London, 1943), 82.

possessing a certain justification. His solution to its evils, against which he inveighed even more forcefully than Renan, was two-degree election, which would join the consultation of all with the ultimate control of government by the upper class.[9]

A further step in the 'intellectual' criticism of democracy was taken some years later by Gustave Le Bon. In his writing any vestigial ties with Liberalism had been severed, and in its place was a thoroughly elitist outlook, totally hostile to democracy. His chief work, *The Crowd* (1895), made an implicit equation between democracy and 'the rule of the crowd', and then analysed the psychology of the crowd as irrational and unconscious. Democracy was not for him merely the rule of the less educated or less intelligent; it was the domination of unconsciousness over consciousness. Le Bon illustrated the extreme development of the intellectual criticism of democracy; democracy was to him, and to his wide public, a negation of rationality, a reversion to the mental conditions of primitive society.

In Germany, Liberal anti-democracy was less important than further west, for Liberalism itself was much weaker. Here democracy was only very partially realized, and conservatism dominated. Yet in spite of a situation in which Liberals had more reason than in France or England to lean to the left, they were less in sympathy with democracy than their counterparts in the West. The philosophic basis of German Liberalism— the Hegelian identification of liberty with the rule of Reason—made it especially easy for Liberals to deny support to democratic movements. What was essential for them was not *who* ruled, but *how* he ruled, whether arbitrarily or by general, known, rationally-arrived-at and justified laws. With both interests and rights replaced by Reason as the criterion of liberal government, the entry of the masses into politics easily appeared menacing. Clearly, the masses were not going to be as rational as the existing upper classes.[10] In Imperial Germany, as in the France of the Third Republic and the England of Gladstone, former Liberals formulated an 'intellectual' critique of democracy that in practice joined hands with the older Conservative criticism.

England differed from the Continent in one important respect, however. Its politics and its political thinking were decidedly less polarized than across the Channel. The proverbial English 'moderation' reflected an underlying consensus, forged by the revolutions of the seventeenth century

---

[9] See Soltau, op. cit., 243.
[10] See Leonard Krieger, *The German Idea of Freedom* (Boston, 1957), especially pp. 459-60. Also see Ralf Dahrendorf, *Society and Democracy in Germany* (Garden City, New York, 1967).

and the long stability of the eighteenth century. This consensus was broad enough to preclude extremism either of right or left. English Liberals, radicals, and even Socialists were, to left-wing Continentals, remarkably conservative, while English Conservatives must have seemed 'crypto-Liberals' to their European counterparts. There was, in consequence, room for a viable middle ground in England; on the Continent, the middle ground was usually an untenable no-man's-land. This fundamental national difference made it possible for Wallas to develop as he did and occupy a special role—that of the committed democrat who yet could appreciate and develop the insights of anti-democrats. Wallas drew upon an English tradition of criticism of democracy that did not demand the rejection of basic Liberal assumptions. This did involve a mental tension, but the tension was not intolerable, because the two traditions, though divergent, were not irreconcilable.

Wallas had the proper background to play this mediating role. He had received a traditional, 'Establishment' education, and yet his 'conversion' to a faith in science and acquisition of a sense of social injustice had made him into a radical. He could understand and sympathize with both democrats and anti-democrats. Further, where 'old Liberals' turning to Conservatism had almost invariably identified intelligence with property, and meritocracy with the *status quo*, Wallas's Fabian experience enabled him to move beyond this limited view, and examine democracy's faults without thereby praising the political virtue or ability of the existing upper classes.

His 'inventory' of the stock of democratic ideas began in November 1890, when he was appointed a University Extension Lecturer. He continued Extension lecturing even after becoming part of the founding faculty at the London School of Economics in 1895, but on an occasional basis. He was, Beatrice Webb noted, 'an admirable and most popular University Extension lecturer'.[11] As he developed a course on 'The English Citizen—Past and Present' (a combination of civics and history), he found himself evaluating as well as describing modern English government. Compelled, as many a university teacher has found himself, to clarify his own thinking in order to teach successfully, Wallas began to see a conflict between his fervent belief in democracy and his conviction, only strengthened by experience and reflection, of the need for intellectual excellence and the most considered judgement in the affairs of government.

This conflict was symbolized by the long-standing problem, made

[11] *Our Partnership*, 38.

freshly acute by the rise of the 'caucus', of the role of the representative in a democracy. It was fitting that Wallas should have constructed his concluding lecture upon J. S. Mill's *Representative Government*, for Mill had been troubled by much the same difficulty in combining democracy and intelligent, expert government.[12] This problem appeared in simple form in Mill's time in the controversy over the 'pledge'.

What ought to be the function of representatives? Were they to be nothing but delegates, 'pledging' themselves to a previously approved programme, or were they to exercise independent judgement? Wallas, following Mill, came down firmly against the delegate theory, as inimical to effective and capable government.[13] To Wallas, the question really was 'should the Electors expect the Members to think?'

This question of representation versus delegation became a leitmotive of Wallas's writings, reappearing with regularity, for it symbolized a basic dilemma of modern politics, of which Wallas was particularly aware: how to reconcile popular control and participation in government with the ever more urgent need for expert, effective government. Two strands of Wallas's Fabianism, his belief in democracy and his recognition of the need for the most capable and expert government possible, were now in conflict.

There had been no such conflict for the early nineteenth-century radicals, the forebears of the Fabians, for whom democratic machinery combined with a sufficient level of public information would inevitably produce the public good.[14] Wallas could not accept this comfortable faith. He now saw no necessary relation between the wishes of the electorate and the public good. Government was more than an arrangement for registering the wishes of the electorate; it was a difficult art, requiring special abilities.

---

[12] See the syllabuses for these lectures, 1891-4 (WP).
[13] See J. S. Mill, *Utilitarianism, Liberty and Representative Government* (New York, 1951), 426-7.
[14] Against this accepted view, for which Wallas has in part been responsible, D. C. Moore has argued that the Benthamites were not so simple-mindedly radical. Their 'individualism' and 'intellectualism', he has tried to show, were conditioned by largely unspoken conservative social assumptions. The populace could be trusted with the vote because they did *not* in fact behave as individuals but as members of groups, and did *not* 'think for themselves' but were guided by their 'natural' leaders. See 'Political Morality in Mid-Nineteenth Century England'.
If Moore's interpretation proves sound—and that will require a fresh study of the Benthamites—it would give an added significance to Wallas's reappraisal. Benthamite political principles could seem so false to Wallas because the unspoken social assumptions on which they rested were no longer held. Wallas's generation, then, would be the first to confront Utilitarian political theory 'naked', shorn of its 'conservative' girding. With this change in the social and intellectual climate, the time would have necessarily arrived for a revaluation of political Utilitarianism.

This view was strengthened by Fabian collectivism: with the sphere of government ever expanding the difficulty of governing effectively became every day more pressing. Thus the very collectivism being brought about by democracy seemed to intensify its weaknesses.

This problem also began to concern other Fabians, but they found it more easily soluble. Sidney Webb placed his faith in expertise to make up for the inadequacies of the *demos*. In a series of lectures on 'The Machinery of Democracy', in 1896,[15] he agreed that the effective administration of society required division of labour, with the most important tasks going to the best qualified. Selection of these persons ought, he argued, to be made by examination and not by election. The popular will could not govern. It could only express broad general principles in non-technical language on matters affecting the whole nation. Much modern legislation was detailed, technical, and dealt with matters affecting only a section of the nation. Following from this, Webb utterly dismissed the 'delegate theory' of representation. For Webb the chief problem of modern government was how to secure the services of the expert while making him subject to popular control, and he had little doubt that this could and would be done. His own career, one of rapid rise into the upper Civil Service solely through outstanding success on examinations, demonstrated to him the possibility and the value of 'government by experts'. The implication of this view of government for democratic theory did not interest him.

Bernard Shaw was also moving away from 'classical' democracy. As early as 1891, he began to emphasize the importance of leadership:

... we who have to submit to majorities ... make it blasphemy against democracy to deny that the majority is always right, although that, as Ibsen says, is a lie. It is a scientific fact that the majority, however eager it may be for the reform of old abuses, is always wrong in its opinion of new developments, or rather is always unfit for them. We shall never march a step forward except at the heels of 'the strongest man, he who is able to stand alone' and to turn his back on 'the damned compact Liberal majority'. All of which is no disparagement of parliaments and adult suffrage, but simply a wholesome reduction of them to their real place in the social economy as pure machinery ... which has ... no motive power in itself whatsoever.[16]

---

[15] These lectures seem to have been influenced by Wallas's Extension lectures. See the syllabuses of Wallas's lectures 1891–4 (WP) and the report of Webb's lectures in *Fabian News*, Nov. and Dec. 1896, and Jan. 1897. Wallas read and criticized at this time the first draft of the Webbs' *Industrial Democracy*, especially the parts on political democracy. See letter from Beatrice Webb, probably 1896 (PP).

[16] *The Quintessence of Ibsenism* (New York, 1913), 104–7. Shaw and Wallas, both bachelors in the early 90s, saw a great deal of each other.

Shaw felt that he was carrying out the same task in politics as in drama—deflating romanticism, in this case the romanticism of democracy. As he had subjected English Marxism and Anarchism to 'exposure' in the eighties, so he turned his critical eyes in the nineties upon his own earlier beliefs.

By the middle nineties, Shaw found democracy an actual obstacle to progress. 'The wage earners', he observed in 1896, 'are far more conventional, prejudiced, and "bourgeois" than the middle-class ... there is not a single democratically constituted authority in England, including the House of Commons, that would not be much more progressive if it were not restrained by fear of the popular vote.'[17] The chief obstruction to the advance of Socialism was not, he argued, 'the wicked machinations of the capitalist, but ... the stupidity, the narrowness ... of all classes, and especially of the class which suffers most by the existing system'.[18]

This loss of faith in democracy and the capacity of the masses led Shaw even further than the Webbs towards a non-partisan, elitist collectivism.[19] His faith in collectivism was not affected; the means and not the end had to be altered. As Webb stressed the importance of the expert, Shaw stressed the vital role of the leader.

By the middle nineties, after a series of discouraging elections in London and in the nation, a mood of disillusionment with that idol of radicalism, 'the people', had entered the upper echelons of Fabianism. 'Whether the English nation', Beatrice Webb reflected after the Tory victory in the general election of 1895, 'desires the change [to collectivism] or can be brought to desire it, whether if it does desire it, it will have the patience to work it out, is to my mind still an open question. In any case it will be a long business—and mainly dependent on the levelling-up of character and intelligence in the mass of the people.'[20] The *demos* could not be relied upon, at least in the short run, to carry forth the banner of collectivism. This discouragement helped turn Shaw and the Webbs away from their former attachment to the radicals, and towards 'flirtations' with the Conservatives and the Rosebery Liberals. As Fabianism detached itself from the conventional 'left', the original meaning of 'permeation'—turning radicals into Socialists—gave way to that of winning over the ruling classes to collectivist measures.

[17] 'Illusions of Socialism', in *Forecasts of the Coming Century*, ed. Edward Carpenter (London, 1897), 160.
[18] Ibid., 161.
[19] See Shaw's essay in *Politics in 1896*, ed. Frederick Whelan (London, 1897), 92.
[20] *Our Partnership*, 127 (10 July 1895).

Wallas's examination of democracy was thus begun at a time when other Fabian leaders were also revising their early faith. He shared his colleagues' sense of the importance of intelligence and expertise, and their impatience with the electoral process. However, he could not let the matter rest at that. If the inadequacy of elections for securing good government was dealt with, as Webb wished, by severely limiting their importance, Wallas felt that democracy would become a sham. Democracy for both Webb and Shaw was a means of procuring *consent* by the populace to the measures of an *élite*. For Wallas it had to be a means of securing at least some popular *understanding* and intelligent participation in government. 'If we cannot be experts ourselves', he wrote in a tract for the London School Board election of 1894, 'we can at least learn to distinguish between the expert and the charlatan.'[21] 'Self-government' he defined in a Fabian lecture as 'collective action preceded and controlled by collective thought'.[22] The electoral process had to be the means for generating that collective thought.[23] As Webb never ceased to be a bureaucrat at heart, so Wallas never ceased being a teacher in his outlook.

Seeking to strengthen 'self-government', Wallas began to study electoral machinery and electoral psychology, and the relation between the two. Nor were his studies merely academic. In 1894 he actually took to the hustings, standing for election to the London School Board.

An official in the London school system since 1887, he had even earlier exhorted Socialists to involve themselves in local school administration and politics.[24] The London School Board had fallen into the hands of the Conservative-clerical party, known as the 'Moderates', which pursued a policy of keeping expenditure down to a minimum in the interests both of economy and of protecting the relative position of the Church schools. The 'Progressive' organization had been rejuvenated by Annie Besant's successful campaign for the Board in 1888, but the well-financed Moderates retained control and won back their losses in 1891. Here was a fertile field for cultivation. A well-organized campaign for better education had good prospects of success, for only 30 per cent of the electorate had voted in 1891.[25] Wallas's Fabian philosophy had always emphasized education

---

[21] *The Case Against Diggleism*, a 200 page tract for the Progressive campaign (co-authored with Harold Spender, a Liberal publicist), xi. The title referred to the 'Moderate' (conservative) chairman of the L.S.B., the Rev. J. R. Diggle.

[22] Lecture on 'The Nature of Self-Government', reported in *Fabian News*, April 1892.

[23] The duty of electors, Wallas insisted, was 'to take anxious thought on a certain group of questions'. Ibid.

[24] Lecture on 'Education' (WP).

[25] 'The Coming School Board Election', reported in *Fabian News*, April 1894.

FROM SOCIALISM TO SOCIAL PSYCHOLOGY

as the prime engine of social improvement. 'It is easy for the State to supply material wants', he pointed out to his fellow Fabians, 'but it is not so easy for it to supply moral and intellectual needs. Yet it must be done.'[26] To seek a place on the London School Board would be a natural outgrowth of Wallas's Fabian views. In December 1893, he was elected to the twelve-member Executive Committee in charge of organizing the Progressive School Board campaign, and in the spring decided to stand for election.[27]

This School Board campaign was Wallas's initiation into the heart of democratic politics—the election. His commitment to 'ordinary political methods', to Socialism through gradualism, depended, at bottom, on the efficacy of the democratic electoral process. Yet a relatively democratic franchise had resulted in a reactionary administration of the schools in the interest of a minority. What was the flaw in democracy that had allowed this to happen? Wallas found it in the fact of public indifference, in the 70 per cent who had not bothered to vote.[28]

It is an ancient experience that, whenever the public becomes indifferent, a public body falls into the hands of those who have a strong private motive for energy. Public mismanagement, in other words, always means public indifference. There is nothing on which London is so indifferent as education.[29]

How could this indifference be explained

The London public are occupied, it may be said, with many other problems—with all the problems of municipal and imperial politics. Their power is hampered by the cumulative vote—a harassing and perplexing electoral anomaly, which gives every advantage to a small, well-organised party, and which calls upon enthusiasm to manifest itself in the restriction, rather than the multiplication of candidates. Again, the difference between the political and educational electoral areas confuses the plans of the Progressive party; while their opponents have ready to hand a gigantic parochial machine which can be applied with the least possible expenditure of energy and money. Last, but not least, there is the ever-lasting excuse, always possessing a certain amount of truth, that education is a subject for experts, on which the average man cannot be expected to speak to any profit or use.[30]

These explanations, however, were inadequate; they were really just an expansion of the original accusation. In the last analysis, the Evangelical in Wallas saw the psychological problem as the deeper-rooted one: 'these

[26] 'The Coming School Board Election', reported in *Fabian News*, April 1894.
[27] Fabian Society Executive Minute Books, 1893–4 (Fabian Society Office).
[28] 'The Coming School Board Election', *Fabian News*, April 1894.
[29] *The Case Against Diggleism*, viii.
[30] Ibid., ix–x.

things are a barrier and a burden to Londoners precisely because of their indifference. If we all really cared for education, we should find in them merely a spur to our energy, and an impulse to our enthusiasm'.[31] How could enthusiasm for education be aroused? 'We must', he urged, 'educate ourselves unto the need of education.'[32] The present campaign, Wallas felt, offered an excellent opportunity; every Progressive candidate should become a missionary. Elections were not merely opportunities to register preformed opinions, but an educational process of forming opinions.

Wallas's 'missionary campaign' was a psychological solution to a psychological problem, but far too simple for the situation.[33] The actual campaign was difficult and somewhat disillusioning. The high moral tone with which it began soon degenerated into ugly party strife. Though Wallas won his seat and the Progressives made gains, the Moderates retained a small majority.

This collision with political reality seems to have brought home forcefully to Wallas how slender a reed democracy was. Just how forcefully can be seen from his account of one such contact a few years later, when he spent the half hour before the close of the vote in one of the polling stations of a very poor district:

The voters who came in were the result of the 'final rally' of the canvassers on both sides. They entered the room in rapid but irregular succession, as if they were jerked forward by a hurried and inefficient machine. About half of them were women, with broken straw hats, pallid faces, and untidy hair. All were dazed and bewildered, having been snatched away in carriages or motors from the making of match-boxes, or button-holes, or cheap furniture, or from the public house, or, since it was Saturday evening, from bed. Most of them seemed to be trying, in the unfamiliar surroundings, to be sure of the name for which, as they had been reminded at the door, they were to vote. A few were drunk, and one man, who was apparently a supporter of my own, clung to my neck while he tried to tell me of some vaguely tremendous fact which just eluded his power of speech. I was very anxious to win, and inclined to think I had won, but my chief feeling was an intense conviction that this could not be accepted as even a decently satisfactory method of creating a government for a city of five million inhabitants....[34]

[31] *The Case Against Diggleism*, xi.
[32] Ibid., xi.
[33] In 1897 the Progressives improved their position over 1894 with a much lower turn-out of voters. Wallas was compelled to discard his equation of public indifference with reactionary and ineffective government, and his initial remedy of simply 'bringing out the 70 per cent'. The behaviour of a democratic electorate was proving more complex than he had thought.
[34] *Human Nature in Politics* (1908; Lincoln, Neb., 1962), 243–4.

Wallas's experience with the workings of democracy gave a new significance to the biography he was writing of Francis Place, the Benthamite radical of the early nineteenth century. This study of Place had developed out of his work in the Fabian Society, for Wallas had found himself far more attracted by 'the history of the Socialist idea' than by the economic arguments that preoccupied contemporary Socialists.[35] His lectures on Chartism (not yet then a subject of historical study) during 1888 helped to introduce a new measure of historical self-consciousness into Fabianism. These lectures, Shaw later recalled,

> wrought a tremendous disillusionment as to the novelty of our ideas and methods of propaganda; much new gospel suddenly appeared to us as stale failure; and we recognised that there had been weak men before Agamemnon, even as far back as in Cromwell's army. The necessity for mastering the history of our own movement and falling into our ordered place in it became apparent.... [36]

In 1892, while working in the British Museum on Chartism, Wallas discovered a large uncatalogued collection of papers of Francis Place. This rich find led him to postpone his planned book on the Chartists and write a biography of Place first. Place's life intrigued Wallas as an example of the practical effect of the ideas of the Philosophic Radicals.[37]

As he immersed himself in Place's career, however, he began to see its relevance for the wider political questions he was simultaneously pondering. Place, in Westminster, 'almost alone among the English politicians of his time', had had 'an intimate and practical acquaintance' with the actuality of democracy.[38] Like Wallas, Place had experienced the difficulties and shortcomings of democracy. 'There is one danger', Wallas observed, 'to which those who are in close contact with the actual facts of political work are peculiarly liable, but which Place entirely escaped. He did not become cynical.'[39] He explained:

> It often happens that a politician, having started with the idea that he is following the rushing current of popular enthusiasm, and having found that his real work consists in creating, by all sorts of ingenious shifts, a poor semblance of interest among a deeply indifferent public, comes to think of himself as a charlatan, and of his work as rather disreputable amusement. Place however, understood the machinery of politics without despising it.[40]

[35] Letter to Pease, 10 Jan. 1916 (WP).
[36] In Pease, op. cit., 277–8. See the summaries of these lectures in *Our Corner*, Aug. and Sept. 1888.
[37] Letter to F. C. Miers, 14 Nov. 1892 (WP).
[38] *Life of Francis Place*, 154.
[39] Ibid., 192.   [40] Ibid., 192.

What had enabled Place to understand politics without becoming cynical? What gave him his faith in democracy, despite his complete awareness of the political ignorance and indifference of most people? The source of Place's confidence, Wallas discovered, was Utilitarian psychology in its earliest and simplest form. Place, coming under the influence of Bentham and James Mill, completely accepted their psychology and its political application. According to his psychology, when men were informed, they always sought their own interest, and the majority of men, once their ignorance had been sufficiently overcome, naturally sought the majority interest. The public good and the good of the majority of the public were synonymous. As Place wrote in 1830:

the vulgarity . . . make fewer mistakes than other men are apt to do. The reason for this is, they have fewer sinister interests to induce them to do wrong; their choice is influenced by the desire to do good to themselves, and it so happens that their good must always be the public good. . . . [41]

Wallas found himself wondering: did this image of 'political man' fit his experience? A decade earlier he and his friends were finding the image of 'economic man' held by Place and his circle to be out of touch with reality, a misleading abstraction based on false assumptions about human behaviour. Yet Place had felt his economics and his politics to be two sides of the same coin; perhaps he had been right. Perhaps they were both based on the same false psychology. In this puzzled 'second look' at Place, the seeds of *Human Nature in Politics* began to germinate.

At the same time, then, that the School Board campaign stimulated his political inquiry, it and the study of Place encouraged the development of a psychological approach. During the campaign and his subsequent sitting on the Board, Wallas came increasingly to view the problems of modern life as fundamentally psychological. The role of education in social progress, he felt, was to stimulate and nurture the intellect, imagination, and emotions of what we would today call 'culturally deprived' children—to alter their psychology. Education did not merely 'open eyes', it 'opened hearts', an even more important function.[42] Wallas wanted to 'teach that the teacher is not merely a dead channel by which information is given to the children'. The children had to 'have not only knowledge but motive behind them'.[43]

[41] *Life of Francis Place*, 155.
[42] *The Case Against Diggleism*, xi.
[43] Talk on 'The Task of London's Education System', Philadelphia, 9 January 1897 (WP).

FROM SOCIALISM TO SOCIAL PSYCHOLOGY 43

Wallas's commitment to education, as we have seen, was more deeply rooted than his Socialism. He felt he had discovered in Socialism the necessary means to that sort of education which was the foundation of the 'good life'. The socialization of material life, he believed, would lead to the socialization of spiritual life; the elimination of the profit motive would foster the creation of social motive. His municipal Socialism had envisaged municipal ownership and services as the means whereby municipal spirit would be developed. This spirit would be first developed in the struggle for this ownership and these services, and then confirmed and strengthened by the new environment thus created.

In the 1890s this identification of education and a change in human psychology with Socialism loosened, as Wallas's interests expanded and as human psychology appeared ever more complex. In organizing an election campaign, in standing as a candidate himself, and later in educational administration, Wallas found it ever more difficult to believe that any programme of structural reform alone would solve the real psychological problems, or that any doctrinaire philosophy was capable of grasping the complexities of human behaviour and social life. His disillusionment in this way spread from the questioning of democracy as an adequate political means to the loss of faith in collectivism as a complete and sufficient programme.

Modern urban society, as he observed it in London, seemed to Wallas to provide a new environment for human beings—not only materially but psychologically as well. In the 1890s, in his educational work, in the settlement work he engaged in,[44] and in his electioneering, this latter environment loomed larger and larger—complex, subtle, and unexplored. Ever since his days as a schoolmaster, the 'human material' of society had interested him more than institutions. The answers to social questions now seemed to lie in these building-blocks of society, individual human beings. He now became convinced that what was most needed was a practical science of psychology.

Wallas's political questioning came to a head on a trip to America in the winter of 1896–7. In order to raise money for his next School Board campaign, he accepted an offer to lecture in Philadelphia from December 1896 to February 1897.[45] Under the auspices of the American counterpart

---

[44] See letters from Mrs. Humphrey Ward to Wallas from 1891 on (WP), *New Weekly*, April 1894, and testimonial to Wallas upon his marriage in 1897 (WP). Besides taking part in the work of Toynbee Hall, Wallas also participated in the founding of a settlement house in Hoxton in 1897. See *Fabian News*, Oct. 1897.
[45] Letter to F. C. Miers, 20 Nov. 1896 (WP).

of the University Extension movement, he gave his regular two series of lectures, on 'The Growth of English Institutions' and 'The Story of English Towns', and also some individual talks to various groups. The two problems he had become concerned with were further developed in these lectures: the problem of creating the conditions for the 'good life' in the modern urban environment, and that of the weaknesses of democracy.

Wallas's concern with the first problem grew out of an ardent civic idealism. His starting-point was Aristotle's famous passage from the *Politics*: 'Men come together in cities in order to live and remain together in order to live well.' He asked his American students, as he had his English students, to explain and comment on this passage.[46] Wallas was anxious to spread this 'civic gospel' in a country where individualism and lack of public interest had made city governments a disgrace. He told his American audience,

We have in London determined to assume that city life is not a mere unfortunate existence in civilisation, for the abolition and forgetting of which we should aim; that city life on the whole, if rightly understood, does offer the finest opportunities for the noblest and most active human life, therefore we are not ashamed to spend money in trying to make things beautiful and elevating, as well as merely healthy or useful.[47]

Modern city life was, in the long sweep of human history, in a sense 'artificial', and thus posed difficulties for ordinary human beings.[48] The complication of modern life made it much harder, as Wallas saw it, for individuals to cope with its demands than the simpler existence of the past. 'We are', he remarked to a group of Bryn Mawr students, 'compelled to live in new and untried circumstances.'[49] Yet, with the will, and armed with an understanding of this new environment, men could realize the 'noblest and most active human life'.

Modern government, too, Wallas found far more complex than in the past. It required 'slowly acquired skill and continuous thought' to function.[50] This need could not be satisfied by direct democracy or by purely delegative representation. It could only be fulfilled by representatives free to exercise their judgement and by the establishment and development of a

---

[46] Syllabus for American University Extension course on 'The Story of the English Towns', Jan.–Feb. 1897 (WP).
[47] Lecture on 'History of London', U.S.A., December 1896 (WP).
[48] Syllabus for 'The Story of English Towns', lecture on 'Education' (WP).
[49] Talk on 'Representative Government' at Bryn Mawr College, 13 Feb. 1897 (WP).
[50] Syllabus for 'The Growth of English Institutions', Jan.–Feb. 1897, lecture on 'Civil Service' (WP).

Civil Service. The ordinary democratic electorate, declared Wallas, was utterly inadequate to the task of running a modern state.[51] How, then, was democracy to survive and function? Only, he concluded, by scientifically re-examining both its theory and its practice.

Observations in America stimulated his own re-examination. America was the democratic nation *par excellence*, and the ideal laboratory, he felt, for the study of democracy. Here could be found democracy undiluted by an aristocratic admixture as it was in Europe. Having determined upon landing to commit himself to no generalizations about America, he told a group of Bryn Mawr students that at the end of six weeks he found himself 'already bubbling over with them'.[52] One generalization he offered: 'A thing that strikes a stranger very forcibly is that a certain set of political assumptions is taken for granted in this country that is not found prevailing in European countries.' He went on to explain,

It is assumed everywhere, predominantly in the newspapers, that society is composed of single individuals, each of whom is equally well informed on all matters of which he is supposed to know anything. The assumption implies that all eyes can see the stage of public action, and, consequently, that each voter can at any moment, pronounce an unbiased opinion on any point required.[53]

This assumption that each and every citizen was informed, interested and competent at every moment, Wallas argued, was false, and had dangerous consequences in an era of transition from rural, localized society to a society of great urban concentrations. In truth, most people were politically ignorant and indifferent, with few clearly thought out opinions. An election, therefore, he pointed out in another American lecture, 'is not the mere mechanical and spontaneous expression of an already existing popular will, but a long and painful process of education by which the knowledge from which alone will can result is slowly matured'.[54] For this educational function to be carried out, experience had taught Wallas that electoral machinery would have to be altered to fit the facts of human nature. Frequent and complicated elections defeated their own purpose by making democracy too difficult for the large majority of people. 'The results of democratic government', he had told the Fabians in 1895, 'show

---

[51] His American host, C. A. Brinley of the American Society for the Extension of University Teaching, objected that Wallas was 'no democrat but an oligarchical socialist. You may think', he went on, 'that you are going to rule the world with your handful of highly trained men, but I doubt it.' Letter, 29 Mar. 1897 (WP).
[52] Talk on 'Representative Government' (WP).
[53] Ibid.
[54] Lecture on the 'History of London', December 1896 (WP).

that there is a great danger of elections coming so often that the electorate ceases to trouble itself about them, and they fall into the hands of wire-pullers and party bosses.'⁵⁵ Long and complicated ballots were another obstacle to effective elections. To the Twentieth Century Club of Boston he argued that 'the first requisite in dealing with politics is concentration of public thought—everybody should know everybody for whom he votes.'⁵⁶

The 'educational process' of an election required, Wallas insisted, not only the improvement of the conditions in which the electorate learned, but also an effective teacher:

The great skill and energy of our eminent politicians have been too long neglected. The influence of political chiefs lies in employing in a scientific way methods that are based on observations of popular conditions, desires and tendencies. These men inject will, free will, into voters.⁵⁷

'The most effective election', he concluded, 'is the election of one widely analysed man, who administrates with the advisory aid of experts.'⁵⁸ Only in this way could the requirements of the maximum possible effectiveness in administration and the maximum possible public understanding and participation in government both be satisfied. In this conclusion Wallas shared Webb's interest in the expert and Shaw's in the leader, but not to bypass or down-grade democratic procedures; rather to make these procedures as effective as possible in the light of a realistic understanding of the facts of politics and human psychology.

The most important task, in Wallas's view, beyond specific improvements in the machinery of democracy, was to improve our understanding of politics. A true science of politics had to be developed, beginning with the demolition of false beliefs and confusions. He urged his Bryn Mawr audience to apply 'searching criticism' to 'the loose phrases of today', to 'cut through the mists that hedge the science of politics, and get to that state of acknowledged ignorance from which the beginning of wisdom may spring'.⁵⁹ The 'real title' of his Bryn Mawr talk, he revealed, was 'Some Prolegomena to a Possible Future Science of Politics'. He then proceeded to suggest lines of research leading to an exact quantitative science of

⁵⁵ Lecture on 'The Issues of the County Council Election', reported in *Fabian News*, April 1895. In the early nineties government in London was divided among a number of different elective bodies, with usually several elections in one year.
⁵⁶ Lecture on 'Democracy', reported in *Boston Herald*, 21 Feb. 1897 (WP).
⁵⁷ Ibid.
⁵⁸ Ibid. This is the direction in which most democratic governments have developed since 1897.
⁵⁹ Talk on 'Representative Government', Bryn Mawr, 13 Feb. 1897 (WP).

politics, pointing to the current tendency on the part of the moral sciences to borrow the methods so successful in the natural sciences. Such research, he predicted, would produce reliable answers to questions of public interest now hopelessly in dispute.

By 1897 Wallas had found democracy, particularly in its American form, to be based on 'abstract ideas' and 'an arbitrary psychology'.[60] The task he set before himself (and before others) was to replace abstractions with knowledge, arbitrary psychology with a scientifically verifiable psychology. His work on the life of Place, his electioneering for the School Board, his teaching, and his visit to America all led to this decision. As he remarked many years later, when asked by Beatrice Webb why he had launched off into psychology when they had stuck to the study of institutions, he had discovered himself pondering the question, '*did he or did he not believe in the psychological basis of democracy* as set out by the Utilitarians? He found that he did *not* believe in the democratic theory of life and his books are the result.'[61]

AN ENDING—THE FABIAN SOCIETY

Hand in hand with Wallas's increasing interest in the study of democracy and political psychology went his gradual estrangement from the Fabian Society and from the Webbs. These two related developments set the pattern for the rest of Wallas's career as an independent social thinker.

As Wallas's interests shifted toward political psychology, the intellectual distance between him and the Webbs widened. The Webbs, concerned only with social and political structures and mechanisms, were not receptive to his new work. Although aware of the inadequacies of democracy, they were satisfied with the existing situation, content to work for reform chiefly from above. Expecting less of democracy, they did not share Wallas's sense of crisis.

Wallas had felt uneasy after the early years of the Society, for his concern had from the first tended to expand beyond the confines of strict Fabianism.[62] His Evangelical upbringing impelled him to take a position on virtually every public issue, on pain of moral irresponsibility. Even more, this upbringing, together with the classics he studied at Shrewsbury and Oxford, instilled in him a distaste for 'pure' collectivism as materialistic,

---

[60] See letter from Sidney Webb to Wallas, 26 Oct. 1898 (PP).

[61] *Beatrice Webb's Diaries 1924–32*, ed. Margaret Cole (London, 1956), 74. Wallas, in 1925, dated this disillusionment in 1898, but, as we have seen, it had developed by early 1897.

[62] See 'Socialism and the Fabian Society' (1916), *Men & Ideas*, 105–6.

unless firmly tied to the goal of a 'higher and nobler' life. As the Society became more and more a narrow 'pressure group' for collectivism, ruthlessly excluding from its purview all wider issues, Wallas, though remaining one of the Society's most popular leaders,[63] found his mind and spirit increasingly cramped.

This self-imposed narrowness of the Society tended to remove the Fabians from the position on the left wing of the Liberals which they had taken up in the late eighties, and move them towards an independent political position. Wallas, however, became more deeply rooted than ever in their original position. As a result, he found himself drifting away from the Society.

From 1890 onwards, with Fabian theory more or less worked out, the Society turned its full energies to propagating rather than developing ideas. Two courses were open: to pressurize existing parties or to join in forming a new party. In the context of the early nineties, the first course meant pushing the Liberal party, more amenable to left-wing prodding than the Conservatives.

After the electoral failure of the Social Democratic Federation in 1885, the idea of a separate party received little attention from the Fabians for several years. The 'Fabian Conference' of all reform groups in 1886 illustrated the new attitude: 'parliamentarism' and 'permeation' were seen as two parts of the same programme. The Fabians construed political action as action to capture the Liberal party for a Socialist policy. However, it was not long before disillusionment with the Liberals set in. By the end of 1888, opinion was shifting within the Society. Hubert Bland's contribution to *Fabian Essays*, when delivered as a lecture, provoked heated discussion. Bland had asserted that from a Socialist standpoint, the Liberals were hopeless, and that the Fabian Society should promote the formation of a separate Socialist party, while Webb had reaffirmed the 'permeationist' view.[64] Webb's views prevailed for the moment, but as the success of the *Fabian Essays* brought in many new members, Bland began a campaign to win these recruits to his policy. This campaign against 'Webbite opportunism' came into the open by the beginning of 1891, and 'stormy debates' over political tactics characterized Fabian meetings during 1891 and 1892.[65]

---

[63] Wallas was placed near or at the top of the poll in the annual elections for the Executive Committee. See *Fabian News*, May of the years 1891–5.

[64] *Today*, xi (Jan. 1889), 54–5.

[65] See McBriar, *Fabian Socialism* . . . 246, and letter from Shaw to Sydney Olivier, 16 Dec. 1890 (WP).

FROM SOCIALISM TO SOCIAL PSYCHOLOGY 49

Wallas emerged as Webb's chief supporter.[66] He had been an active permeator for some years, for in addition to being chairman of the Fabian Parliamentary League in 1887-8, he was active and influential in the Metropolitan Radical Federation, struggling within it against the propagandists for the Social Democratic Federation.[67] In November 1890, he had worked out with the then Beatrice Potter the Fabian negotiating position for a meeting with Richard Haldane to arrange an alliance between the progressive Liberals and the Fabian Society.[68] In pursuit of this aim Wallas dined a number of times with leading progressive Liberals.[69] Wallas's support for permeation was anything but 'opportunist'. It arose from a deep commitment to Liberal principles which Webb did not share, and remained after Webb had changed policies.

The disappointing performance of the Liberal Government elected in 1892, together with the rise of the Independent Labour Party, seemed to discredit permeation, and led to the publication of 'To Your Tents, Oh Israel!', a sharp attack upon the Liberals. Wallas opposed the tract, claiming, with some justice, that the Society was rushed into it by fear of being thought complacent by the Independent Labour Party.[70] The decision of the Trade Union Congress of 1893 to establish a fund to support independent Labour-Socialist candidates at both local and parliamentary elections promised to make the development of a powerful independent left-wing party practicable.[71] Though the hopes thus raised were dashed at the Trade Union Congress of 1894, and the Fabian Society refused to join with the I.L.P., there was, to Wallas's disappointment, no real reconciliation with the Liberals. The alternative to Fabian merger with the I.L.P. was coming to be 'independence'. Wallas, the only Liberal at heart among the leaders of the Society, alone held firm to the majority view of 1888-92.

Meanwhile, Wallas found his new position on the London School Board drawing him away from the Society and from Socialism. The election of 1894 had resulted in Progressive gains which, however, fell just short of a majority. With the parties nearly in balance, Wallas set out to follow

[66] 'As Wallas says', Shaw advised another Fabian, 'Postulate, Permeate, Perorate.' *Bernard Shaw: Collected Letters 1874-97*, ed. Dan H. Laurence, (London, 1965), 390 (24 Apr. 1893).
[67] Letter to Sir Charles Russell, 18 Jan. 1887 (WP). Also see McBriar, 237.
[68] See Beatrice Webb's Diary, 1 Dec. 1890 (PP). While these negotiations were going on, Wallas was hoping for Bland's departure from the Society, since he was the greatest obstacle to such an alliance. See letter from Shaw to Wallas, 16 Dec. 1890 (WP).
[69] See letter from Wallas to Beatrice Potter, 1891 (PP), and letter to Sidney Webb, 30 Nov. 1892 (WP).
[70] *Our Partnership*, 110.   [71] McBriar, op. cit., 251.

the example of Webb on the London County Council and to 'politic' among the more open-minded Moderates. Beatrice Webb approvingly watched him 'making friends with the "left wing" of the enemy in the hope of detaching the majority of them from the educational policy of Diggle [the leader of the "Moderates"] and turning the scale'.[72] She went on to note,

It is very curious that both Sidney and Graham, though very advanced in their views, are better liked by the Moderates of the L.C.C. and the L.S.B. than by other members of the Progressive Party. 'Wily Webb', as Sidney is called on the L.C.C., is always colloguing with the more sensible of the Moderates with a view of getting them to agree to things *in detail* which they could hardly accept in bulk. That seems to be Graham's policy which he is carefully beginning on the London School Board.[73]

However, Wallas began to carry this practical approach further even than the Webbs. In a talk to the Fabian Society in the spring of 1895, he contrasted two methods of advocating political or social changes—'religious' and 'scientific'. (This nomenclature was significant; School Board struggles with Churchmen were making him daily more anti-religious.) The first method, typified in his eyes by the attitude of the I.L.P., he condemned as fanatical, proposing instead the application to politics of the 'scientific method'—open-minded and experimental. The scientific approach was more difficult than the religious, but it was the only one that ultimately produced concrete results. The Fabian Society, he declared, had been characterized by the scientific habit of mind. Apparently the purpose of his lecture was to 'inoculate' the Society against any rise of emotionalism or tendency to dogmatism.[74] Wallas spoke here, as he had for several years, as a representative of the 'liberal wing' of the Fabian Society; but now the methods of practicality, open-mindedness and 'piecemealism', no longer clearly served any specifically Socialist ends. In his work on the Board he seemed to find Fabianism no less an ideological encumbrance than Progressivism. 'The triumphs of the [London County] Council had been obtained by ingenuity and by good administration.' Fabians 'should get above the mere consideration of the Fabian and anti-Fabian methods of approaching political questions, and see the problem as it presented itself to the millions who would be called upon to vote'.[75] As a motive for action, he offered instead the consideration of 'the results of human activity on human happiness'—an unideological, but also unhelpful, guide.

[72] *Our Partnership*, 67 (1 Dec. 1894).   [73] Ibid., 67–8.
[74] 'The Issues of the County Council Election', reported in *Fabian News*, Mar. 1895.
[75] Ibid.

FROM SOCIALISM TO SOCIAL PSYCHOLOGY

The new burdens of administrative responsibility and the lack of a Progressive majority on the School Board clearly contributed to Wallas's drift away from Socialism. He found,

> It was difficult when one had been holding up the banner of the ideal during the course of an election, after the victory to come to the first committee meeting and to begin to examine the ideal, and inquire whether it could be carried out or not.[76]

This experience led Wallas to accept and value compromise. 'In an administrative body', he discovered, 'the man who becomes a martyr for his opinions, who insisted upon standing by the whole of his accepted principles, without doubting... was entirely out of place.'[77] The *limits* of compromise, however, were left undefined. How much of Wallas's Socialism survived, after doubt and compromise, was increasingly uncertain. Harold Laski observed, many years later, that 'Wallas was not, by nature, the fighting party man. He could rarely be interested in tightness of doctrine or symmetry of institutions. His genius was for dealing with persons and their relations.' His dissatisfaction with the Fabians was part of what Laski called 'his lifelong inability to tread a narrow path'.[78]

Wallas's drift away from the Fabian Society came to a head in August 1895, when he visited the Webbs at their summer place. Beatrice Webb noted,

> He is going through a crisis... wants to leave the Fabian Society and be free of all formulas and intellectual ties so as to give himself over as he thinks to empirical administration and 'untrammelled' thought. It is interesting to watch the struggle in his mind. He says, as I think truly, that he has not changed his mind and that he is still an economic collectivist of an empirical kind. And he admits that the Fabian Society has explicitly and implicitly declared its creed to be purely empirical or hypothetical. But he complains that some of the members and the greater part of the public identify the word Socialist with a cut-and-dried formula held with theological fervour and that on the one hand he is treated as a traitor by the extreme section, and on the other hand as a fanatic by the outside public—that his position is misunderstood. Behind this are the facts: in his present life on the School Board, and in his University Extension work he is constantly associating with cultivated sceptics either with the purely practical or with the purely academic mind. To these men the Socialists are either irritating or contemptible; and Graham naturally resents the feeling he is arousing. He lacks patience to quietly persist and live the misunderstanding down; he wants to cut the whole thing away and start fresh in the world.[79]

[76] 'The Issues of the County Council Election', reported in *Fabian News*, Mar. 1895.
[77] Ibid.   [78] *Economica*, xxxviii (Nov. 1932), 406.
[79] Diary, 25 Sept. 1895 (PP).

Reluctant to let him go, the Webbs argued that either his leaving the Society would not be noticed, or, if it were, it would be understood to mean that he had gone back on his faith in democratic collectivism and greater economic equality. He was already committed, they reminded him, and at the age of forty it was a little late to start afresh.[80] As a result, Wallas agreed to remain in the Society but resigned from the Executive.[81] 'Wallas presented an anxious problem', Shaw wrote to one of his actress friends, 'as he is getting very uneasy in the bonds of socialism, and we all had fearful and prolonged arguments and pleadings which had to be steered carefully clear of ending in strained bonds and possibly broken ones.'[82] Beatrice Webb reflected,

Poor Graham, he is one of those sensitive, self-conscious men who will always be in trouble about his soul. Anyway his present attitude makes him restless and unsatisfied with us. He is lonely and overworked and wants a little mental coddling—and we are inclined to douche him with cold water! Perhaps we do not fully recognize the worth of his work—he is finding appreciation elsewhere—men like Arthur Sidgwick and Lyulph Stanley are waking up to his fine qualities and we are taking them all for granted. No wonder our influence is waning![83]

The lack of appreciation and encouragement coming from the Webbs is understandable in view of Wallas's diverging outlook. While their attention remained centred upon the progress of collectivism, Wallas was becoming more than ever interested in the whole range of political questions. Wallas was, unlike the Webbs, a Socialist *and* a Liberal, and in London government was being cultivated by Liberals like Sidgwick and Stanley. At the same time, as we have seen, he was becoming even more sceptical of the self-sufficiency of collectivism.

The distance opening up between Wallas and the Webbs was greatly widened by differing views on education. Here Wallas was the 'dogmatist', protesting against the violation of 'principles' by Webb and the Society. Between 1897 and 1904 both Wallas and Webb held leading posts in the educational administration of London. While Webb was chairman of the Technical Education Committee of the L.C.C., Wallas held the key position on the L.S.B. of chairman of the School Management Committee.[84] They worked together on many issues—on the general expansion and improvement of public education they were as one against the argu-

[80] Diary, 25 Sept. 1895 (PP).
[81] *Fabian News*, Nov. 1895.
[82] *Collected Letters*, 549 (to Janet Achurch) (24 Aug. 1895).
[83] Diary, 25 Sept. 1895.
[84] See Sidney Webb, *Economica*, xxxviii (Nov. 1932), 403-4.

ments of economy and 'individualism'. However, the question of state aid to the voluntary (Church-run) schools drove an ever-widening wedge between them.

Though not decidedly anti-clerical in the eighties, Wallas became, after election to the School Board, an ever more enthusiastic secularist. The School Board, after all, was in direct competition with the voluntary schools, and the clerical party was the chief obstacle to any expansion or improvement of its activities. It was not surprising, then, that Wallas came to regard the voluntary schools as 'the enemy'. Also, for one who saw the chief task of public education, not in providing skills or useful knowledge, but in 'opening the eyes and the heart', the dogmatism and sectarianism of the voluntary schools were intolerable. If education had had a less exalted role in his thought, he would not have been led to take the secularist position which did much to make co-operation with the Webbs impossible.

Webb, from the wider vantage-point of the London County Council, felt no hostility towards the voluntary schools. Having more narrowly collectivist and utilitarian educational aims, he saw no necessary opposition between the voluntary and the Board schools. Whether religion were taught or not mattered little to him, as long as the 'three Rs' were also taught. Webb had shared the early Fabian opposition to religious instruction in the Board schools, but had never felt strongly about it; and, in any case, the voluntary schools were a different case. He was determined on education reform to raise the level of efficiency and widen the scope of London education, and with a Conservative Government entrenched in Whitehall, knew it could be attained only by winning over the Church interest. He was ready, indeed eager, to buy unification and expansion of public education in London with public aid for the voluntary schools.[85]

The conflict between Wallas and Webb over educational policy began with the Conservative Government's abortive Education Bill of 1896, combining administrative reform and a 'reward' for the Anglicans whose support had been vital to the Conservatives in the elections of 1895. It provided for the extension of the powers of the County Councils over education, for state assistance to the voluntary schools, and for the allowance, in certain cases, of separate religious instruction in the Board school buildings. Wallas was completely opposed to the Bill, writing and lobbying for its withdrawal. Webb, on the other hand, did not want to lose its

[85] See Elie Halévy, *Imperialism and the Rise of Labour* (London, 1926) (2nd revised edn., 1951) pt. II. § i. For a discussion centred on the role of the Fabians, see McBriar, cp. cit., 206–18.

reform provisions, and advised Wallas to concentrate on trying to improve it by amendments.[86] Shaw registered his strong support for the Bill and blamed the anti-Church fanaticism of the Liberals for its withdrawal.[87] From this point on, Wallas found himself in constant opposition to his two colleagues.

For the next several years, Wallas continued to argue educational policy with other Fabians. He agreed that educational authority was divided among many bodies with too little co-ordination, but his solution was to expand the authority of the School Board over all levels of education and, ultimately, over all educational institutions.[88] In education he proved more of a collectivist than Webb, who accepted the political necessity of educational diversity, and, apart from this necessity, favoured diversity over complete unification in education.[89]

By May 1899, when Webb proposed that the Society advocate abolishing the School Boards, Wallas had come to agree that control of education by the London County Council would be better than control by an *ad hoc* body like the London School Board, but he still had his doubts. The L.C.C., he objected, might be overloaded with work, and education would suffer from being only one of many issues demanding the attention of the councillors. His chief objection, however, was to the state aid to voluntary schools which would accompany administrative reform in the scheme Webb was working out with the Government's Education Department. The voluntary schools at this time were declining both in expenditures and in number of students enrolled relative to the Board schools, and a secularist could reasonably hope for their continued decline if only the state did not step in to save them. Webb's arguments, based on administrative efficiency, carried the Society, and plans were made for a tract on the subject.[90]

Wallas eventually came out for the abolition of the School Board, the sole Progressive on the Board to do so, but his opposition to religious education only became more intense.[91] During a visit to the Webbs, he argued his views with Beatrice, who went much further than Sidney in her

[86] See letter from Webb, 8 Sept. 1896 (PP).   [87] *Politics in 1896*, 100–2.
[88] Lecture on 'The Issues of the School Board Election', reported in *Fabian News*, Nov. 1897. The L.S.B. had authority only over non-private, elementary education. Wallas's position was basically the same as when he first became interested in educational policy, if more fervent. He had approvingly noted in his lecture on Aristotle's *Politics* in 1887 that Aristotle had advocated universal state education and opposed religious education.
[89] See Webb's recollections on this period, written in 1928, quoted by McBriar, op. cit., 215.
[90] *Fabian News*, June 1899.   [91] See Wallas's letter to Pease, 5 Feb. 1916 (WP).

sympathy with religion. He recognized but deplored the growing tolerance of, if not sympathy with, religious teaching on the part of confessed agnostics.

He distinguished with some subtlety [Beatrice recorded] between the old broad Church party, who wished to broaden the creed of the Church to one which they could emphatically accept, and those religious-minded agnostics, who accept Church teaching, not because they believe its assertions to be true, but lest worse befall the child's mind in the form of a crude materialistic philosophy. 'I cannot see the spirit of genuine reform, if there is no portion of the Church's teaching which you object to more than any other; if you cease to discriminate between what you accept and what you reject, denying all and accepting all, with the same breath, denying the dogmas as statements of fact accepting them as interpreting a spirit which pleases you. [92]

Accepting the passage of the Education Act of 1902, Wallas hoped to continue fighting against religious education on the London County Council, and tension deepened between him and the Webbs.[93] Beatrice observed that

he has a deeply-rooted suspicion that Sidney is playing false with regard to religious education. He wants all religious teaching abolished. As Sidney is not himself a 'religionist', Graham thinks that he too should wish it swept away. Politically, this seems to Sidney impossible, whilst I do not desire it even if it were possible. So between us, we are prepared for a working agreement with the mammon of ecclesiasticism. Poor dear Wallas consequently sees this working agreement writ large in every act of the T.E.B. [Technical Education Board], however irrelevant it may be to the religious issue.... This suspicion makes frank co-operation between Sidney and our old friend impossible—and though personal relations remain affectionate and appreciative, I fear there must be some official friction if not actual hostility. As Sidney's side is bound to win, ... it is to be hoped that Graham will retire from educational administration.[94]

Mrs. Webb was on strong ground in criticizing Wallas's political realism. Though he had argued for open-mindedness in pressing Socialist aims, Wallas changed horses when it came to one of his Liberal principles, particularly anti-clericalism. Here he revealed himself as a preacher and

---

[92] *Our Partnership*, 241–2 (5 June 1902). For another rationalist's argument over religion with Mrs. Webb around this time, see Leonard Woolf, *Sowing* (London, 1960), 54–5.
[93] See letter from Webb to Wallas, 4 Dec. 1902 (PP).
[94] *Our Partnership*, 256–7 (16 Jan. 1903). Wallas tried to win over Shaw, but failed. Beatrice noted that 'G.B.S. is too rootedly sceptical about all alternative philosophies to be inclined to oust Christianity by *force majeure*'. Ibid.

not a politician, driven by moral imperatives rather than by political judgement. The progress of public education in England had already been greatly retarded by religious conflict, and the Webbs no doubt were right in seeing Wallas's preoccupation with this as essentially regressive. However, the Webbs' position was not based solely on realism. Mrs. Webb's powerful sympathy with religion made her deeply hostile, apart from political reasons, to anti-clericalism and militant secularism.

In any event, Wallas retired from neither educational administration nor criticism. He complained to the Fabian Executive that Webb's draft Tract on the machinery of the Education Act, promised to be non-controversial, was in fact, a polemic against the opponents of the Act. He maintained,

I myself have every desire so to work the new Act as to get the greatest public advantage from it. I shall be engaged in the next few years in an attempt to amend it—and, if I have any share in administering it, I shall desire, where in my judgement such a denominational monopoly of education opportunities exists as to create hardship, to diminish that hardship.

It would be impossible for me to do either of these things with any effect if I were responsible for a Tract denouncing and sneering at that policy.[95]

The campaign for the L.C.C. in February 1904 found Wallas and the Webbs on opposite sides. Beatrice admitted

it is an uncomfortable fact that we are convinced that on the Council he will obstruct our side of things without promoting his own—one has, in this ruthless world, to accept uncomfortable facts and act on them. We try to persuade ourselves that it will be better for him if he drops out for the next three years—or at any rate has the minor position of a co-opted member.[96]

Wallas and the Progressives won, however, and he found himself together with Sidney Webb on the County Council. Neither of them possessed the power they had had before the storm aroused by the new Act. Henceforth Wallas was to devote less of his time and interest to educational administration and more to his political and social studies. But the break with the outlook of the Webbs was definitive.

The education issue was by no means the only question on which Wallas found himself opposed to the position of the Fabian Society. Imperialism and tariff reform were two other such questions, and it was disagreement over Shaw's Tariff Tract that precipitated his decision to sever ties. Wallas was critical of Shaw's *Fabianism and the Empire*.[97] Shaw, it seemed to him,

[95] Letter to Pease, 16 March 1903 (Fabian Society Office).
[96] Diary, 27 Feb. 1904 (PP).
[97] Letter to Pease, 5 Sept. 1900 (Fabian Society Office).

ignored the non-white races and attacked the idea of local self-government. Wallas, though not a pro-Boer,[98] held views fairly close to those of anti-imperial Liberals, while Shaw, ridiculing 'Cobdenism', as he had 'the damned compact Liberal majority', could not have been further from them. As the leading representative of the 'Liberal wing' of Fabianism, Wallas struggled on imperial as on domestic issues against the Society's increasingly strident repudiation of Liberalism.

The final break came over the tariff question. Shaw was not, he felt, the proper person to draft a tract, since he was an ardent protectionist.[99] The resulting tract, *Fabianism and the Fiscal Question*, while pretending to be impartial, and containing free trade modifications by other members of the Executive, was Protectionist in underlying assumptions and phraseology. Wallas's objections went beyond the fiscal question to the general political outlook of the tract. 'On the questions which divide the Liberal and Conservative parties', he maintained, 'I am a Liberal.' Shaw's draft, however, implied

that the Liberal Programme in education, etc. is (and by implication in Free Trade) not insufficient but actively *reactionary* as compared with the Tory Programme. . . . I am still a 'permeator' and not a follower of ILP tactics. But the effective phrases . . . are pure ILP.[100]

Wallas moved that Shaw's draft not be printed, but was defeated by a large majority. He thereupon submitted his resignation.[101]

[98] *Our Partnership*, 188–9 (30 Oct. 1899).
[99] Letter to Pease, 21 Jan. 1904 (Fabian Society Office). [100] Ibid.
[101] *Fabian News*, Feb. 1904. The letter of resignation went as follows:

'Dear Pease—I am resigning my membership of the Fabian. For a good many years past, in fact, since I left the Executive, I have, as you know, been able to give very little time to the Society. I have drafted almost nothing myself, and when I have disagreed with the form or substance of any tract I have come forward as a very unhelpful critic of work already done.

'I have, for instance, disagreed with some minor points in the London Education Tract which is about to appear, and with many important points in the Tariff Tract which was passed last Friday. On that occasion it was clear that the vast majority of the Society was in agreement with the Executive and against me.

'If I were an independent student I might give up criticism and content myself with showing by my membership a general sympathy with the cause of social reform. But I am an active politician, and even such matters as election tactics or the details of administrative machinery, which are of small importance to a student, do create real difficulties for any man who has, day by day, to adopt and defend a position of his own on these very points.

'I have therefore determined to go. Those who, like yourself, have been fellow members of mine for these last eighteen years will understand the regret with which I do so. I should like you, even now, to think of me as an unattached friend of the Society, and to allow me to help the Local Government Information Bureau on any questions connected with my work.'

In the years since Wallas had given up his seat on the Executive, the Fabian Society had moved further away from his type of radicalism. Already somewhat alienated from the Liberals in 1895, it became positively anti-Liberal by 1903. Elie Halévy, a close friend of Wallas's in later years, described the Webbs at this time as 'convinced imperialists . . . looking to a national and militarist state to realize their programme . . . [feeling] contempt for every formula of Liberalism and free trade.'[102] The meetings of the Society were addressed by imperialists and anti-Liberals like Bland, Benjamin Kidd, Cecil Chesterton, and W. G. Hewins. In this Society Wallas saw no place for himself. Taking an active part in the work of the 'advanced' political groups, he felt himself compromised by this anti-Liberalism.[103]

However, there were other, less immediate causes for this divergence. Wallas remarked in reviewing Pease's *History of the Fabian Society*,

I always, after the first few years, felt rather restless in the Society. I can explain my own difficulties best by quoting a few facts from Pease's book. Tract 70 in 1896, for instance, declared that the Fabian Society 'has no distinctive opinions on the Marriage Question, Religion, Art . . . or any other subject than its own special business of practical Democracy and Socialism'. In 1899 the Executive argued that the question at issue between the Boers and the British Government was one 'which Socialism cannot solve and does not touch'. I do not think that the Society has ever published a word on its own responsibility about India. In the present war the Society 'has made no pronouncement and adopted no policy'. In my case other things than our own 'special business' were always breaking in, and disturbing the 'practical' problems of democracy and equality. I could not decide on a policy as to educational administration without bringing in my views as to the effect of ecclesiastical control, or on free trade without considering its influence on international relations, or on such a manifesto against a Liberal Government as To Your Tents, O Israel (1893), without considering the probable influence of a Conservative Government on a number of matters which lay outside our 'special business'.[104]

The narrow concentration of the Fabian Society reflected the outlook of the Webbs. This outlook was quite different from Wallas's as their portrait in Wells's *New Machiavelli* suggested. Where Wallas was (perhaps excessively) open to every new problem, pondering and inconclusive,

---

[102] *Imperialism and the Rise of Labour*, 365.

[103] Pease, in his *History*, over-emphasizes the importance of the educational issue by making it virtually the sole reason for Wallas's departure. McBriar, on the other hand, gives too great a role to the disagreement over tariff reform.

[104] 'Socialism and the Fabian Society', (1916), *Men & Ideas*, 105–6.

FROM SOCIALISM TO SOCIAL PSYCHOLOGY

they strictly defined their interests, and their views within that sphere were definite and determined; in matters outside they took no interest.[105] Wallas and the Webbs were far apart not only in their approach to problems, but in the kinds that interested them. The Webbs were interested in social organization, believing that the 'good society' could be attained by constructing the appropriate institutions. They were concerned with the structure and functions of government, not with individuals.[106] Wallas, from his early Socialist days, had been interested in social psychology, and in the individuals that make up society, and this interest grew ever more dominant. As Wallas later observed to Alfred Zimmern, the Webbs were interested in town councils, while he was interested in town councillors.[107]

Wallas's mental development led him away, not only from the Webbs and from the Fabian Society, but from the purely economic and structural approach to social improvement, which they had come to represent. By the time of his resignation he had come to feel, strongly and clearly, that social and political problems were fundamentally psychological in nature.[108] He had felt something of this as early as the 1880s, but as this

[105] Leonard Woolf, whose mind was similar in many respects to Wallas's, observed of the Webbs:
'They had drawn for themselves a circle which enclosed certain subjects and departments of human life. Those subjects were *their* subjects: they studied them closely and continually; they had a theory and a policy with regard to them; there were certain things which they wanted done with regard to them. . . . Anything outside the circumference of their circle was treated differently. It belonged to a "subject" which was not theirs. Their opinion upon it was therefore irrelevant, and in some way or other the subject itself was irrelevant.'
The Webbs and Their Work, ed. Margaret Cole (London, 1949), 260.
[106] The Webbs seemed to Kingsley Martin 'absurdly to over-simplify all the psychological factors. . . . they did not recognize the intractable complexity of individuals'. *Editor* (London, 1968), 71. Perhaps a partial exception should be made for Beatrice, who did have a curiosity about social behaviour which 'never reduced itself to a study of the institutions merely as social *mechanisms* apart from the motives that drove them on'. (G. D. H. Cole, in *The Webbs and Their Work*, 282). However, Beatrice kept this curiosity largely confined to her diaries and followed her husband's lead in public work. It was this psychological interest that made her more sympathetic to Wallas's work than Sidney, though still not very understanding. See, for example, her diary for 9 Aug. 1932.
[107] Zimmern, *Nationality and Government* (London, 1919), 87–8.
[108] See H. G. Wells, 'The Great Community', *Nation*, xv, 531 (review of Wallas's *The Great Society*). Wallas helped Mrs. Humphrey Ward in writing *Marcella* (1894), a novel dealing with Socialism and social reform, in which the Fabian Society (under the name of the 'Venturist Society') does not come off well. Marcella's conclusion perhaps reflects something of Wallas's mind: 'Not in mere wealth and poverty, she thought, but in things of quite another order—things of social sympathy and relation—alterable at every turn, even under existing conditions, by the human will, lie the real barriers that divide us man from man.' (vol. ii, p. 488.)

view developed and became more definite, he found it increasingly incompatible with Fabianism.

In the early years, Fabianism was still loosely defined and broad enough to include men of varying approaches, but as it became more and more sharply defined, and as it narrowed its scope, Wallas became progressively more uncomfortable, wanting to leave as early as 1895. Wallas's alienation from the Fabian Society was a mutual process; as he developed away from the Society, it was developing away from him.

The Fabian neglect of psychology left it, in Wallas's eyes, without any philosophical coherence. In spite of its claims, Fabianism rested, he began to see, neither on a coherent philosophy nor on a true science of political or social life. Wallas's political studies led him to find Fabianism, like all other existing approaches to politics, inadequate. He left the Fabians, not for another political organization, but to pursue a career as a 'free thinker', searching for a science and a philosophy of politics. 'How is it', he asked in 1899, 'that there exists no party today whose political opinions are based to the same degree as those of the Utilitarians and the Painites upon a complete system of political philosophy?'[109] Wallas's dominant passion was now intellectual as well as practical—'to see human society as an intelligible whole'.[110] 'In the midst of a bustle of activity, politics appeared to have no centre to which its thinking and doing could be referred.' Political science as then known, was 'a science of human relationships with the human beings left out'.[111] Wallas resolved to find the missing centre by returning, in a sense, to his master Aristotle, and putting the human beings back into political science. To accomplish this, he turned from political action to reflection, from Fabian Socialism to social psychology.

[109] *Speaker*, 21 Oct. 1899 (WP).   [110] Ibid.
[111] Walter Lippmann, *A Preface to Politics* (New York, 1913), 72. Lippmann, Wallas's student, was discussing Wallas's contribution to political science.

CHAPTER IV

A NEW VIEW OF POLITICS

THE chief problem of politics, as Wallas came to see it, was one of psychology. He found a great gap between democratic theory and democratic reality in the realm of behaviour; people did not think and act politically as they were 'supposed' to. Classical democratic theory, particularly in its 'purest' American form, assumed a view of human nature and of human motivation which conflicted with Wallas's experiences in London government and his observations in America. In so far as the inadequacy of classical democratic theory had been recognized, it had only discredited any attempt to rest political thought on a definite view of human nature. As a result, Wallas found contemporary thinking about politics to be based either on false assumptions or on nothing whatsoever.

Unwilling to accept either error or confusion, Wallas, with Benthamite determination, sought a way out. The young Kingsley Martin was struck by this determination some years later when walking with Wallas and Lowes Dickinson in Cambridge. Suddenly extending his hand, 'as if striving to grab something that danced, tantalising, before him', Wallas turned to Dickinson and asked, 'Don't you sometimes feel that the solution of the problem of democracy is just *there*, almost within reach, if only you could see more clearly, and grasp more firmly?' Dickinson's eyebrows arched ironically.[1]

Wallas set himself a twofold task: first, to clear the ground by exposing the falsity of the old assumptions about the effect of human motivation on political behaviour; second, and most important, to lay the foundations for a realistic science of politics. This 'Prolegomenon to Politics', as he referred to it, would introduce a new 'scientific' method and a new psychological content. He wanted to stimulate a return to the aims of Bentham, while bringing the Benthamite conception of method and of human nature up to date.

The purpose of Wallas's new science was eminently practical. Following Bentham, he saw the political thinker as a social physician or engineer, using the knowledge gained from political science to solve immediate

[1] Kingsley Martin, *Harold Laski*, 49.

problems—to treat the 'diseases of democracy' or to calculate the psychological strains involved in a given political structure. With this aim in mind, Wallas set out to reconstruct political thought.

I

Wallas's endeavour sprang from the temper of his time. The dominant mood of Edwardian political thinking was disillusionment and a sense of lost bearings.² Wallas had remarked in 1899 on the contrast, vividly brought home to him by his study of Francis Place, between the certainty and confidence of the political reformers of the early nineteenth century and the lack of these attributes among their latter-day successors.³ The former, he noted, had possessed a coherent and comprehensive political philosophy, whereas the latter did not. This contrast became even more marked as the twentieth century opened. An increasing awareness of the frustrating complexity of reality had eroded the simplistic assumptions of the Painites and the Benthamites without replacing them with any others. The *Nation* remarked in reviewing C. F. G. Masterman's pessimistic *Condition of England* (1908),

What is peculiar to the modern reformer is that the dawn which he greets in his sanguine hour is so very grey and ambiguous a twilight. This is the chief difference between him and his ancestors, the change from confidence to misgiving, from hope to a brooding doubt. All the certainties of politics seem to have melted away in the interval.⁴

'It is a grey moment', another observer noted. 'So many of our cherished watchwords are being reconsidered. . . . What is wrong? We don't quite know.'⁵

The unforeseen problems of democracy stood out most clearly in America, the model of 'pure' democracy, unalloyed by aristocratic, monarchic, or bureaucratic elements.⁶ Wallas's visit in 1896–7 was a decisive step in his intellectual development, for the problems which had begun to bother him in London appeared in magnified and more disturbing form across

---

² See C. H. Driver, 'Political Ideas', in *Edwardian England*, ed. F. J. C. Hearnshaw (1933), 231–76. Driver's is the best general account of Edwardian political thought. See also Samuel Hynes, op. cit., for a general account of Edwardian thought. Hynes's work further supports the characterization of this era as one of uncertainty and anxiety.
³ *Speaker*, 21 Oct. 1899. See *Francis Place*, 362–3.
⁴ *Nation*, i (1909), 357.
⁵ *The Commonwealth* (a Christian Social magazine), Feb. 1909 (review of *Human Nature in Politics*).
⁶ See Wallas's article, 'The American Analogy', *Independent Review*, i (1903), 505.

A NEW VIEW OF POLITICS

the Atlantic.⁷ That democratic government could be the worst enemy of good government, seemed to be an inescapable conclusion to an observer of the corruption and inefficiency existing in America. Why was this? Democratic government, Wallas became aware, presupposed two assumptions: a 'theatre simile' of public opinion—'that all eyes can see the stage of public action', as he noted in 1897—and a rationalistic conception of human motivation—that each voter, seeing his interests, would naturally seek these interests. Neither of these assumptions, upon observation, seemed to hold up. Public opinion and political behaviour were in practice far less simple and understandable than Wallas had been led to believe in his youth. In America this divergence appeared sharper and more disturbing, since it could not be attributed to continued pre-democratic influences.

This problem was also, of course, agitating those in the United States, and Wallas soon became acquainted with the work of E. L. Godkin, the foremost American writer on the subject.⁸ To Godkin the gap between democratic theory and democratic practice was largely one of scale. The men who first began to write on democracy towards the close of the eighteenth and the beginning of the nineteenth centuries, he pointed out,

had really a very small notion of its working on the scale which the modern world witnesses. . . . Their democracies all met in the forum or market place; their leading men were known to every citizen. Nothing seemed easier than to fill the public offices by a mere show of hands. Every man was supposed to be intensely occupied with public affairs, to be eager to vote on them, and to be quite able to vote intelligently. The work of management had not a prominent place in any former democratic scheme.⁹

Management, however, was indispensable in a modern mass democracy, since the size of the polity made 'the work of bringing the popular will to bear in filling the offices of the government, or in performing any act of government' one of great difficulty, requiring almost constant attention from a large army of professionals or semi-professionals.¹⁰ With political

---

⁷ In his lectures at the London School of Economics during 1898 he talked of this danger. Letter from E. F. Carrington, a student, 19 Jan. 1899 (WP).

⁸ Exactly when he first encountered Godkin's work is unclear; the first explicit reference to Godkin in Wallas's writings is in 1903. However, the similarity between Godkin's essay 'The Real Problems of Democracy', published in the *Atlantic* in July 1896, and Wallas's lectures in America from December 1896 to February 1897 is such that I suspect Wallas read it at that time, or at the end of 1896, when it was published in a collection of Godkin's essays.

⁹ 'The Real Problems of Democracy' (July 1896), *Problems of Democracy* (New York, 1896), 287.

¹⁰ Ibid., 288.

machinery necessarily complex and government necessarily remote from the average citizen, political interest in a mass democracy had to be constantly and 'artificially' stimulated, and those who worked the machinery came to form a special group. Godkin concluded that 'the reluctance of a democracy to vote at all, or to vote right was not foreseen'. 'The greatest mistake of the theoretical democrats' was that they 'did not anticipate the necessity of organizing and directing the suffrage, or of the intervention of the boss and his assistants.'[11]

Prodded and coaxed, 'public opinion', the ultimate source of power and authority in democracy, appeared far less autonomous and rational, and far more ambiguous than had been assumed. 'What is it', Godkin asked, 'that moves large bodies of parties in a democracy like ours . . . to say that its government should do this, or should not do that, in any matter that may happen to be before them?' He concluded,

Nothing can be more difficult than an answer to this question. Every writer about democracy from Montesquieu down, has tried to answer it by *a priori* predictions as to what democracy will say or do or think, under certain given circumstances. The uniform failure naturally suggests the conclusion that the question is not answerable at all, owing largely to the enormously increased number of influences under which all men act in the modern world.[12]

It was this crucial question that Wallas, younger and more hopeful than Godkin, set out to answer. Democratic government, Wallas decided, would be only as effective as public opinion was competent to meet the demands placed upon it. The low quality of American government, he felt, reflected the inability of American public opinion to cope with the responsibilities assumed by democracy.

This revaluation of public opinion in a democracy was beginning to make its way among Wallas's English contemporaries. The rise of jingoism and the ebbing of interest in reform was forcing Liberals and Socialists to reassess their faith in 'the people'.[13] Three years after Wallas's visit to America and his criticism of American assumptions about political psychology, Ramsay MacDonald wrote:

The faith that the voice of the people is the voice of God is now about thirty years out of date. Those who held it assumed that an enfranchised democracy

[11] 'The Real Problems of Democracy' (July 1896), *Problems of Democracy* (New York, 1896), 289-90.
[12] *Unforeseen Tendencies of Democracy* (New York, 1898), 210.
[13] The importance of imperialism in forcing English progressives to rethink their political ideas is brought out in Bernard Porter, *Critics of Empire* (London, 1968), 93, 140, 145-6, 211, 222.

would be wide awake to every political issue, would take a constant and continual interest in matters of government, would form opinions which, by reason of the mass holding them, would be best for the nation, would steadily uphold humanity as apart from caste ideals, and would speak and move in such a way that their wishes, whatever their quality, would be easily known and could give rise to no ambiguity in their statements.[14]

The experience of the last thirty years, however, he continued,

goes to show that the democracy took infinitely more interest in getting the vote than they have taken in using it, that parties have largely abandoned political principles for which they won majorities by hard work and educational propaganda, and have drifted more and more into the hands and state of mind of the skilled election agent whose business is not to build and maintain the fabric of a party, but to win elections, that democratic opinion is neither clear nor determined, and that manhood suffrage does not guard the country against some of the most degrading forms of class ascendency.[15]

Leonard Hobhouse pointed out the superficiality and volatility of public opinion:

the man-in-the-street ... is now the typical representative of public opinion, and the man-in-the-street means the man who is hurrying from his home to his office, or to a place of amusement. He has just got the last news-sheet from his neighbour; he has not waited to test or sift it; he may have heard three contradictory reports, or seen two lying posters on his way up the street, but he has an expression of opinion ready on his lips, which is nonetheless confident, because all the grounds on which it is founded may be swept away by the next report he hears. The man-in-the-street is the man in a hurry; the man who has not time to think and will not take the trouble to do so if he has the time. He is the faithful reflex of the popular sheet and the shouting newsboy.... To this new public of the streets and the tramcars it is useless to appeal in terms of reason; it has not time to put the two ends of an argument together; it has hardly patience to receive a single idea, much less to hold two in the mind and compare them.[16]

MacDonald placed the blame for the 'subversion of the democratic instincts' upon the capitalist economic system. Yet, however much he tried to explain away his disappointment in democracy, he finally had to admit that 'if the moneyed interests have undermined some of the democratic virtues, it must be said, on the other hand, that those virtues have not always been so robust as they were imagined to be'. It was no longer

---

[14] 'The People in Power', in *Ethical Democracy: Essays in Social Dynamics*, ed. Stanton Coit (London, 1900), 70–2.
[15] Ibid., 61.   [16] *Democracy and Reaction* (London, 1904), 70–2.

possible, MacDonald had to conclude, to continue in the delusion that the instincts of the average man could be trusted 'to keep up within him political enthusiasm, and indicate to him the most desirable line of political advance'.[17] He urged reformers to turn from exclusive concern with institutions and deal with human nature, by 'the education of the individual citizen in civic virtues'.[18]

Slowly and reluctantly, Edwardian political thinkers were becoming aware of the unforeseen difficulties of democracy. To solve these difficulties they proposed either 'mechanical' or 'ethical' remedies, or a combination of both, as Lord Bryce did in *Hindrances to Good Citizenship* (1909). Some, like Hobhouse, concentrated on improving the structure of democratic government; others, like MacDonald, emphasized improving the character and spirit of the people. Yet all these proposals came down in practice to little more than some 'tinkering' with the machinery or vague ethical exhortations. Hobhouse's suggestions were largely to increase still further the democratic element in government, thus evading the problem. Others, who like MacDonald and Bryce called for 'education in civic duty', never spelled out exactly what this would mean in practice. The remedies proposed for the flaws of democracy showed far less realism than the perceptions of these flaws.

At root, most Edwardian political thinkers were still 'Victorian' in their reluctance to separate facts and values.[19] Wallas's contemporaries, even those who were baring the problems of democracy, refused to carry their questioning to their own preconceptions; indeed, they often responded by a redoubling of their commitment to their rationalist ideals.[20] To turn from laws and formal institutions to the constituent elements of politics— human nature and human relations—was an advance; but if it was only to preach 'education in civic duty', then little had been gained.

His contemporaries were uneasy and uncertain, Wallas felt, because they inhabited a half-way house. Their experience had invalidated their conclusions without affecting their values; their realism was only very partial. For Wallas the times demanded not still more idealism but less. The problems of democracy would only find their solution, not by un-

---

[17] Op. cit., 67-8.   [18] Ibid., 73.
[19] On this fusion of fact and value, which has been labelled 'Positivism' (one of the many uses of this term), see Noel Annan, 'The Curious Strength of Positivism in English Political Thought', *L. T. Hobhouse Memorial Lecture*, no. 28 (London, 1959). Also see J. W. Burrow, *Evolution and Society* (Cambridge, 1966).
[20] Even the economic theory of Imperialism of Wallas's friend, J. A. Hobson, for example, can be seen as an attempt to preserve a faith in human rationality in the face of seemingly irrational behaviour. See B. Porter, op. cit., 207-27.

considered exhortation, but by the development of an objective science of man and politics.

The aim of a science of politics was to be practical; Wallas had little interest in pure knowledge. He was, after all, very much a part of that moralistic tradition he thought he was rebelling against. For all his self-conscious modernity, Wallas, an active supporter of the South Place Ethical Society, only partially escaped his Evangelical upbringing. He rejected the fusion of ethics and social science, but not their intimate connection, and the ultimate subordination of the latter to the former. His approach to the study of politics and society, like that of most of his friends and associates, was always that of a reformer and moralist, not of a pure scientist.[21]

Wallas's moralism was typically English. As Noel Annan has observed, in no other country was 'the passion . . . for laying down how men ought to behave' so irresistible, moral relativism so intolerable.[22] Relativism, which has proved to be an essential precondition for the development of the social sciences, flourished exuberantly on the Continent, but failed to take root in England before the First World War. Perhaps because of the lack of fundamental social conflict, attaining a position of detachment from accepted values and standards was extremely difficult for English intellectuals.

Yet Wallas was not wrong in thinking he was breaking with the past. He did put behind him the later Victorian tradition, shared by 'materialists' like Spencer and 'idealists' like Green, of political and social thought as a total philosophy of life, a substitute for religion.[23] Wallas sought to rebuild political science stripped of ethical assumptions and conclusions, far more limited in its role, but far more effective within those limits. Political science so reconstructed could serve moral ends, but be itself independent of ethics. The political scientist was to be not a philosopher but a social engineer.

This reconstruction would never, he knew, be accomplished without a great change in English methods of thinking about politics. English political thought, particularly in Wallas's time, tended to revolve around the two opposite poles of idealism and empiricism, virtually ignoring the all-important middle ground. Wallas was well acquainted with both poles. His years at Shrewsbury and Oxford had instructed him in the idealist

[21] For a discussion of the 'moral' motives guiding the work of J. A. Hobson, also an active supporter at South Place, see Porter, op. cit., 158–78.
[22] 'Curious Strength', op. cit., 18.
[23] See Burrow, op. cit., on this tradition.

outlook, in the all-pervasive form of classicism as well as in the more specific version of T. H. Green's philosophy. His years in Fabianism, as it came more and more under the dominant influence of Sidney Webb, had imbued Wallas with the empiricist viewpoint. Both left a permanent mark on his thinking, but neither satisfied him any longer.

The abstractions that were the stock-in-trade of the political philosophy which Wallas had learned at Oxford, dealing as they did with 'universal truths' and 'the State' instead of existing states, had little relevance to actual political life. A few years later, he was to recall a discouraging conversation with a group of Oxford tutors and professors:

> I was pleading that greater reality and force would be given to the characteristic studies of the University if the students were encouraged from time to time to deal with such problems as, e.g., the Referendum (which was at the moment a burning question), and to use the ordinary methods of science in collecting and arranging their material. I felt that I had the spirit of the place against me. The most distinguished man present argued that it was only a high degree of abstraction in the subject matter which made teaching possible. The question as to what a particular State should do in a particular case brought in, he said, the whole concrete world, and knowledge of the concrete world was unteachable at a university; it must come from later experience. Others seemed to me to hold, more or less consciously, the Platonic view that the fleeting phenomena of fact were mere shadows, which would confuse philosophy if they were taken too seriously.[24]

For Wallas, however, political philosophy existed 'for the sake of action, and action, unfortunately for us, does deal with the whole concrete world'.[25] In so far, therefore, 'as our thought fails to give an adequate picture of that world, our most carefully considered actions will miscarry'.

The alternative way of thinking about politics, the starkly empirical, was just the other side of the idealist coin, for, by disparaging theory, it too denied the essential connection between thought and action. The two worked together to maintain a wall of separation between 'philosophy' and the everyday world of politics. The last attempt to break down that wall was that of the Benthamites, who attempted to make a science of human nature the basis of political thought. Their discrediting had led virtually to the discrediting of the possibility of a science of politics, and, even more, to the abandonment of psychology as a starting-point for political thinking.

Wallas set out to resurrect the aims and approach, if not the conclusions,

---

[24] 'Oxford and English Political Thought', *Nation*, xvii (15 May 1915), 227.
[25] Ibid.

A NEW VIEW OF POLITICS

of Bentham. Sharply criticizing Leslie Stephen's disparagement in his *English Utilitarians*, he urged renewed study of the Benthamite movement as 'providing possible guidance for an attempt to create and make effective similar [political] forces today'.[26] The present situation he characterized as one of 'vague political opportunism', which could not last. Wallas claimed,

In every nation there still are some for whom the desire to see human society as an intelligible whole is a lifelong passion.

They know that the old easy formulas have been broken up, and that in Europe and America statesmen are facing, with helpless bewilderment or a dull reliance on habit and prejudice, the urgent questions which arise from the contact of stronger and weaker races, from the claims of property, and the unsolved difficulties of representative government. For themselves they may have given up any desire for the confident assurance of the eighteenth century. They may expect much more from specialised study and much less from deductive reasoning, but they are compelled to hope for the coming of a school of politics in which there may at least be so much agreement on first principles that each can feel that he is working on a plan understood by all.[27]

Wallas looked about and saw a far greater *quantity* of political investigation going on than ever before, but this world-wide activity lacked a focus—'missing is any attempt to deal with politics in its relation to the nature of man.'[28] All the great political thinkers of the past had had a distinct conception of human nature upon which they had based their speculations on government. Now, however, he complained, political treatises simply refused to discuss the question. In fact, in most cases, 'one cannot even discover whether the writer is conscious of possessing any conception of human nature at all.'[29]

This retreat from psychology had not at all, Wallas acutely saw, eliminated the influence of psychological assumptions; on the contrary, it had allowed unexamined assumptions unjustified influence. Though now no longer exactly believed in, the eighteenth-century conception of human nature, 'because nothing else has taken its place, still exercises a kind of shadowy authority in a hypothetical universe'.[30] Such unverified and unacknowledged half-beliefs, he pointed out, were immensely harmful intellectually. He realized, as a later generation has come to see, that the student of politics must, consciously or unconsciously, form a conception of human nature, and 'the less conscious he is of his conception, the more likely he is to be dominated by it'.[31]

[26] *Speaker*, 2 March 1901.
[28] *Human Nature in Politics*, 35.
[30] Ibid., 146.
[27] *Speaker*, 21 Oct. 1899.
[29] Ibid., 35.
[31] Ibid., 38.

Thus, the first principle of Wallas's prospective science of politics was that it should be rooted in an explicit psychology. He wanted to return to Bentham, but with a vital difference. Bentham's 'science of politics' had foundered on an over-simple deductive psychology; now, Wallas felt, the advance of the natural sciences had made possible a far more sophisticated psychology, truer to the complexity of reality.

The era of reductionism was past. Wallas urged the adoption of the more humble method of the biologist, who tried to discover how many common qualities can be observed and measured in a group of related beings, rather than that of the physicist, who constructs ('or used to construct', he emended) a science out of a single quality common to the whole material world. The 'biometric' work of Karl Pearson, aimed at making biology statistical and quantitative, was attracting attention at the time, and seemed to Wallas a promising model for political science. 'We must', he insisted, 'aim at finding as many relevant and measurable facts about human nature as possible, and we must attempt to make all of them serviceable in political reasoning.'[32]

'Measurable facts'—here was the second principle of Wallas's science of politics: quantification. Again, Wallas was returning to Bentham, but on a more advanced level. Bentham had seen that a true social science had to have at least some degree of quantification, but the mathematical and statistical methods that could make it so did not exist in his time. Thus, his effort to establish a psychological 'calculus' was doomed to failure.

The nineteenth century, however, had seen a great development of mathematics and statistics, and the beginning of their application in at least one social science. Wallas was the first in England to propose as a general rule that political thinkers follow the example of the economists, who had radically altered their methods of reasoning in the previous half-century. The method of deduction from generalizations based on abstractions, which characterized 'classical' political economy, had been largely abandoned for a more complex and less absolute, but more useful, statistical and empirical method. More and more, Wallas saw verbal statements and abstractions being translated into quantitative terms, graphs and curves replacing syllogisms and black-and-white assertions. The result seemed to be a far greater fidelity to the complexity of reality and a greatly increased practical utility. In every case in which a political thinker was able to adopt the quantitative approach,

[32] *Human Nature in Politics*, 140.

his vocabulary and method, instead of constantly suggesting a false simplicity, warn him that every individual instance from which he deals is different from any other, that any effect is a function of many variable causes, and, therefore, that no estimate of the result of any act can be accurate unless all its conditions and their relative importance are taken into account.[33]

Wallas compared the methods of the Edwardian Commission on the Poor Law with those of the Commission that drew up the New Poor Law of 1834. The Report of the earlier Commission had been based on a set of *a priori* syllogisms devoid of any attempt at careful verification, whereas the current Poor Law Commission 'is being driven, by the mere necessity of dealing with the mass of varied evidence before it, onto new lines'.[34] He concluded,

Every year larger and more exact collections of detailed political facts are being accumulated; and collections of detailed facts, if they are to be used at all in political reasoning, must be used quantitatively. The intellectual work of preparing legislation, whether carried on by permanent officials or Royal Commissions or Cabinet Ministers takes every year a more quantitative and a less qualitative form.[35]

II

Wallas's dual dissatisfactions—with democracy in practice and with the existing state of political thought—were not unique. Both were increasingly shared by thinkers in Europe and America. Critiques of democracy were on the rise in all leading Western countries. These critiques were coming to be associated with wider criticism of the psychological tradition stemming from the Enlightenment. At the heart of this tradition had been the assumption of the fundamental rationality of men. This assumption, though not in its origin democratic, became intimately associated with democracy in the course of its rise. Thus, the fate of the Enlightenment conception of man and the fate of democracy, though logically independent, became historically interdependent. Dissatisfaction with either rebounded upon the other: the perception of flaws in the working of democracy stimulated reassessment of human rationality, while intellectual criticisms of rationalistic psychology undermined support for democracy. Elitist political ideas and irrationalist psychology, drawing sustenance from the same attitudes and experiences, tended to merge.

On the highest level, philosophical developments, as H. Stuart Hughes has shown, contributed to this change in political thought. The discarding in the 1890s of what Hughes calls 'Positivist' epistemology, with its

[33] *Human Nature in Politics*, 166.   [34] Ibid., 174.   [35] Ibid., 173.

assumption of the possibility of objective and certain knowledge in human affairs, encouraged thinkers like Sorel, Pareto, and Mosca to look underneath the surface of politics, to 'penetrate behind the fictions of political action'.[36] They realized that a man's political behaviour rested not on any real perception of the outside world (which they deemed philosophically impossible), but on the way in which his mind perceived that world. The key to political science then was to study the mind rather than the world. Here was an example of the new psychology calling forth a new view of politics.

Moving in the opposite intellectual direction, hostility to democracy stimulated the development of a highly influential genre of irrationalist psychology—the 'crowd psychology' made famous by Gustave Le Bon.[37] This current of thought had little connection with the first, except as they both were indications of the breakdown of the assurance of liberal-democratic rationalism. For a scientific basis, the crowd psychologists drew upon Darwinism, with its revelation of the animal nature of man. Other than substituting irrationalism for rationalism, they remained completely 'Positivist' in epistemology and method.

In theoretical approach Wallas belongs more with the crowd psychologists than with Hughes's subjects. The philosophical critique of Positivism made no impression upon him. Partly this lack of influence was due to Wallas's own intellectual limitations; his mind was not at home on the rarified plane of pure philosophy. However, it also reflected the English intellectual climate, which, with its combination of moralism and moderation, stifled for a long time the emergence of any radical scepticism. Thus the founding fathers of modern social science—Durkheim, Weber, Pareto, and the others—had no counterparts in England, and Wallas's very real advance towards a science of politics was to be permanently flawed by his lack of a clear break with nineteenth-century Positivism.

On the other hand, the Continental philosophy implied that the problem of mis-perception of the political world arose inevitably from the nature of mind, and was in the last analysis insoluble. Perhaps this is why the great Continental thinkers were not often political activists. The English, precisely because of their philosophical naivety, did not give up the effort to solve these problems and could, with less tension, unite the lives of political thinker and participant.

[36] *Consciousness and Society* (New York, 1958), 65.
[37] See Robert Merton's introduction to Le Bon, *The Crowd* (new edn., New York, 1960), and Gordon Allport, 'Historical Background of Modern Social Psychology', in Gardner Lindzey (ed.), *Handbook of Social Psychology* (Reading, Mass., 1954), 29–30.

Wallas never broke with his nineteenth-century faith in democracy, in spite of his growing awareness of its flaws. Unlike many of his contemporaries on the Continent who were also exposing democratic illusions about human behaviour, Wallas was too deeply committed by moral conviction and by years of practical labours to turn against democracy. While Le Bon, Pareto, Sorel, and others were laying the bases for twentieth-century anti-democratic ideologies, Wallas, reflecting the chasm in political thinking between the English-speaking world and the continent of Europe, placed his faith in the capacity of democracy to overcome its own weaknesses.[38]

The difficulties of democratic government had, naturally enough, been discussed mainly by the opponents of democracy. Wallas sought to right this imbalance; it was time, he argued, for the democrats themselves to consider these difficulties, 'just as it is the engineer who is trying to build the bridge, and not the ferry-owner, who is against any bridge at all, whose duty it is to calculate the strain which the materials will stand'.[39] To 'calculate the strain', Wallas sought to develop a quantitative political psychology.

In his attempt to create a psychology of politics, Wallas was not without predecessors. Bagehot's *Physics and Politics* (1872) had been on the reading list for his University Extension lecture on 'Political Forms' as early as 1891, and no doubt the even more famous work on *The English Constitution* (1867) was equally well known to him. Bagehot had, in these books, set forth a new view of 'human nature in politics'—partly a restatement of some aspects of Burkean conservatism, partly an effort to work out the political implications of Darwinism. His neo-Burkism and his application of Darwin had worked together to undermine the intellectualist psychology of Liberals, Radicals, and democrats.

From Darwin, Bagehot had drawn an evolutionary conception of human nature, which had led him to the view that the 'modern' politics of representative government had to work with 'primitive' human material. Human nature could be permanently and fundamentally changed only biologically, and since biological change was necessarily very slow compared to social change, there was inevitably a gap between men's nature and their nominal

---

[38] National differences certainly played a role in determining attitudes to democracy: of the 'crowd psychology' of the 1890s, the one work written by an American, Boris Sidis's *The Psychology of Suggestion* (New York, 1898), shared the same premises that led Le Bon and Sighele to reject democracy, yet drew opposite conclusions from them. Though he held 'suggestion' to be a basic evil, Sidis felt that democracy could combat its effects through education. See Allport, op. cit., 30.
[39] *Human Nature in Politics*, 253.

political institutions. Representative government, the most recent and advanced form of government, Bagehot had concluded, far from being 'natural', was an artificial contrivance. The theory of representative government, he felt he had discovered, was largely imaginary; it did not and could not, given the present state of human nature, work as it was 'supposed to'. Representative government, as it existed in mid-Victorian England, operated on lines different from those that anyone had been aware of, and Bagehot had tried to uncover these lines.

Following from an evolutionary view of human nature was the observation that political behaviour, like human behaviour generally, was far more 'primitive' than was usually assumed. The most powerful motivations were neither rational nor conscious. Bagehot had found the most important political motive in 'the propensity of man to imitate what is before him'.[40] This imitation was neither voluntary nor conscious. On the contrary, 'it has its seat', he insisted, 'mainly in very obscure parts of the mind, whose notions, so far from having been consciously produced, are hardly felt to exist; so far from being conceived beforehand, are not even felt at the time.'[41]

Thus, men were not and could not be governed by their conscious reason. In actuality, their unconscious propensities governed them. Government, as Bagehot had viewed it, had to reckon with the intellectual weakness of the average man, and the form of government that did so best was monarchy.

The best reason [he explained] why Monarchy is a strong government is, that it is an intelligible government. The mass of mankind understand it, and they hardly anywhere in the world understand any other. It is often said that men are ruled by their imaginations; but it would be truer to say they are governed by the weakness of their imaginations. The nature of a constitution, the action of an assembly, the play of parties, the unseen formation of a guiding opinion, are complex facts, difficult to know, and easy to mistake. But the action of a single will, the fiat of a single mind, are easy ideas: anybody can make them out, and no one can ever forget them. . . . A Republic has only difficult ideas in government; a Constitutional Monarchy has an easy idea too; it has a comprehensible element for the vacant many, as well as complex laws and notions for the inquiring few.[42]

Bagehot's work, a penetrating criticism of 'intellectualist' psychological assumptions, was the first attempt to restore the study of human nature, with an awareness of its complexities, to the centre of political thinking. It

[40] *Physics and Politics* [1872], (Boston, 1956), 135.
[41] Ibid., 68.
[42] *The English Constitution* [1867], (Garden City, New York, n.d.), 89, 93.

A NEW VIEW OF POLITICS

was only a sketch, however, and had not been taken up by others. Yet Bagehot, having been the first seriously to concern himself with the psychological problems faced by representative government and the shortcomings of democratic psychology, very likely took on new significance for Wallas as he struggled to resolve these questions in the late 1890s.

Between Bagehot and Wallas there intervened one other political writer who attempted to take a psychological approach. Sir Henry Maine, in *Popular Government* (1885), criticized democratic political thought for ignoring psychological realities. Democracy, Maine insisted, was the most difficult and least satisfactory of all forms of government. The 'will of the people' on which it was supposedly based he found to be an illusion. Maine argued that a very large proportion of the people cannot have a will, except on the simplest and most definite issues. In practice, most people accept the will of another, be it a politician or a newspaper. He warned of the debasement of thought thus produced by mass politics. Democracy, for Maine, could only result in the rule of demagogues working on the irrational and ignorant emotions of the masses.

Maine criticized Bentham for greatly over-estimating the intelligence of the mass of men; most men, he felt, did not know their own interest, nor did they act so as to secure it. The dominant psychological characteristic of human nature was not the rational calculation of pleasure and pain, but habit. Societies could not progress, nor even be adequately governed, through habit, and thus the mass of men were unfit for rule. Government, Maine concluded, had to rely on the special few, whose intelligence and ability enabled them to overcome the reign of habit.[43]

The tradition of psychological analysis of representative government typified by Bagehot and Maine, in spite of its conservative-elitist bias, was a crucial part of the background to Wallas's work. Led to a psychological critique of democracy independently, Wallas could find in this tradition many suggestive insights. Bagehot and Maine had prepared the way for a 'natural history of politics'.[44] 'He who acts', Wallas noted in 1899, 'must deal with the whole man', formed by 'habit, heredity, tradition', instead of an eighteenth-century or Romantic abstraction.[45] To this realization Conservatives like Bagehot and Maine contributed.

Before 'the whole man' could be understood, the false conceptions of

---

[43] See Robert H. Murray, *Studies in the English Social and Political Thinkers of the Nineteenth Century* (Cambridge, 1929), Benjamin Lippincott, *Victorian Critics of Democracy* (New York, 1938), and K. B. Smellie, 'Sir Henry Maine', *Economica*, xxii (March 1928), 64–94.
[44] Notes for 'Prolegomenon to Politics', 1899 (WP).
[45] Ibid.

'political man' in democratic thought had to be exposed, as Wallas had told his American student audience in 1897. In notes written in 1899 for his 'Prolegomenon to Politics' he identified three such fallacies. First there was the 'theatre simile' he had observed in America in 1897; the assumption that 'all eyes can see the stage of public action', that all citizens can thus pronounce an opinion on all subjects, that consequently there was an informed, reasonable 'public opinion' on any given subject at any moment. Wallas had come to realize through his political activity in London, as Godkin had in New York, that 'public opinion' was a very mysterious and elusive thing. At any given moment few persons, he had discovered, had well-informed and rationally formulated political opinions; an election, rather than being a means of giving expression to public opinion, was a process of creating one. The 'theatre simile' further erred in assuming that all citizens of a polity shared a common mental environment in forming opinions. Actually, it seemed now to Wallas, each person 'walks through life with his head locked within a lighted box painted with the picture of the world by which he guides his steps'.[46]

A second fallacy was that of much of what passed for political science, and it was derived from Benthamism—the assumption that the 'perfect selfishness of the voter' would, by the proper mechanical arrangements, yield the 'perfect unselfishness of the representative'.[47] Like classical political economy, this assumption foundered on the reef of abstraction. The election mechanism, Wallas now was convinced, was no more a panacea than the market mechanism had proved to be; there was no 'hidden hand' in representative government, bringing public spirit out of selfishness, or wisdom out of ignorance. Political problems would have to be faced as economic problems were beginning to be, with a due regard for their complexity.

The third fallacy that Wallas perceived was that of political romanticism. In his historical work, Wallas had encountered this attitude in Chartism. The 'Chartist hopes' had been belied by the facts of democratic life—by the reality of canvassing, and the necessity of management and manipulation. The *demos* had proved itself apathetic instead of public-spirited, roused by emotion, not reason, prejudices, not interests, appeals to base motives, not to altruism. It was no longer possible to 'trust the people'; romanticism had to give way to realism.

[46] *Our Social Heritage* (New Haven, Connecticut, 1924), 79, explaining a brief note written in 1899. Walter Lippmann, in *Public Opinion* (1921), developed this idea of a 'painted box' into the notion of 'stereotypes'.
[47] Notes for 'Prolegomenon'.

A NEW VIEW OF POLITICS

The political implications of this exposure of democratic assumptions, Wallas found, were far-reaching. Ordinary human nature stood revealed as undynamic and incompetent, politically helpless without the leader and the expert. Government appeared an art relying on advertisement and acting, rather than a clear and reasonable proceeding. Gladstone's great popular success, for example, appeared in this light to have rested more on his ability as an actor and self-advertiser, than on his policies. Policies, necessarily complicated and difficult, were in general less important than slogans, 'political cries', and symbols—emotional focal-points like 'Unity of the Empire', 'Peace, Retrenchment, and Reform', and 'Rum, Romanism, and Rebellion'. Political ideas had to have emotional force to be effective, had to move 'the whole man' and not just the rational faculty.[48] Politicians, consequently, had to shape opinion, for there usually was no pre-existing opinion for them to respond to; they had to shape this opinion, moreover, by means other than pure rational argument.

In the light of these discoveries, what was left of traditional democratic theory? Very little, certainly. Yet it was unclear what was to replace it.[49] At this uncertain juncture Wallas came across a series of articles in the *Fortnightly Review* by a man hitherto known only as a writer of imaginative fiction. These articles by H. G. Wells were published during 1901 and in book form at the end of the year under the formidable title of *Anticipations of the Reaction of Mechanical and Scientific Progress upon Human Life and Thought*. Wallas found them remarkably attuned to his own thinking, and by the late spring of 1901 had made Wells's acquaintance.[50] 'I know of no case for the elective Democratic government of modern States that cannot be knocked to pieces in five minutes', Wells had written, and Wallas agreed.[51] However, Wells did not leave the problem at that; he went on to examine the necessities and possibilities of political reconstruction. This was what Wallas too was seeking.

Wallas and Wells became good friends and intellectual comrades in the early Edwardian years. Wallas co-proposed Wells (with Shaw) for membership of the Fabian Society, and nominated him for membership

---

[48] Notes for 'Prolegomenon'.
[49] A student at the School of Economics complained around this time that Wallas's lectures 'lack constructive ability. . . . I receive nothing but fragmentary thoughts. . . . You seem to wander in a circle'. Letter from N. G. Bacon, 5 Dec. 1901 (WP).
[50] See H. G. Wells, *The New Machiavelli* (London, 1911), 134, where Wallas is thinly disguised as 'Willersley'. In May 1901, Shaw wrote to Wallas asking for Wells's address (WP). The Webbs, too, were impressed with *Anticipations* and took Wells up. See *Our Partnership*, 226, 230-1, 289 (Dec. 1901 and Feb. 1902).
[51] *Anticipations* (Leipzig, 1902), 136. Quoted in *Human Nature in Politics*, 217.

of the National Liberal Club.[52] He read and criticized early drafts of Wells's *Mankind in the Making* (1904), *A Modern Utopia* (1905), and *New Worlds for Old* (1908), and Wells did the same for *Human Nature in Politics*.[53] In 1902 the two spent a fortnight in Switzerland, tramping in the mountains. These weeks were filled, Wells later recalled, with discussions of 'our common doubts of contemporary democracy' and 'the problems of mental and social organization that open upon one directly one abandons a mystical faith in the mind of the masses'.[54]

Wallas's 'Prolegomenon to Politics' was already well under way, but the stimulus of Wells's mind helped him to clarify his thoughts and place them in a broader perspective. In *Anticipations* Wells had put forward a conception of future social and political development towards a new world order, in which democracy as then existing was merely a transitional phase.[55] The nineteenth century, in Wells's conception, had witnessed the rise of new socio-economic forces which had necessarily come into conflict with the old political order. Still incoherent and unorganized themselves, these forces had been powerful enough to destroy, but were not yet capable of rebuilding. Democratic ideas had been taken up as a counter to the existing oligarchical order, for lack of any 'formula of definite reconstruction'. Democracy arose in the gap between the fall of the old rulers and the emergence of the new. In a transitional period, when no clear order and no conscious ruling class existed, democracy was the only viable principle of organization, but, based as it was on social confusion, it could not be permanent.

Wells perceived the new ruling class emerging in the form of a scientific-technological-managerial *elite*, at present almost indistinguishably mingled with the rest of society. The existing political scheme ignored these vital 'functional men', operating as if they did not exist, as if nothing existed between 'the irresponsible wealthy on the one hand, and the great grey politically indifferent community on the other'.[56] Yet a polity which

---

[52] *Fabian News*, Feb. 1903, and letters from Wells, 14 and 15 Oct. 1903, and undated (WP).

[53] See letters from Wells to Wallas (WP), and from Wallas to Wells (H. G. Wells Collection, University of Illinois Library, Urbana, Ill.). Wells later reflected on this 'rather slovenly, slightly pedantic, noble-spirited man', and concluded that Wallas had influenced him 'very considerably'. This influence had been both in the content of his thought and in the direction of his thought towards public service and general social philosophy. See Wells, *Experiment in Autobiography* (New York, 1934), 509–11, and obituary article in *Literary Guide and Rationalist Review*, Sept. 1932.

[54] H. G. Wells, in *Literary Guide and Rationalist Review*, Sept. 1932.

[55] For the following, see *Anticipations*, 138–43.

[56] Ibid., 143.

A NEW VIEW OF POLITICS

recognized only these two groups was doomed in a world of ever-increasing complexity. Wells has an autobiographical character observe, in a thinly fictionalized account of his Swiss trip with Wallas,

> We got it more and more definite that the core of our purpose beneath all its varied aspects must needs be order and discipline. 'Muddle', said I, 'is the enemy.' ... 'We build the state', we said over and over again. 'That is what we are for—servants of the new reorganization!'
> Willersley [Wallas] and I professed ourselves Socialists but ... Socialism as a simple democratic cry we had done with for ever. We were Socialists because Individualism for us meant muddle. ... [57]

They felt that society and politics as they were then were a 'muddle', and so were the ideas they were based upon. 'There had to be some firmer basis', they agreed, 'a better-thought-out system of ideas, for social and political activities than was available at that time.'[58] The reconstruction of social and political thought appeared to be the first necessity. 'We have got to think out', Wells had 'Willersley' urge, 'just what we are and what we are up to. We've got to do that now.'[59] The most urgent sphere of activity, 'Willersley' decided, was 'Social Service—education'. 'Whatever else matters or doesn't matter, it seems to me there is one thing we *must* have and increase, and that is the number of people who can think a little—and have an adequate sense of causation.'[60] This conviction, mutually agreed upon, was reflected in Wells's next book, *Mankind in the Making*, written during 1903:

> Thought [Wells declared] is the life, the spontaneous flexibility of a community. A community that thinks fully throughout its population is capable of a thousand things that are impossible in an unthinking mass of people. ... Thought is the solvent that will make a road for men through gigantic rocks of custom and tradition that loom so forbiddingly athwart all our further plans. ... If our present civilization collapses, it will collapse as all previous civilisations have collapsed, not from want of will but from the want of organisation for its will, for the want of that knowledge, that conviction and that general understanding that would have kept pace with the continually more complicated problems that arose about it.[61]

From this Swiss summer in 1902 onwards, Wallas's attention and efforts were concentrated upon the task of developing a new intellectual basis for social and political action. Until then, his public activities had

[57] *The New Machiavelli*, 141. [58] *Experiment in Autobiography*, 511.
[59] *The New Machiavelli*, 134. [60] Ibid., 138.
[61] (New York, 1904), 331-2. In the preface, Wells acknowledged Wallas's great help in reading and criticizing the draft.

absorbed a great part of his time and prevented him from making much progress on his 'Prolegomenon', as they had delayed completion of *Francis Place* before that. As Chairman of the School Management Committee, he had felt it his duty, Sidney Webb recalled,

not only to peruse the voluminous agenda at the almost daily meetings, and know every detail, but also to make up his own mind before each meeting exactly what each subcommittee ought to decide on each issue. It generally did so decide. His friends sometimes reproached him for lying awake at night worrying over the problem of which of the scores of assistant teachers, all of whom were to be promoted to the scores of vacant headships, might be expected best to cope with the peculiar difficulties of each particular school. This exceptional conscientiousness ... his friends thought more praiseworthy in intention than prudent in the way of economy of effort.[62]

Wallas had been well aware of the dilemma, and had sympathized with the similar fate of Adam Smith. Smith, he had observed in 1895, had planned a work of political science to follow his *Wealth of Nations*, but an appointment to a permanent government post prevented its realization. 'Public work', he concluded, in an accurate self-assessment, 'is the worst of all snares to a kindly and procrastinating man, since he can always represent to himself that work for others is more important than work for himself.'[63]

After the end of his elected career in London government, in 1908, Wallas reflected,

now that I am fifty years old, whether I have been entirely 'futile' [as Shaw had implied in a letter], I am blessed if I know. If I had done a day's work every day at writing I could have produced more books and perhaps it has been stupid of me not to have done so. But I have never looked upon myself as a professional writer.

[62] *Economica*, xxxviii (Nov. 1932), 404. See letters from Webb to Wallas, 3 Mar. and 3 July 1907, after Wallas's defeat, urging him to devote his full time to writing (PP). Also see letter from Wells to Wallas, 1907, and Shaw's letter, 24 Aug. 1899, giving similar advice (WP). Shaw had been exasperated for years at Wallas's sacrifice of his intellectual abilities, and had urged him, to no avail, to quit the School Board. 'All this committee work', he wrote, 'is nothing but being lazy by public machinery.... What on earth is the use of spending eight hours a day as a petty magistrate disposing of cases of drunken schoolmistresses, and perpetuating a system that ought to be abolished? Jackson the Sage said to me the other day when I said something about keeping in contact with life and experience by public work and the like. "Why, man, you're *bilious* with a surfeit of life and experience. Go and use your imagination whilst it's still in its prime." I pass the admonition on to you, and heartily wish you a necrossed foot or something equally effectual to detach you from that foolish democratic mistake, the adhocious [a pun intended here] School Board. You'd much better write another book, without any preparation.' Letter to Wallas, 24 Aug. 1899 (WP).
[63] Review of John Rae, 'Life of Adam Smith', *Daily Chronicle*, 28 May 1895.

A NEW VIEW OF POLITICS

My 'Works of Charles Lamb' have been the bound volumes of committee minutes and the notebooks of people who have been to my lectures. I have helped to keep the School of Economics going, and every elementary school in London is really different in its looks, the size of its classes, its medical inspector, the selection of its teachers and its general efficiency from what it would have been had I not gone bald-headed into the School Board in 1894. The books which I did not write would I think have been about as good as J. A. Hobson's. It may be that I should have got more done by means of them than by direct administration. But I am not at all sure.[64]

Unwilling to cut back voluntarily on the demands of public service, Wallas was given partial release by the death sentence pronounced on the School Board in the Education Act of 1902.[65] 'He is more in his old form', Beatrice Webb noted, 'than I have seen him for years. The approaching abolition of the School Board, in which he acquiesces . . . has detached his mind from the minute details of school management and left it freer to turn back to the student's life.'[66]

In 1901 he had been excited by Wells's *Anticipations*; the huge treatise on *Democracy and the Organization of Political Parties* by Moisei Ostrogorski, published in two volumes in 1902, had a similar impact. Wallas was 'greatly impressed' by this 'break towards realism in political science'.[67] In this work Ostrogorski pointed out and dealt with at length many of the 'unforeseen tendencies of democracy' which had been hidden by a preoccupation of political thinkers with forms instead of substance. Many of the flaws in democratic theory that had been bothering Wallas—the excessive faith in elections, the lack of provision for the necessity of organizing the electorate, the lack of foresight about the increasing difficulty of generating public interest in an ever larger and more complex society, —were illustrated in detail.

Sweeping aside legalistic conceptions of government by a frank treatment of parliamentary actuality, Ostrogorski seemed to have produced the first major work of Wallas's 'new science'.[68] Yet, impressive as

---

[64] Letter to Shaw, 13 Dec. 1908 (BM).
[65] His activity in public education continued, as a member of the L.C.C. until 1907, and then as a non-elected member of its Education Committee until 1910, but it was activity on a greatly reduced scale and he wielded less power.
[66] *Our Partnership*, 241 (5 June 1902). [67] Wells, *Experiment in Autobiography*, 511.
[68] The noted political sociologist S. M. Lipset claims that Ostrogorski 'was the first to argue for the need to go beyond the analysis of formal political institutions, to study the actual political behaviour of men and institutions outside the governmental sphere'. Introduction to abridged edition of *Democracy and the Organization of Political Parties* (New York, 1964), xi.

Ostrogorski's achievement was, Wallas found it unsatisfactory. As far as he went, Wallas felt, Ostrogorski was excellent; the trouble was that he did not go far enough. 'Realistic acid', Wallas saw, 'might be made to bite still deeper into political conventionality.'[69] A thorough-going revision of political theory required a psychological examination of mass political reactions, an examination conducted in a rigorously scientific spirit. This requirement was not supplied by Ostrogorski, who remained, for all his path breaking, bound to certain cherished ideals and psychological assumptions.

Ostrogorski provided Wallas with a foil for the development of his own ideas. Wallas offered to write a review article on Ostrogorski for the newly founded *Independent Review*,[70] and the result was as much a statement of *his* political thought as an assessment of Ostrogorski's. Passing over the bulk of the work, with its description and analysis, Wallas immediately turned to consider Ostrogorski's conclusion and proposals. In Ostrogorski's view, he noted, the diseases of nineteenth-century democracy, fully developed in America, and inevitable, if present tendencies continued, in England, were due to the increasing submission of the individual citizen to permanent, monolithic party organizations. These organizations, with their ideal of discipline and 'regularity', undermined the basis of democracy, individual moral and intellectual freedom. Real democracy was for Ostrogorski compatible only with 'free' political organizations such as the Anti-Corn Law League, associations appealing to the independent judgement of individuals, on a single point of policy, competing with, but not absorbing, other organizations, and disappearing at the moment of victory.

To reverse the existing tendency of political development, Ostrogorski relied largely on the intellectual changes resulting from a recognition of the evils he described, and to a lesser extent on certain changes in political machinery which would, he hoped, increase political freedom and undercut the power of parties. However, Wallas could see little justification in Ostrogorski's description and analysis for confidence in his proposed remedies. Ostrogorski, Wallas decided, had not fully faced the implications of his work: determined to retain his faith, Ostrogorski had kept his philosophy apart from his experience. Wallas explained:

After hundreds of pages showing how ignorant and passionate men are, and how easily their opinions can be formed and exploited by any one who will take the

---

[69] Wells, *Experiment in Autobiography*, 511.
[70] Letter from G. M. Trevelyan, one of the editors (WP).

A NEW VIEW OF POLITICS

trouble to surround them with crude illusions, he is still able to use the words 'free reason', and 'individual conscience', in an almost religious sense.[71]

'Moral liberty', that is, thinking and acting as 'free reason' dictated, Ostrogorski admitted, had yet to be achieved. Yet, he insisted, 'men must be taught to use their judgment and to act independently'.[72] For the lack of reason and liberty in present democratic politics, Ostrogorski concluded, 'the remedy is obvious: reason and liberty, and a double dose of reason and liberty!'[73] This failure to analyse the concept of 'free reason' was pin-pointed by Wallas as the chief defect of the book, 'a defect', he declared, 'which renders futile much of the work, not only of M. Ostrogorski, but also of many others who, in England and America, are attempting to restate the problem, and to reform the machinery, of democracy'.[74]

The concept of 'free reason', to Wallas, was part of the fallacious view of 'the public' at the root of democratic theory, which he had first remarked upon in America in 1897. Each man, in this view, as an equal spectator of the political drama, could, once freed from the blinders of fear and custom, 'draw for himself the plain conclusion from what he saw, and act upon it'.[75]

In the last half-century, however, Wallas observed, the trend of modern science had made 'free' the most difficult of words to use in any exact sense. Further, Darwin, and the biologists and psychologists who had written since Darwin, by showing man's connection with the animal world, had made it difficult also to use the word 'reason' of any state of mental activity without narrow and careful definition. Above all, practical experience had shown clearly that 'the "reasoning" of the citizens of great nations deals, not with a single-world seen by all of them with equal clearness, but with views and memories and imaginations of things, so varied as to constitute a million different worlds'.[76]

The original intellectual basis of contemporary politics thus lay in ruins. What was to replace it? As a dedicated liberal reformer, and youthful convert to rationalism, Wallas firmly rejected irrationalism, whether the 'high' form espoused on the Continent by Bergson and Sorel, or the popular 'Darwinian' version represented in England by W. H. Mallock and Benjamin Kidd. Both forms saw the subconscious, the intuitive, the passionate not merely as important, but of higher value than the rational

---

[71] 'The American Analogy', *Independent Review*, i (1903), 507.
[72] Quoted ibid., 507.
[73] Moisei Ostrogorski, *Democracy and the Organization of Political Parties*, ii (New York, 1902), 729.
[74] 'The American Analogy', 508.   [75] Ibid., 508.   [76] Ibid., 508.

and reflective. Instead, Wallas proposed a 'new rationalism', taking account of the power of the non-rational without surrendering the commitment to reason:

> There are thinkers who rely as absolutely as M. Ostrogorski himself upon reason—the painful process of conscious inference from consciously co-ordinated premises—as the ultimate guide in politics. They would claim perhaps for themselves the name of 'scientific', not as advocating a habit of confident and easy deduction from the 'few simple principles' of the 'classical' or any other Political Economy or Political Philosophy, but as hoping in statecraft for some of the success which has attended Bacon's 'ministration and interpretation of Nature' in the natural sciences.[77]

Wallas's Baconian thinkers (Wells and himself, presumably) would not be daunted by Ostrogorski's charge of 'forgetfulness of the best traditions, contempt for the noblest ideals' of the nineteenth century. Wallas explained,

> They would never ask the citizen who is to use reason in politics to take 'a double dose' of 'liberty'. They might even say to him: 'It is a small matter whether your reason is "free" or not, or indeed whether the word "freedom" means anything at all or not. Your duty is, to secure that your conclusions, and the conclusions of those whom you can influence, free or unfree, shall be right; and on that you must concentrate every fibre of your being.'[78]

These new thinkers, calling for self-discipline instead of liberty, were 'followers of Carlyle'—and, he might have added, of Matthew Arnold and John Stuart Mill as well.[79] In his critique of Ostrogorski and of American democrats, Wallas spoke for a long English tradition of elitism. In his own life, this tradition had been reinforced by devotion to the Greek philosophers, who had defined 'liberty' as the capacity to act rightly, and by the Fabian creed of remaking society through expertise.

Wallas now sought to replace the false and dangerous idea of 'reason' held by liberals and democrats. Reason, Wallas insisted, must be seen 'not as a divine gift which acquires supernatural efficiency when made "free" by an act of the moral will, but as a difficult process, whose success depends on time, and discipline, and organisation'.[80]

From this point of view, Wallas criticized the reform in machinery advocated by Ostrogorski. Reforms aimed at increasing 'freedom' might

---

[77] 'The American Analogy', 509.   [78] Ibid., 509.
[79] Both Arnold and Mill were important influences upon his thinking. For Mill, see ch. III, § I; for Arnold see ch. VIII.
[80] 'The American Analogy', 510.

have a very different effect on 'rightness'. Further, reforms based on ideal assumptions might have quite different results in the real world. 'A "Baconian" democrat', Wallas stated, 'would try to found his electoral system, not on any conception of what the voter ought to be, but upon as exact an estimate as he can form of what the voter is, and can in the near future become.'[81]

But how could 'an exact estimate' of what the voter is be arrived at? Wallas had formulated his approach, but had not yet found the means by which to carry it out. At this critical point, Wallas discovered the basis for the 'scientific psychology', which could rescue political thought, in the work of his old hero, Darwin. Darwin, he now saw, had transformed the study of psychology by breaking down the wall dividing the human mind and human behaviour from the rest of the natural world. *The Descent of Man* (1871) and *The Expression of the Emotions in Man and Animals* (1872) had carried naturalism into the realm of what had come to be defensively called 'the distinctively human'. With them, human phenomena had been freed for the application of the scientific method.[82] Wallas first felt the excitement of this liberation at Oxford, and now its less immediate implications presented themselves to him.[83]

With Darwin, psychology became a branch of the natural sciences. Having brought the human mind into the natural world in the *Descent*, he proceeded to study it as such, in *The Expression of the Emotions*. Here Darwin initiated the field of comparative psychology. The same principle was revealed at work in the human mind as in the rest of the organic world. Mind, in the Darwinian universe, it has been pointed out,

has evolved like every other piece of organic equipment; it is subject to the laws of variation and inheritance; it is one means by which organisms adapt themselves in the struggle for existence and reveal their fitness to survive. The process of natural selection, nature's way of sifting the fit from the unfit, operates upon mental no less than upon physical qualities.[84]

---

[81] 'The American Analogy', 513.
[82] See Fay B. Karpf, *American Social Psychology* (New York, 1932), 150–1. See also the classic work by John Dewey, 'The Influence of Darwin on Philosophy', in *The Influence of Darwin on Philosophy and Other Essays* (New York, 1910). Wallas (and Dewey) perhaps overstated Darwin's importance in this regard, ignoring other developments in Darwin's day that were working towards this transformation of psychological studies. But this very overestimation attests to the great importance of the Darwinian image for these men.
[83] See 'Darwinism and Social Motive', (1906) *Men & Ideas*, 89–94.
[84] L. S. Hearnshaw, *A Short History of British Psychology, 1840–1940* (London, 1964), 36.

In order to study men and animals together, there had to be a common method. The traditional psychological method of introspection, applicable only to the human mind, was obviously of no use here. In order to study emotion comparatively, therefore, Darwin approached it from the standpoint of 'expression' rather than the traditional one of 'states of mind'. Both men and animals exhibited behaviour; only through the observation of behaviour could a universal scientific psychology be developed.

Hitherto human psychology had been explained by the workings of reason, and animal psychology by that of instinct. The new-found biological continuity between man and animal, however, meant a continuity of explanation as well; there could no more be a mental than a physiological divide between man and the animal world. The realms of reason and instinct yielded up their distinctiveness and merged. Man could no longer be regarded as a mainly rational creature carefully considering before he acted; he seemed often to act impulsively 'from instinct or long habit, as does probably a bee or ant, when it blindly follows its instincts'.[85]

This 'new psychology' of instinct and unconscious mental processes reached Wallas most fully through William James. *Human Nature in Politics*, Wallas wrote to James, was the result of the reading of his psychology by a practical political thinker.[86] James's *Principles of Psychology* (1890) was a remarkable success as high-level popularization, introducing the 'new psychology' to an audience beyond professional psychologists, and providing just what Wallas was seeking. James, remarked William McDougall, the leading instinct-psychologist of his day, in 1910, 'humanised' psychology, 'brought it out of its corner' as a 'neglected and somewhat despised branch of metaphysics', into the centre of social and political inquiry.[87]

James's 'new psychology' broadened the conception of 'human nature' beyond the rational consciousness. The discovery of mental processes outside the sphere of consciousness, he declared, was the 'most important step forward' in his time, revealing as it did 'an entirely unsuspected peculiarity in the constitution of human nature'.[88] The *Principles* drew a

---

[85] Darwin, quoted by Hearnshaw, ibid., 36. The twentieth century has, to a degree, restored the uniqueness of man by substituting 'culture' for 'reason'. This restoration is the basic difference between Wallas and the social thought of today. See the discussion of this difference in Chapter V.
[86] Letter, 1908, in Houghton Library, Harvard University.
[87] 'The Work of William James, II: As Psychologist', *Sociological Review*, iii (1910), 314.
[88] Quoted by J. C. Flugel, *One Hundred Years of Psychology* (London, 1933; 2nd rev. edn., 1953), 155-6.

picture of human behaviour as the product of the interaction of a relatively fixed human nature, composed of a great number of inherited non-rational impulses, with its social and physical environment. To understand why people acted as they did, it was necessary, James showed, to know not only their experience but also the instincts they carried with them as the shared inheritance of the species, beyond the reach of reason or reflection.[89]

The impact of Darwinism, in addition to stimulating the rise of an instinct psychology, reinforced the trend towards a genetic approach in place of a static one in the study of human behaviour.[90] This evolutionary viewpoint linked up with comparative psychology to show 'primitive' instincts and impulses surviving, in large part, within present human nature. Human nature, like the rest of nature, evolved under the pressure of natural selection, struggling to adapt to its environment.[91] Biological evolution, however, was very slow, whereas man's environment, his self-created social environment, changed much more rapidly. Consequently, existing human nature was not fully adapted to existing society. Existing political and social arrangements could not work properly if they assumed an unreal harmony with human nature.

James, following Darwin, had argued that man's behaviour was the resultant of an interaction between his nature and his environment; if this nature was more 'primitive' than this environment, the resulting behaviour would fall that far short of expectations. Bagehot had realized this and its political implications: 'Civilised ages', he had written, 'inherit the human nature which was victorious in barbarous ages, and that nature is, in many respects, not at all suited to civilised circumstances.'[92] If this interpretation of Darwin was correct, it was this 'primitive' nature, and not a hypothetical 'civilised' one, that political thinkers would have to come to terms with.

However, Bagehot did not develop this theme, nor did anyone follow it up until Wallas. Drawing out the psychological implications of Darwin, Bagehot and Wallas both saw that the relation between human nature and its political environment was the central question of politics. Wallas, with the advantage of a generation of 'Darwinian' research in psychology to draw upon, was able to go far beyond Bagehot's tentative foray into this new field of thought, and to begin to open it up for scientific study and for practical application. Darwinism, he noted, offered to the social reformer

[89] See W. James, *Principles of Psychology*, ii (London, 1891), 383-93.
[90] For the origins and history of this trend in England, see Burrow, *Evolution and Society*.
[91] See L. S. Hearnshaw, op. cit., 36-40.   [92] *Physics and Politics*, 135.

'some guidance in his life-long search for those social motives which are the fulcrum of social change'. Wallas explained,

Unless he is prepared to study undismayed the nature of man as evolution has for the moment left it, the reformer who is also a politician will find his life one of constant and cruel disillusionment. Even if, like Disraeli, he is against Darwin and on the side of the angels, he may learn, against his will, that his efforts to check the brutalities of Chinese indentured labour are only successful when they are backed by the instinctive hatred of the West European man for the Mongolian racial type. He may recognize in the shouting crowd who applaud his election the same instinct which shocked him at a great football match. He may realise with disgust but without understanding, the professional skill by which his agent and the agent on the other side work up the driving force of a great political contest, by playing on those facts in human nature which he most desires to forget.[93]

The only way out of this helpless disillusion was the clear-sighted examination of human nature 'as evolution has for the moment left it', in its relation to its environment. Wallas felt that the eugenicists, who were at this time rising to the crest of their vogue, were correct in emphasizing the scientific study of human nature; they erred, however, in making the biological inheritance all-important, and in confining their interest to this inheritance. Human behaviour, as James had observed, was produced by an interaction between biological inheritance and environment—social as well as physical. To appreciate the significance of human nature for politics one would have to study human nature *in* politics. He agreed with the eugenicists against conventional opinion that 'it would be necessary to learn man's instinctive organisation, the series of impulses that lead to action'. But he cautioned,

it would be equally necessary to ascertain the medium in which these impulses manifest themselves; how they have been maintained in the past; whether a purpose could be discovered in their organisation. For instance, there was the common saying that a man loved his country. What was his country to him? He had the impulse of love; was it a name, or was it a conception, or again, was it a generalisation? Only recently, they had all been suffering from waves of emotional fancies about party—all their instincts had been aroused by either the Conservative or the Liberal party. What was that party to them—a party they had never seen? He only wished to impress the fact that, if they were to proceed from the breeder's point of view, it would be necessary to have a clear idea of the natural impulses and their relation to society.[94]

[93] 'Darwinism and Social Motive' (1906), *Men & Ideas*, 93-4.
[94] Comment on J. A. Thomson's 'The Sociological Appeal to Biology', delivered 14 March 1906 before the Sociological Society. Reported in *Sociological Papers*, iii (1906), 187.

A NEW VIEW OF POLITICS

'The natural impulses and their relation to society'—here was to be the focus of Wallas's 'new view of politics'. His disillusionment with the unrealistic assumptions of Liberal-democratic thought had found a resolution in a new approach to politics based on 'Darwinism' and the 'new psychology'. The 'exact estimate . . . of what the voter is' on which Wallas's 'Baconian' democrat would found his polity could be supplied by the application of modern psychology.

Modern pedagogy, a field in which Wallas was deeply involved, by basing itself on the most recent psychology, was already altering the process of education for the better. 'Under the leadership of men like Professors William James, Lloyd Morgan, and Stanley Hall', Wallas pointed out, 'a progressive science of teaching is being developed, which combines the study of types of school organisation and method with a determined attempt to learn from special experiments, from introspection, and from other sciences, what manner of thing a child is.'[95] *Human Nature in Politics* (1908) was intended as a plea for a corresponding change in political science.

III

Wallas based *Human Nature in Politics* on the 'Darwinian' assumption that 'man's impulses and thoughts and acts result from the relation between his nature and the environment into which he is born'.[96] He approached it first from the side of man's nature, and then turned to study man's political environment.

The first effect of modern psychology upon political thinking, Wallas decided, was destructive, revealing as baseless the common tendency to exaggerate the rationality of mankind. Before political behaviour could be understood, this 'intellectualist fallacy' had to be abandoned. 'Impulse', psychologists now agreed, 'has an evolutionary history of its own earlier than the history of those intellectual processes by which it is often directed and modified.'[97] The operation of natural selection, as seen by the new psychology, had given men inclinations to react in certain ways to certain stimuli, inclinations which resulted not from conscious forethought but from evolutionary development.

These inclinations or impulses varied in strength, Wallas concluded, in proportion 'not to their importance in our present life, but to the point at which they appeared in our evolutionary past'.[98] The more 'primitive' the

[95] *Human Nature in Politics*, 40. [96] Ibid., 81.
[97] Ibid., 48. [98] Ibid., 63.

impulse (provided it still served an evolutionary purpose), the more powerful it was. The past experience of the race, and not the present experience of the individual, was the fundamental determinant of political behaviour.

The pre-rational and determinate character of many human impulses was, Wallas pointed out (following James), disguised by their modification during the lifetime of every individual by experience, acting through memory, habit, and thought. Thus, it was not surprising that political psychology had been slower to develop than educational psychology. In politics such clear-cut, separate instincts as might be found in animals and in children were rare. Political impulses were, rather, 'tendencies often weakened by the course of human evolution, still more often transferred to new uses, and acting not simply but in combination or counteraction'.[99] Still, it was necessary to attempt a description of some of the more important of these political impulses, and this Wallas set out to do.

He began with his old mentor, Aristotle, for whom political society had been made possible by the existence of a hereditary instinct of 'affection' among men. Wallas's electioneering experience had confirmed for him the existence of this instinct, and had given him insight into its use in contemporary politics. He now saw election tactics as consisting largely of 'contrivances by which this immediate emotion of personal affection may be set up'.[100] The candidate's appearances were managed so as to create the greatest personal familiarity and friendliness in the electorate, under circumstances offering little or no opportunity for the formation of a reasoned opinion of his merits. All efforts were directed toward shaping and propagating a 'public image' of the candidate which would stimulate 'affection'.

Another crucial instinct in political and social life, if indeed it was an instinct, was the desire for property. Almost the whole of the economic question between socialism and individualism, in Wallas's view, turned on the nature and limitations of this desire. Citing evidence of child and animal psychology for its instinctual nature, Wallas urged that 'some economist ought therefore to give us a treatise in which this property instinct is carefully and quantitatively examined.'[101]

[99] *Human Nature in Politics*, 53.   [100] Ibid., 54.
[101] The sort of questions Wallas wanted asked about the property instinct were:
'Is it, like the hunting instinct, an impulse which dies away if it is not indulged? How far can it be eliminated or modified by education? Is it satisfied by a leasehold or a life-interest, or by such an arrangement of corporate property as is offered by a collegiate foundation or by the provision of a public park? Does it require for its satisfaction material and visible things such as land or houses, or is the holding, say, of colonial railroad shares sufficient? Is the absence of unlimited proprietary rights felt

A NEW VIEW OF POLITICS

He saw other instincts important in politics demanding similar examination, among them the fighting instinct, the instinct of suspicion, of curiosity, and the desire to excel. He himself did not carry out these examinations. Wallas's concern was with pointing out this entirely new area for investigation, and in reorienting the direction and scope of political studies.

Wallas's chief concern was the practical implications of this new view of human nature. For these he turned to the actual workings of inherited impulses in political life. He found, first of all, that the immediate effectiveness of these impulses was greatly increased when they were 'pure'—unaccompanied by competing or opposing impulses—and unmodified. However, in real life these impulses always appeared in mixed and modified form. Only as a result of deliberate contrivance, as in art, did 'pure' impulses make an appearance. Politicians and political agents, however, practised an art as well; contriving to provide artificially 'pure' emotional stimuli for the greatest immediate impact. Yet the last influence of impulses depended on their connection with the earlier stages of human evolution, with the most primary needs and experiences—what might be called their 'first-hand' quality. Since, in modern politics, the emotional stimulation which reached the electorate through the newspapers, the most important medium, was generally 'pure', but 'second hand', it was both artificial and transient.

The process of communication in modern political society appeared far more difficult and unsatisfactory than had hitherto been imagined. In coming to grips with Godkin's question concerning the nature of that crucial entity, public opinion, Wallas was uncovering some unsettling facts. Modern political society was foundering, Wallas now believed, on the inability of valuable and necessary political ideas to acquire, for the average citizen, that 'pungent sense of effective reality' spoken of by William James.[102] His political campaigns had brought home to Wallas 'the enormously greater solidity for most men of the work-a-day world which they see for themselves, as compared with the world of inference and secondary ideas which they see through the newspapers'.[103] Political ideas and issues were remote and 'second-hand', based on a relatively weak reason, and consequently demanded great effort. Mass politics, as a

---

more strongly in the case of personal chattels (such as furniture and ornaments) than in the case of land or machinery? Does the degree and direction of the instinct markedly differ among different individuals or races, or between the two sexes?' Ibid., 60.
This was quite a different way of looking at the prospects for socialism from that which Wallas had learned in the 1880s, though it was foreshadowed even then in Wallas's concern for fitting social reforms to human nature.
[102] Ibid., 65.   [103] Ibid., 66.

result, came to rely increasingly on the 'pure' emotional stimuli of advertisement and 'stage-managing'. It was, in short, very difficult to make politics part of the 'first-hand' reality of a mass electorate in modern society, and, when reaching the voters through 'second-hand' media, artificially contrived emotional stimuli had far greater immediate impact than complex and demanding ideas and issues.

If the mass of the electorate did not see 'the stage of public action' equally and clearly, if it was not motivated politically by reflection upon the events taking place on that stage, what did it see and what did move it to opinion and action? Wallas now had an answer. People saw and were moved by symbols and images. Men's political environment was populated by these self-created entities, by which political relations were established and maintained, and political communication carried on. It was, Wallas observed (applying his Darwinism), to changes in this environment only that all human political development had been due. The human biological inheritance, changing only over vast stretches of time, was for practical purposes fixed. However, the environment into which men were born, increasingly social instead of natural, was rapidly and indefinitely changing. Thus, for the source of the enormous political changes that separated modern men from their ancestors, they must look to new facts in their environment. One important group of facts, Wallas found, were new entities about which men could think and feel. These entities were established by a non-rational process of 'creating artificial and easily recognizable political likenesses'.[104]

Wallas traced symbol-making from the animal world to the primitive human world, and thence to civilized society. Recognition, he noted, often attached itself to certain special points in the thing recognized. These points then became symbols of the thing as a whole, evoking a particular impulse or impulses. Emotional associations acquired over a period of time cemented the process of recognition into an automatic reaction. In early political society, the importance of 'symbolic recognition' was clear. As political society developed, conscious reasoning began to encroach on the realm of symbols, but without displacing it. The process of symbolic recognition came, however, to be intellectualized. Particularly when the symbol was actual language, it was very difficult 'not to confuse acquired emotional association with the full process of logical inference'.[105]

Because [Wallas explained] one of the effects of those sounds and signs which we call language is to stimulate in us a process of deliberate logical thought we tend

[104] *Human Nature in Politics*, 85. [105] Ibid., 87.

A NEW VIEW OF POLITICS

to ignore all their other effects. Nothing is easier than to make a description of the logical use of language, the breaking up by abstraction of a bundle of sensations—one's memory, for instance, of a royal person; the selection of a single quality—kingship, for instance,—shared by other such bundles of sensations, the giving to that quality the name king, and the use of the name to enable us to repeat the process of abstraction. When we are consciously trying to reason correctly by the use of language all this does occur, just as it would occur if we had not evolved the use of voice-language at all, and were attempting to construct a valid logic of colours and models and pictures. But any text-book of psychology will explain why it errs, both by excess and defect, if taken as a description of that which actually happens when language is used for the purpose of stimulating us to action.[106]

The habit of giving intellectual explanations of emotional experiences, Wallas pointed out, showed itself in many areas, such as religion, morals and education. It was far strongest, though, in politics, where, as he had seen, the impulsive and pre-rational character of much mental activity was disguised by a superstructure of individual experience and rational thought. For most men the central political entity was their country. 'When a man dies for his country', Wallas asked, 'what does he die for?'[107] Here was the most basic political act, and it could not be explained rationally. What seemed to happen in the crisis of battle was 'not the logical building up or analyzing of the idea of one's country, but that automatic selection by the mind of some thing of sense accompanied by an equally automatic emotion of affection' that Wallas had just described.[108]

As it was with states, so also with other types of political entities. As soon as any body of men was grouped under a common political name, that name might take on emotional associations in addition to an intellectually analysable meaning. Within the modern national state, the most effective political entity was the party, which represented 'the most vigorous attempt which has been made to adapt the form of our political institutions to the actual facts of human nature'.[109] Carrying forward his earlier criticism of Ostrogorski's treatment of parties, Wallas analysed their function under the conditions of modern political life:

> In a modern State there may be ten million or more voters. Every one of them has equal right to come forward as a candidate and to urge either as candidate or agitator the particular views which he may hold on any possible political question. But to each citizen, living as he does in the infinite stream of things, only a few of his million fellow-citizens could exist as separate objects of political

[106] *Human Nature in Politics*, 87–8. [107] Ibid., 93.
[108] Ibid., 93. [109] Ibid., 103.

thought or feeling, even if each one of them held only one opinion on one subject without change during his life. Something is required simpler and more permanent, something which can be loved and trusted, and which can be recognized at successive elections as being the same thing that was loved and trusted before; and a party is such a thing.[110]

A particular party might originate in a deliberate intellectual process, but once in existence it was dependent upon facts of human nature of which deliberate thought was only one. A party was 'primarily a name, which, like other names, calls up when it is heard or seen an "image" that shades imperceptibly into the voluntary realization of its meaning'.[111] As with other symbols, emotional reactions could be stimulated by the name and its automatic mental associations. Party managers strove to ensure that these automatic associations 'shall be as clear as possible, shall be shared by as large a number as possible, and shall call up as many and as strong emotions as possible'.[112] For this purpose they employed such means as colours, music, and phrases.

To illustrate the relation between party entities and political impulse, Wallas turned to the art of advertisement, in which the psychological process could be observed apart from its ethical implications. Advertisement and party politics, he felt, were becoming more and more alike in method. Both were more and more directing their appeal towards the 'weaknesses' of human nature—not only towards the instincts directly, but also towards the non-rational character of much mental association, or, as Wallas called it, 'non-rational inference'.

Unconscious or half-conscious associations, fixed by habit, not reasoning tested by experience, constituted the source of most of the political opinions of most men. In ordinary life non-rational inference was more or less satisfactory, since this sort of association usually corresponded to some reality. In politics, however, as in advertising, certain people had an interest in using non-rational inference for their own ends. In commercial advertising, the development of techniques of psychological manipulation was bad enough, but in political advertising, it posed a grave threat to the very possibility of real democracy. 'The empirical art of politics', Wallas warned, 'consists largely in the creation of opinion by the deliberate exploitation of sub-conscious non-rational inference.'[113]

---
[110] *Human Nature in Politics*, 103-4.   [111] Ibid., 104.   [112] Ibid., 104.
[113] Ibid., 18. This 'new electioneering' was making rapid advances. A year after the publication of *Human Nature in Politics*, Wallas raised a new warning against the exploitation of the instincts and emotions of the masses by the new breed of political agent and their wealthy clients. He perceived something 'new in English Democratic politics' in:

Political psychology thus had grave practical implications. It revealed, underneath the simple façade of rational democratic politics, 'an organized system of mental suggestion', whose dimensions and dynamics were as yet uncharted.[114] Such a prospect was frightening to a dedicated Liberal and democrat such as Wallas, and impelled him to spend much of the rest of his life seeking ways to combat it.

In turning away from formalistic and idealistic political thinking towards an examination of the actual workings of politics, Wallas earned an important place among the founders of modern political science. Almost alone in England, he tried to turn the study of laws, ideals, and 'official' institutions into the study of behaviour. Wallas was the first to direct attention specifically to the 'unconscious', non-rational side of politics in a scientific rather than polemical and ideological way. In place of the sweeping generalities of Conservative writers, Wallas sought to subject patterns of non-rational behaviour to specific, and if possible, quantitative examination. This unorthodox approach can be seen in a suggestion that

some professor of experimental psychology ... arrange his class in the laboratory with sphygmographs on their wrists ready to record those pulse movements, which accompany the sensation of 'thrill', and would then introduce into the room without notice, and in chance order, a bishop, a well-known general, the greatest living man of letters, and a minor member of the royal family. The resulting records of immediate pulse disturbances would be of real scientific importance, and it might even be possible to continue the record in each case say, for a quarter of a minute, and to trace the secondary effects of variations in political opinions, education, or the sense of humour among the students.[115]

'the almost open way in which rich men are now urged to pay for the winning argument whether they believe in it or not. ... Equally new and even more sinister is the actual delight with which some of our electioneering "overmen" contemplate the process of manufacturing opinion for the advantage, not of those who vote, but of those who pay. Mr. A. A. Baumann, in the "Fortnightly" for October first says: "I rejoice at the power of money in politics", and then, quoting a sentence from a book of my own as to the skill in the production of opinion now to be bought, urges that the English rich men should buy that skill more lavishly and so "use their enormous money power in a scientific manner". He apparently no more feels anything disgraceful in the suggestion than would Juvenal's "Graeculus Esuriens", or a fifteenth-century condottiere. In a circular issued last August, appealing for support for the Budget Protest League, that body professes to have "introduced the true twentieth century note in the *ever-fascinating* art of political propaganda". The word which I have italicized is quite horribly significant.'
'The Money-Power at War', *Nation*, i (1909), 454.
[114] *Human Nature in Politics*, 124.   [115] Ibid., 57.

Today this suggestion sounds impractical and somewhat naïve in its adoption of the paraphernalia of physiology. In 1908 it was a revolutionary and valuable break with the accepted idea of political study.

Wallas's 'new science', while a great change from the older conception of political study, did not mark a complete break with tradition. Rejecting idealism, Wallas retained the notion of a science of politics tied to moral concerns. His passionate attachment to Liberalism, and his determination to reform society led him to subordinate political thought to political values and action. For this link with Victorianism, he was to be criticized by his successors.

Wallas, though a pioneer in the study of political behaviour, unfortunately held too narrow a conception of behaviour. Like most of his 'advanced' contemporaries, including one of the greatest minds of the age, Sigmund Freud, Wallas thought the key to behaviour lay within the individual, in the relation between his biological inheritance and his environment. This assumption led him to explain non-rational behaviour by means of 'instincts'. Today this 'individualism', or 'biologism' (to use Robert Nisbet's apt term) has been superseded by a 'social' interpretation of behaviour, making a good deal of Wallas's work obsolete.[116]

Further, Wallas preached the quantitative approach more than he practised it. Apart from some stimulating suggestions, he contributed little to the actual quantification of political science. This lack was part of a more general lack of specific content in his political psychology. *Human Nature in Politics* was an introduction to the psychological study of politics rather than an example of it; programmatic and suggestive, but not really a scientific monograph. 'He has not produced a political psychology', his student Walter Lippmann wrote, 'but he has written a manifesto for it.'[117]

We must look for Wallas's place in the history of political thinking not in the specific but in the general. Wallas contributed to a change in the orientation of this thinking towards the study of behaviour, towards psychology, towards quantification. His importance 'in supplying political science with a new outlook' Edward S. Corwin told the American Political Science Association in 1929, 'would be hard to overestimate'.[118] He was, in a sense, Moses rather than Joshua: he showed the way out of the desert, but did not himself enter the land of modern political science.

[116] This is discussed in more detail in Chapter V. See Nisbet's *Emile Durkheim* (Englewood Cliffs, New Jersey, 1965) for these terms.
[117] *Preface to Politics* (New York, 1913), 78.
[118] 'The Democratic Dogma and the Future of Political Science', *American Political Science Review*, xxiii, no. 2 (Aug. 1929), 582.

A NEW VIEW OF POLITICS

In part his failure to go beyond this 'manifesto' and give a positive content to his political psychology can be attributed to age (he was over fifty, when *Human Nature in Politics* appeared), to his intellectual limitations, and to the limitations of the English climate of opinion he lived in. Much of it, however, is clearly due to his character as a reformer, publicist, and would-be social engineer. His interest was focused, not on theoretical questions, but on the very practical problem of making democracy work under the actual conditions of modern life. The role of political science was to provide the knowledge without which that problem could not be solved.

He came more and more to see himself in the role of the 'engineer' of modern politics and society, or, as he put it in his critique of Ostrogorski, the 'physician' treating the 'diseases of democracy' and of modern society in general. 'Pure' value-free political science was as alien to Wallas as to the Greeks he had studied for so many years. His early comrades in the Fabian Society, too, had viewed the development of the social sciences as a means of effecting practical improvements in society. Socialism, they had been sure, was inseparable from social science, and the two would advance arm in arm. This aspect of Fabianism, harmonizing as it did with other sources of his outlook, remained always with Wallas.

By 1908, with *Human Nature in Politics*, Wallas had worked out his new view of politics, a view he did not henceforth change substantially. His attention began to turn to the practical problem of adjusting his hopes and ideals to the realities revealed by this new view—of harmonizing human nature and democratic government under modern conditions, or, as he put it, of 'increasing the margin of safety in our democracy'.

His intellectual horizons, however, did not remain restricted to politics. Even while he was working out his new view of politics, the problem of democracy began to appear to him as only part of a larger, more general problem. Modern politics had developed beyond the capacities of human nature to cope with it, but this simply reflected the general development of modern society. 'We are compelled to live in new and untried circumstances', Wallas had told his American audience in 1897. If this was true of men's political circumstances, how much truer of their social circumstances! Wallas's experiences in governing London had shown him more than just the difficulties of democracy. They had impressed upon him the vast problems—psychological as well as material—created by the revolution in the nature of society since the eighteenth century.

CHAPTER V

HUMAN NATURE IN MODERN SOCIETY

I

In the later eighteenth century the Western world entered upon a period of accelerated social change, as two 'revolutions'—industrial and democratic—gathered force. A 'new society' took shape in the course of the nineteenth century, while thinkers in every country pondered its character. This body of thought gradually coalesced around a dualism most sharply represented by the concepts, coined by the German sociologist Ferdinand Toennies, of *Gemeinschaft* and *Gesellschaft*.[1] *Gemeinschaft* stood for a traditionalist, group-centred small-scale form of social organization; *Gesellschaft* a rationalistic, individualistic large-scale form. The former was identified with pre-industrial, pre-democratic times, the latter with the advancing new society. There were great differences concerning the exact character, as well as the value, of 'old' and 'new' society, but this general transition was widely agreed upon.[2]

The problems of the new society became more apparent as the nineteenth century drew toward a close.[3] Earlier, it had been merely a promise or spectre, depending on whether one was Liberal or Conservative. Now it was reality, and subject to scrutiny by students of society, both professional and amateur. The closing years of the century saw a new awareness of loss as well as gain in Europe and America, and a new scepticism about the benefits of 'progress'. Materially, it was clear that this social transformation had been, and would apparently continue to be, beneficial. Psychologically, however, the change seemed fraught with dangers.

Emile Durkheim, one of the founders of modern sociology, became more and more concerned in his later work about the disorganizing and alienating effects of this transformation. The essential fact of modern society, as he saw it, was the release of the individual from all unchosen social ties and norms. While in one sense an 'emancipation', this individual-

[1] See *Community and Association* (English translation of *Gemeinschaft und Gesellschaft*, 1887), London 1955.
[2] See Robert Nisbet, *The Sociological Tradition* (New York, 1966), 21-44.
[3] See Nisbet, *Emile Durkheim*, 19-23.

lism imposed a new and, he came to feel, in some ways far heavier, burden upon men—the burden of being totally responsible for one's own life.

This realization developed through his study, first published in 1897, of suicide, which he took as an index of 'the general unrest of contemporary societies'.[4] A certain amount of suicide was natural, but in modern Europe, he felt, 'the exceptionally high number of voluntary deaths manifests the state of deep disturbance from which civilized societies are suffering, and bears witness to its gravity'.[5] And it was precisely in those sectors of society that were most 'modern'—Protestant, urban, industrial, and secular—that suicide was most prevalent. Individualism, Durkheim had to conclude (reluctantly, for he was politically Liberal), could be pathological, dissolving vital human ties and undermining psychic security. 'Progress', whatever benefit it was bringing, was also destroying community and isolating men from one another.

In this state of isolation, even individual identity, the supposed justification for the destruction of tradition and social bonds, seemed threatened. George Simmel, a German sociologist, saw the essence of modern society as 'metropolis', which was not merely a new physical situation but, more important, a new psychological one. The shift from rural and small-town life to the metropolis, wrote Simmel, involved two psychological changes: the 'intensification of nervous stimulation' and the 'objectification of life'.[6] Though Simmel tried to refrain from judging 'metropolitan' life, the picture he drew of its results was disturbing to less Olympian minds. In the interest of inner stability in the face of the barrage of stimulation, the intellect takes command, and feeling and emotion are suppressed. Even with this adaptation, the barrage threatens to 'overload' the psyche; consequently the defence mechanism of withdrawal arises, in the forms of the blasé attitude and 'reserve', increasing the individual's alienation from the general life of society.

Simmel saw this alienation further increased by the widening gap between the growth of 'a purely objective life' in society as a whole, and 'the subjective spirit' of the individual. As a result of this, the individual finds it increasingly difficult to know himself as himself; he sees himself more and more as a mere part of the external, objective culture:

> The individual has become a mere cog in an enormous organization of things and powers which tear from his hands all progress, spirituality, and value in order to transform them from their subjective form into the form of a purely objective

[4] *Suicide* (Glencoe, Ill., 1951), 391.   [5] Ibid.
[6] See Kurt H. Wolff, trans. and ed., *The Sociology of George Simmel* (New York, 1964).

life. It needs merely to be pointed out that metropolis is the genuine arena of this culture which outgrows all personal life. Here in buildings and educational institutions, in the wonders and comforts of space-conquering technology, in the formations of community life, and in the visible institutions of the state, is offered such an overwhelming fullness of crystallized and impersonalized spirit that the personality, so to speak, cannot maintain itself under its impact.[7]

The fundamental concern haunting Durkheim and Simmel, and a growing number of other social thinkers, was the problematic character of modern industrial-urban-'liberal' society. This sophisticated and profound concern among sociologists was paralleled on a more 'popular' plane by a rising mood of dissatisfaction with the fruits of modernity. In every major European country a new current of criticism arose, not simply political or economic but 'cultural', hostile to individualism, to urbanism, to liberalism. Germany, where pre-modern institutions and values persisted alongside the new, led the way in the depth and breadth of dissatisfaction. Fritz Stern's admirable study of Paul de Lagarde, Julius Langbehn, and Moeller van den Bruck has shown us the significance of this state of mind.[8] In France, men like Maurice Barrés and Charles Maurras embodied much the same outlook.

England, the most thoroughly 'modernized' of European countries, provided the least hospitable environment for this new mood.[9] Yet, it *was* present and vital there, even if this presence has been generally overlooked by English historians. Though most social criticism in Edwardian England was of the familiar 'left-wing' type, castigating political and economic inequities and inefficiency, there was another body of criticism—cultural and psychological—running alongside, if beneath, the main stream. This was in part perceived by C. H. Driver, who pointed out a generation ago that the main Edwardian innovation in social thought was a turn to psychology. The better-known economic thinking of that era, on the other hand, largely carried forth questions arising in the 1880s.[10] Cutting across all existing party lines, this new interest in psychology, arising out of

[7] See Kurt H. Wolff, trans. and ed., *The Sociology of George Simmel* (New York, 1964), 422.
[8] *The Politics of Cultural Despair* (Berkeley, California, 1961).
[9] As it provided the least hospitable environment for Marxism, the 'anti-industrialism' of the Left. Adam Ulam has pointed to the similarity in appeal of Marxism and 'reactionary' anti-industrialism, which prospered or failed to prosper together, depending on the strength of attachment to modernity in a country. *The Unfinished Revolution* (New York, 1960).
[10] See Driver, in Hearnshaw (ed.), op. cit.; 'The application of the psychological clue to the riddles of human activity', Ernest Barker observed in 1915, 'has indeed become the fashion of the day.' *Political Thought in England 1848–1914* (London, 1915), 128.

anxiety about modern society, provided the necessary context for Wallas's achievement.

As Samuel Hynes has illustrated, the Edwardian period was not fundamentally a serene epilogue to Victorianism nor was it generally an age of confident new beginnings. More than either of these, it was a time of uncertainty and anxiety.[11] The past was disappearing too rapidly and too completely for mental comfort, leaving many men unreconciled to the idea of a twentieth-century, urban, industrial England. To C. F. G. Masterman, a prominent Liberal, England at the start of the new century was 'a civilisation becoming ever more divorced from Nature and its ancient sanities',[12] becoming emptied of significance. 'The city state, concentrated in such a centre as London, remains as meaningless and as impossible to co-ordinate with any theory of spiritual purposes as the law of gravitation itself.'[13]

The most influential product of this mood of anxiety was Masterman's own *Condition of England* (1909). Quickly surveying the material condition, he found 'little to excite foreboding', though as Parliamentary Secretary to the Local Government Board he was well-informed about poverty and had established himself as a dedicated reformer. 'It is rather in the region of the spirit', he warned, 'that the doubts are still disturbing.'[14] As G. K. Chesterton and Hilaire Belloc were doing, Masterman held 'Progress' up to scrutiny, and denied its automatic value. He pointed out,

In all our mechanical ingenuities we have constructed masters for us, rather than servants; being compelled, immediately such ingenuities have found fruit in invention, to adjust our lives to the new conditions which these, and not we ourselves, henceforth dictate and impose.[15]

It was not the present only that disturbed Masterman, but even more the future. It seemed clear that the path of social development was leading 'towards a life increasing in complexity, and making ever more difficult demands on body and soul'.[16]

In 1902, when British national attention was still focused on the Empire, ten 'New Liberals', among them G. M. Trevelyan, G. P. Gooch, Noel Buxton, and Masterman sought to point out new and urgent problems closer to home. In a collection of essays entitled *The Heart of the Empire* they declared that public opinion 'had by no means kept pace with the

[11] *Edwardian Turn of Mind.*
[12] *In Peril of Change* (London, 1905), xii.   [13] Ibid., xiii.
[14] *The Condition of England* (London, 1909; 1911), 175 and 177.
[15] Ibid., 182.   [16] Ibid., 183.

altered conditions of the world'.[17] Foremost among the changes which had taken place, they wrote, was the 'stupendous growth of cities'. 'The aspect of life has ... been altered; no longer brought into direct contact with the forces of nature, man has carved out for himself new and artificial conditions.'[18]

The symposium dealt with the psychological as well as the economic implications of this new environment. Masterman's essay was the germ for his *Condition of England*, and Reginald Bray wrote one that developed into *The Town Child* (1907), a book Wallas found 'eloquent'.[19] In that full-length study, Bray, a fellow-member of Wallas's on the London County Council Education Committee, drew from the psychology of William James to support his conviction that the influence of environment on men's character and behaviour was overwhelming. Since the general environment of the city differed so greatly from that of the country, Bray concluded that the character, as well as the physique, of the town child could be expected to differ correspondingly from that of the country child. He thus urged greater study of urban conditions as they bore upon 'human nature', and warned that the results would be disturbing.[20]

The Edwardian era, as Hynes remarks, 'had found its new problems but not the answers'.[21] While sharing the anxiety and uncertainty of Masterman, Wallas set out to find these answers. In this quest, he became the foremost practitioner and exponent of the new psychological self-consciousness, raising this sort of unsystematic probing into a scientific and practical inquiry. In him anxiety was balanced by the unquenchable hope of a perennial teacher and reformer.

II

Wallas's life had been an excellent preparation for a psychological study of society. Socialism had taught him in the 1880s that the new industrial society was *the* problem of the age, overshadowing the current controversies over politics, philosophy, and theology. Though the Fabians,

---

[17] *The Heart of the Empire* (London, 1902; 1907), vii.
[18] Ibid., vii–viii. This theme of 'artificiality' was certainly overdone; after all, men had been altering their natural environment and replacing it with an 'artificial' one for thousands of years. The 'natural' countryside beloved of nineteenth-century romantics, for example, was largely the product of centuries of human effort and ingenuity. However, there was an important germ of truth in this argument; the age-old process of replacement of a 'natural' by an 'artificial' environment had greatly accelerated since the eighteenth century, and such a tremendous change in quantity could be regarded as a change in quality.
[19] *Men & Ideas*, 165. [20] See *The Town Child*, 4–5. [21] *Edwardian Turn of Mind*, 86.

and Socialists generally, saw this problem as economic and administrative, Wallas had looked further. 'Under the justest possible social system', he had cautioned his fellow Socialists, 'we might still have to face all those vices and diseases which are not the direct result of poverty and overwork; we might still suffer . . . mental anguish and bewilderment . . .'[22] Modern capitalist society, he had found himself agreeing with William Morris, starved the spirit as well as the body. The goal of Socialism, he had felt, was more than material prosperity, and even more than social justice; it was the establishment of a new consciousness, a new culture. Aristotle's ideal of the 'good life' gave Wallas an aim for which economic and administrative change were only means.

Wallas's Socialism was now becoming based on the ideal of the Greek *polis*—a community of citizenship, co-operation, and common feeling, in which individual and society were in harmony. This harmony, in so far as it had existed, had been established and preserved in ancient Greece by a common public education. He hoped to turn London's common educational system to a similar purpose. On the School Board Wallas's Socialism developed into something broader: what he had earlier attributed to 'capitalism' he began to see as a more general social problem. Modern urban-industrial society, he perceived in London, constituted a new psychological environment as well as a material one. This new environment, far removed from that of the classical Greeks, put the very possibility of a 'good life' as prescribed by Aristotle in doubt. In London Wallas found a lack of community and an 'artificial' environment which failed to satisfy basic human needs. He sought to create common feeling and a sense of citizenship, and to harmonize human nature and the new environment through the public education system. However, though he remained an ardent proponent of education, Wallas's thoughts soon developed beyond the purely educational aspect of modern society.

Even in political thought, he found, it was impossible to exclude a general view of society. The problems posed by 'human nature in politics' were intimately connected to the situation confronting 'human nature' in modern society. As E. L. Godkin had noted, one underlying cause of the present difficulties of democracy was the change of scale which had transformed the nature of all social and political relations. The inadequacies of democracy were more damaging in a large-scale, complex society than in a small one. Since human nature, in Wallas's 'Darwinian' view, had been

[22] 'Property Under Socialism', in *Fabian Essays*, 148.

largely formed in the long period of prehistory, it was better able to cope with the conditions of primitive society than with modern conditions. The incompetent and uncomprehending manipulated voter was but one facet of the alienated individual of 'mass society'. How, Wallas worried, were men to understand and feel part of that which had grown too large, complex, and remote from their instincts, senses, or imaginations?

In this effort to understand and to cope with these new circumstances, the Liberalism which had sufficed for the nineteenth century was clearly inadequate. Examining, in 1901, the causes of the decay of Liberalism, Wallas pointed to the new social conditions that had arisen in the previous century. In the vast and complex new society created by technological advance the old values of individualism, liberty, and non-intervention would not work. The technological revolution, Wallas commented in a letter to Shaw,

has drawn the inhabitants of 'civilised' countries to live in great cities where they are much more dependent than before upon efficient social arrangements and much less upon 'individual' foresight not only for their chance of happiness but for the avoidance of the most tremendous evils.[23]

What had shattered Liberalism, he recorded in his notes, was not its original failure to see clearly the conditions of social problems, but the change in these very conditions brought about by such innovations as the railway and the telegraph. Looked on by Cobden as the triumph of Liberalism, these inventions really destroyed it by creating a world in which individualism and *laissez-faire* were meaningless, a world in which 'each man's life depends on causes he can't understand'.[24]

Wallas's concern with this aspect of modern society, developing out of Fabianism but going beyond it in breadth of inquiry and psychological focus, led him to his second major work, *The Great Society* (1914). Its 'problem' was stated in its opening sentences:

During the last hundred years the external conditions of civilised life have been transformed by a series of inventions which have abolished old limits to the creation of mechanical force, carriage of men and goods, and communication by written and spoken words. One effect of this transformation is a general change of social scale. Men find themselves working and thinking in relation to an

---

[23] Letter in response to Shaw's request for additions to the 'Revolutionist's Handbook' at the end of *Man and Superman*. Wallas felt he couldn't write aphorisms so merely sent some reflections, (probably written 1903) (WP).
[24] Notes for lecture at South Place Ethical Society, Oct. 1901, on 'The Decay of Liberalism'. (WP).

environment which, both in its connection with all sides of human existence, is without precedent in the history of the world.[25]

As economists before him had used the term 'the Great Industry' to describe the economic aspect of this transformation, Wallas called the new environment in its totality 'the Great Society'. The Great Society was urban, industrial, large-scale, impersonal and, world-wide. Its chief characteristic, Wallas felt, was simply its scale—the enormously increased size and scope of the 'reality' with which the average person had to cope. In being extended to the furthest limits of the world, social relations had been 'delocalised', in a phrase of H. G. Wells's, and depersonalized.[26]

This new society would inevitably be increasingly collectivist, but Wallas no longer saw collectivism as beneficent *per se*. While remaining a 'practical collectivist',[27] Wallas, with his tendency to philosophize which had always provoked the more practical Fabians like Sidney Webb, looked beyond the mechanics of economic organization toward a broader social philosophy. If collectivism was, as he believed, inherent in the Great Society, the real question was what sort of collectivism, directed towards what ends, based on what set of values, and with what conception of human needs? While Liberalism had fallen hopelessly out of touch with contemporary realities, Fabianism, while more relevant, was yet too narrow and limited to replace it. Modern society's most fundamental problems, which were psychological, could not be solved purely by applying the Fabian panacea of state expansion and organizational reform.

In this Wallas was more prescient than most of his contemporaries. After more than half a century, we have found that collectivism is only a partial answer to the unprecedented problems of modern society. The extension of the state into more and more areas of life, however necessary, has not by itself been able to deal with—indeed, has been one of the causes of—the growing anxiety over the vast scale of modern life. The new political questions now being raised in every advanced nation—of participation, alienation, the unresponsiveness of institutions—signify the bankruptcy of the 'pure' collectivist tradition. These questions are in a line of descent that in England included Wallas and a few other critics of orthodox Fabianism like the Guild Socialists; after so many years their criticisms have finally entered the general consciousness.

[25] p. 3.
[26] *Mankind in the Making*, 406.
[27] He characterized himself in 1906 to French acquaintances as a 'collectiviste possibliste'. 'Impressions of Paris', *Daily Chronicle*, 13 Feb. 1906.

Wallas's divergence from the approach of his Fabian colleagues was evident in his attitude toward Imperialism. At the time of the Boer War, Shaw, in his draft for *Fabianism and the Empire* (1900), had virtually embraced the extension of British rule overseas as a beneficent necessity. Imperialism, as Shaw saw it, was (or could be, with proper management) the international form of socialism. Technical progress having made the world one interdependent society, Cobdenite Liberalism was as out of date in international relations as it was domestically. Non-interference under modern conditions, he claimed, meant anarchy; Imperialism, in its best sense, meant international order.[28]

Wallas criticized Shaw's approval of Imperialism, but not his critique of Liberalism or his conception of a new world society.[29] Like Shaw, Wallas thought the development of world-empires inevitable, following from 'the enormous improvement in the means of communication', and expected that 'this process will develop on its economic side until the world is organized economically as one place', though, most likely under several political authorities.[30] However, Wallas did not feel as complacent as Shaw in contemplating the new state of affairs. On the contrary, he felt deeply disturbed. While Shaw took for granted the indefinite continuation of the British Empire and European world domination, Wallas foresaw grave, perhaps irreconcilable conflict.

The European nations, in establishing empires, were 'gathering round them bodies of dependent peoples, in many cases greatly outnumbering themselves, but without either political rights or the prospect of assimilation by intermarriage'.[31] How were these disparate elements to be integrated into a society not only economically but psychologically and ethically coherent? Wallas agreed with Shaw that Cobdenite Liberalism had outlived its time, but saw nothing to replace it. The new era of world-politics, he argued, required a 'world-consciousness'. The most important question was 'whether there exists at this moment a "world-ethic", a moral conception of world-relations, corresponding to the new world politics'. Wallas decided that it was 'almost impossible to answer "yes" to that question'.[32] The new world-economy called into being by economic and technological revolution, like the great cities similarly created, represented a leap of organization without a corresponding leap of human imagination, and as such embodied danger as well as opportunity.

[28] Much of this survived into the final version, revised by a committee of Fabians. See *Fabianism and the Empire* (London, 1900), 3–4, 14, 16.
[29] See Wallas's letter to Pease, 5 Sept. 1900 (Fabian Office).
[30] 'Religion and Empire', *Inquirer*, 29 June 1901.   [31] Ibid.   [32] Ibid.

This problem of the rapidly widening gap between social organization and human imagination had been a central theme of H. G. Wells's *Anticipations of the Reaction of Mechanical and Scientific Progress Upon Human Life and Thought*. Reading it in 1901 as a series of essays in the *Fortnightly Review*, Wallas had been immediately struck by its relevance to his concerns. Wells's criticism of democratic theory, which reinforced Wallas's own developing criticism, had been but part of a general critique of the applicability of eighteenth- and nineteenth-century ideas to twentieth-century reality. As a result of technological advance, Wells had perceived, a 'new society' was taking form, fundamentally different from any that had ever existed. The leading 'event' of the previous century, according to Wells, had been 'the sudden transition from a nearly static social organisation to a violently progressive one', a transition from which 'there can never be any return'.[33] This social revolution, and the 'change of scale' that had accompanied it, were to be the basic facts of life in the twentieth century. All social and political conceptions and programmes, Wells had asserted, would have to be re-examined in this light.

The stimulus of Wells's mind during their close association in the early Edwardian years helped Wallas to develop his ideas and clarify his purpose. The two men were equally critical of all existing social and political philosophies, whether Conservative, Liberal, or Socialist; nor was either satisfied with the unphilosophic Fabian approach. As Wells put it in *Mankind in the Making* (1904), a book written with much assistance from Wallas, the need was urgent 'for some general principle, some leading idea, some standard, sufficiently comprehensive to be of real guiding value in social and political matters'.[34]

This need could not be met by any of the existing political parties, absorbed as they were in arguing past quarrels and pitting one interest group against another. It could only be met, they agreed, by individual thinkers, free of partisan commitments, going back to the fundamentals and attempting to reconstruct social and political thought.

However much Wells and Wallas at first felt in agreement, they soon began to diverge. Wells, to whom ideas came in a rush, who was ever impatient for action, envisaged this reconstruction as a rapid thinking-out of the essentials of a new understanding of modern society followed by an immediate effort to bring about general public acceptance of this new view. Wallas, on the other hand, more reflective and thorough, if less energetic than Wells, meant by reconstruction the slow and painstaking effort to lay

[33] *Anticipations*, 69. [34] *Mankind in the Making*, 4.

the foundations for a realistic, scientific social philosophy where none at present existed. This divergence in approach, hardly noticed at first, gradually ended their close association. To Wells, Wallas came to appear lazy and 'academic': 'Essentially', he recalled after Wallas's death, 'Wallas was a talker and a lecturer. He liked picking a case to pieces with a quiet fastidious deliberation far more than he liked the labour of putting things together.' His weakness as a social thinker, Wells continued, lay in the fact that 'he was under no inner compulsion to get things positively done. If he had not had very definite academic ambitions and a real joy in answering questions, he might have sunk altogether into sterile erudite wisdom.'[35]

Wallas, for his part, came to share Beatrice Webb's disapproval of Well's lack of Fabian self-discipline and patience.[36] As Wells began to carve out a career as a social prophet and rebel, Wallas followed his own path of careful intellectual pioneering, clearer in thought and aim for his association with Wells.

III

The greatest challenge to the 'Great Society' seemed to Wallas to be the psychological dislocation it brought. The 'normal social life', as Wells called it, in existence for thousands of years, had suddenly disappeared. Confining and limiting as it had been, it had also been comforting and comprehensible, making few psychological demands beyond the natural capacities of the ordinary person. The Great Society, however, had brought a new set of demands for which men had not been prepared, and from which, as Wells had said, 'there can never be any return'.

The English factory girl [Wallas noted] who is urged to join her Union, the tired old Scotch gatekeeper with a few pounds to invest, the Galician peasant when the emigration agent calls, the artisan in a French provincial town whose industry is threatened by a new invention, all know that unless they find their way successfully among world-wide facts which reach them only through misleading words they will be crushed. They may desire to live the old life among familiar sights and sounds and the friends whom they know and trust, but they dare not try to do so. To their children, brought up in the outskirts of Chicago or the mean streets of Tottenham or Middlesbrough, the old life will have ceased to exist, even as an object of desire.[37]

[35] *Experiment in Autobiography*, 510-1.
[36] See her diary, 15 July 1906 (PP).
[37] *The Great Society*, 5.

Wallas had seen the 'old life' for himself, in his West Country childhood, and had watched its rapid retreat in his lifetime with mixed feelings. What, he pondered, were the costs of progress? To Aristotle, it had been obvious that a society beyond the grasp of the human senses and memory could not be a community. Nowadays, Wallas felt, men were apt to forget that the facts on which Aristotle had relied were still real and important. The quality of life seemed to be bound up with its immediacy. Wallas had observed in the concluding chapter of *Human Nature in Politics*,

> It is now only here and there in villages outside the main stream of civilisation, that men know the faces of their neighbours, and see daily as part of one whole the fields and cottages in which they work and rest. Yet, even now, when a village is absorbed by a sprawling suburb or overwhelmed by the influx of a new industrial population, some of the older inhabitants feel that they are losing touch with the deeper realities of life.[38]

Wallas recalled a conversation with an old Yorkshire schoolmaster, who had told him how, within his memory, 'the old affection for place and home had disappeared from the district'. As the older feeling had gone, the man told his sympathetic listener,

> nothing ... had taken its place, or would take its place, but a naked and restless individualism, always seeking for personal satisfaction, and always missing it. And then, almost in the words of Morris and Ruskin, he began to urge that we should pay a cheap price if we could regain the true riches of life by forgetting steam and electricity, and returning to the agriculture of the medieval village and the handicrafts of the medieval town.[39]

Yet, 'he knew and I knew', Wallas concluded, 'that his plea was hopeless.'

Wallas was similarly struck, as he told a friend,

> with the intense vehemence with which an intelligent Hindoo whom I questioned, protested in favour of the deeper happiness of village life as compared to modern industrial life in India, even although the village life was lived on a money basis of two or three pounds a year per family.[40]

'And yet', he continued, 'we clearly do not want to return to village life.' Men would have to learn to live as best they could in their new environment.[41] To help men accomplish this, Wallas turned to 'Darwinian' social psychology.

The implications of the *Origin of Species*, as they gradually emerged at the end of the nineteenth century, seemed to call for the return of the

---

[38] *Human Nature in Politics*, 283–4.
[39] Ibid., 284–5.
[40] Letter to Alfred Zimmern, 16 Mar. 1909 (WP).
[41] Ibid.

concept of 'human nature' to its former place at the centre of social and psychological thinking. The Enlightenment had been unable satisfactorily to explain the diversity of history and of contemporary 'primitive' societies, and the nineteenth-century attempt to deal with human diversity through overarching evolutionary patterns, lacking a basis in the natural sciences, led only to tautology and unprovable metaphysics.[42] Darwin, however, had made possible an advance beyond that cul-de-sac by providing a view of man evolving, not autonomously, but through a continuous interaction with his environment ('natural selection').Further,this evolution proceeded on a vast time scale, and was thus very slow—imperceptible in the brief span of recorded history. These two contributions appeared to rescue human nature from both relativism and metaphysics by providing both a high degree of fixity and a verifiable mechanism of change.

From this Darwinian foundation arose the instinct psychology and, closely allied with it, the adaptational or 'functional' psychology that characterized Wallas's era. A biological approach necessarily takes the individual as the key unit, and a Darwinian, as opposed to a Lamarckian, biology stresses the short-run fixity of this unit. Thus, 'instincts', lodged within the individual, passed on by inheritance, were postulated as the fundamental, irreducible units of the science of man, like atoms in physics. Individual psychology was largely determined by these instincts, and social psychology was individual psychology multiplied. An extreme version of this biological and individualist reductionism formed the creed of eugenics, which arose and flourished while Wallas was writing his major works; in somewhat more moderate form, it was the theoretical basis of William McDougall's influential *Introduction to Social Psychology* (1908), where the various supposed instincts were listed and discussed, preparatory to an examination of their action in society.

The adaptational, or functional, approach to psychology also flourished under Darwin's wing. Through the process of natural selection, the inherited impulses of man—which constituted his 'nature'—were constantly adapting themselves to the environment and its requirements. This adaptation became the focus of much psychological study—that of William James and John Dewey, among others.[43]

Today the biological approach, together with the Darwinism that underlay it, has been largely discarded by the social sciences. Darwin had

---

[42] By far the best treatment of these attempts is J. W. Burrow, *Evolution an Society*.
[43] See F. B. Karpf, *American Social Psychology*.

left inexact both the character of the interaction between biological inheritance and environment and the precise nature of this inheritance. In addition, 'social Darwinism' assumed continuity between the primeval past and the present; the same laws of development were taken as applying throughout. All of these points eventually fell into dispute.

The relative importance of heredity and environment became a fiercely debated issue, and heredity by itself came to seem less and less decisive. Even within the 'biological' camp, doubts arose as to the specificity of inherited behaviour. Clearly, men did not inherit the kind of elaborately detailed instincts that insects, for example, did. There seemed to be a trend as one went up the evolutionary ladder toward less specific patterns of inherited behaviour. As the term 'instinct' began to yield to terms like 'disposition' or 'tendency', the force of the 'biological' approach to human behaviour waned.[44]

The assumption of continuity between nature and society has also been discarded. Human history, rather than just a continuation of the history of life, now seems to be a new story, with new rules. The development of intelligence and the establishment of society have completely altered man's situation, bringing the billion-year process of evolution by natural selection to an end. The dominion of biology has been broken, and plasticity and possibility have ousted fixity. 'Human nature' has consequently lost most of its meaning.[45]

Along with these specific arguments, and ultimately more important than any of them, went a growing appreciation of the power and influence of society over the individuals that compose it. This appreciation was at the heart of the new social sciences. It underlay the revolutionary concept of 'culture' in anthropology, and the rise of sociology as a science completely independent of biology. More than any single factor, it has transformed our understanding of human behaviour.

The years since Wallas have seen the destruction of 'biologism', in whose climate Wallas lived and thought. However, Wallas's outlook had never been purely 'biological'. In the arguments over the meaning of 'social Darwinism' in the late nineteenth century he had been an environmentalist. Against Herbert Spencer's fatalism, he and other Socialists emphasized the possibilities for improving upon nature by controlling environment. In an early Fabian lecture he had pointed out that

[44] See Karpf, op. cit.; Allport, 'Historical Background', in Lindzey, op. cit.; Mark Haller, *Eugenics* (New Brunswick, N.J., 1963).
[45] For an extreme statement of this, see Edmund Leach's 1968 Reith lectures, *A Runaway World?* (London, 1969).

nearly all of the progress in the physical evolution of the animal or vegetable world in the three or four thousand years of our history has been due to deliberate human care and forethought and not to any mere blind struggle. No man now who wishes to improve his pear trees proposed to shut up his garden and wait two or three hundred thousand years until he can see which variety has developed itself best. He rather digs his ground carefully and prunes, trains and waters each individual plant till all are better.[46]

Wallas took a middle position in the Edwardian debate over 'nature versus nurture', against the 'excesses' of both sides. In his 'trimming' way Wallas interpreted Darwin's legacy as a twofold view of human nature, hereditary *and* environmental. The question that concerned him was the precise nature of the interaction between the inherited and the acquired in human behaviour, the area for study that of the meeting-ground between biology and society.[47]

This focus on the meeting-ground of biology and society was shared by several of the leading minds of the time, including one of the founders of modern anthropology, Bronislaw Malinowski. Malinowski, working as a graduate student under the ethnologist C. G. Seligman, at the L.S.E., read *The Great Society* in proof. 'It deals', he wrote admiringly from Australia, where he was beginning the fieldwork that was to help change the course of anthropology, 'with exactly those problems which for me always were most essential and truly scientific. My greatest ambition would be to draw the ethnological conclusions from your work, to apply these general sociological principles to the special problems of ethnology.'[48]

Like Wallas in political science, Malinowski wanted to move anthropology away from the study of isolated customs, and towards the study of human beings. In attempting this he took the same general approach Wallas had, making the focus of his work the relation between culture and biology. His 'functionalism' was an outgrowth of 'biologism'. Social institutions could only be understood, he insisted, if we take account of the fact that they must satisfy the needs of living human beings. These needs, ultimately biological, were the starting and concluding points of social life. Yet Malinowski also insisted, breaking sharply with Wallas's generation, that there were many different ways of satisfying these needs, all of them valid in their own terms.[49] His successors in turn, were to keep and build upon his

---

[46] Lecture on 'Socialism', 1886 or 1887 (WP).
[47] See *Sociological Papers*, iii (1906), 187.
[48] Letter to Wallas, 27 June 1916 (WP).
[49] See Edmund Leach, 'Frazer and Malinowski', *Encounter*, xxv. no. 5 (Nov. 1965), 24-36.

functionalism and cultural relativism, while playing down or criticizing their original biological basis.[50] Malinowski illustrates the relevance of 'old-fashioned' ideas in the development of newer ones. Rarely is one entire way of looking at things superseded by another, entirely different way. Instead, elements of the older view are rejected, while other elements are continued, and often even given greater importance than before. Only later are these latter elements subject to scrutiny and rejection. This pattern can be seen in the human sciences. Wallas's work formed part of a significant stage in their development, as we have seen in political science. In anthropology, his approach was not only carried on by Malinowski, but used to sweep away older approaches that were blocking advance. An inability to grasp the overwhelming power of society to shape behaviour that we call 'culture' left Wallas with one foot firmly planted in the nineteenth century. Yet his concentration upon the interaction of biology and society was valuable in its time.

In any event, the rejection of 'biologism' may well have gone too far. In recent years many students of human behaviour have had second thoughts. The extreme cultural relativism espoused most vigorously by Ruth Benedict has been toned down under the criticisms of Clyde Kluckhohn and others, who have reaffirmed the ultimate biological foundation of behaviour.[51] A political scientist, James C. Davies, has borrowed the title 'Human Nature in Politics' for his own work which attempts to 'redirect attention to neglected lines of thought'—the relation of biology and political behaviour.[52] In his search for the 'origins of political behaviour', Davies sees no reason for accepting the assumption of the mind as a *tabula rasa* upon which culture writes whatever it chooses to write. Instead, he seeks to discover 'what can and cannot be imprinted on the *tabula non rasa*'.[53]

[50] See Leach's criticism of Malinowski for postulating 'a psychological unity of mankind', ibid., 36, and generally for taking biological needs as the basis of social analysis. 'The Epistemological Basis of Malinowski's Empiricism', *Man and Culture*, ed. R. Firth (London, 1957). For a defence of Malinowski on this score, see R. Piddington, 'Malinowski's Theory of Needs', *Man and Culture*.
[51] See Piddington, op. cit., and Kluckhohn, 'Values and Value-Orientations in the Theory of Action', in *Towards a General Theory of Action*, ed. T. Parsons and E. Shils, (Cambridge, Mass., 1951).
[52] *Human Nature in Politics: The Dynamics of Political Behavior* (New York, 1963).
[53] Ibid., viii. Heinz Eulau of Stanford, in reviewing Davies's book, agreed that 'political behavior, like all human behavior, is rooted in man's organic needs as these interact with situation and environment' and that 'in studying political behavior, we should return to human nature as the point of departure'. 'It has always seemed to me', he went on, 'and

The political experiences of the twentieth century have prompted reconsideration of the idea of 'human nature'. The failure of totalitarian régimes radically to transform behaviour has pointed to apparent limits of human plasticity, limits that may well be fortunate. In re-evaluating Freud, Lionel Trilling has asked us 'to consider whether this emphasis on biology ... far from being a reactionary idea ... is actually a liberating idea. It proposes to us that culture is not all-powerful. It suggests that there is a residue of human quality beyond the reach of cultural control, and that this residue ..., elemental as it may be, serves to bring culture itself under criticism and keeps it from being absolute'.[54]

The depressing persistence and even intensification of conflict in this most modern century has revived speculation that this sort of undesirable behaviour may be rooted in our biological inheritance. The noted ethologist, Konrad Lorenz, in *On Aggression* has sought to cast light on human behaviour by examining man's particular place in the animal world. This approach has become popular in recent years, and a host of less reliable works than Lorenz's have found a wide readership.

Yet, even after separating out the element of fashion, it seems that the repudiation of biologism was too complete, and its funeral perhaps premature. 'The principal antinomy that haunts us today', Gordon Allport has pointed out, 'is the incontestable truth that there are, on the one hand, biological and psychological laws governing the conduct of the individual, while at the same time, there are incontestable social, societal, and cultural laws of equal constraint.'[55] To arrive at a complete view of man, Allport concludes, we will sooner or later have to bring together biology and sociology. In this endeavour Wallas, though outdated, is far from irrelevant.[56]

[this] book confirms it that what I would call the "great deviation" in the study of politics occurred when human nature was left out of its equations. Graham Wallas was the first to call our attention to what had been lost in the decades after John Stuart Mill, but his call for the study of human nature in politics was largely ignored for more decades to come.' Eulau, however, also pointed out the enormous practical difficulties confronting the biological approach to the study of behavior. *American Political Science Review*, lviii (1964), 118–20.

[54] *Freud and the Crisis of Our Culture* (Boston, 1955), 48.

[55] 'William James and the Behavioral Sciences', *Journal of the History of the Behavioral Sciences*, ii (1966), 146.

[56] Discussing the new interest in primate behaviour, a sociologist has drawn implications that take us back to Wallas's programme. 'We must be far more open', Lionel Tiger has cautioned American liberals, 'to the possibility of biological or "animal" control of the infra-structure of our social arrangements. We must learn about the real facts of human mutability and the relationship between genetic program and cultural ex-

The adaptational viewpoint deriving from Darwinism gave Wallas the key he was seeking to the 'discontents' of the 'Great Society'. Adaptation was necessarily imperfect, since the environment was always changing. This fruitful gap provided the motive force of evolution. However, when viewed not from the macrocosmic standpoint but from that of individual human happiness in the modern world, this evolutionary gap was a painful one.

The hereditary drives making up human nature, it was assumed, had originally come into existence to perform a necessary or useful function. When, due to a change in the needs of the environment, their function was no longer advantageous, they would disappear and new impulses would arise. This change-over, however, took a vast length of time by the standards of human history. Until the rise of civilization, the slow pace of biological change had not been a great problem for man, since the environment also changed very slowly, and there was usually adequate time to adapt to new conditions. Now, however, there was little time for adaptation. The basic problem of modern life was the 'maladjustment' of man to his self-created environment, the 'disharmony' between human nature and the new society.[57]

This problem, of which Wallas had been imprecisely aware for years, was probably clarified for him by two articles by Dr. Wilfred Trotter appearing in the *Sociological Review*, the journal of the Sociological Society, during 1908 and 1909. In these articles, which Wallas, as an active member of the Society, read, Trotter postulated an instinct of gregariousness to explain human social behaviour. This 'herd instinct', according to Trotter, had enabled men to live together and to develop civilization, but at the same time it had become a source of profound psychological tension. The demands of society, he warned, given force within the individual by gregariousness, inevitably came into conflict with the demands of individual desires. The development of organized human society, though a great step forward, was not an unmixed blessing, for social life necessarily

---

pression. To know the biological constants, which is to say the non-cultural ones, sharpens our appreciation precisely of cultural differences. Thus a new Fabianism might involve research on these constants—biologically grounded research as a preliminary ground for conscious attempts at social change.' *The New Republic*, clviii. 16 (20 Apr. 1968), 37.

[57] Konrad Lorenz has echoed Wallas's concern, noting that 'the extreme speed of ecological and sociological change wrought by the developments of technology causes many customs to become maladaptive within one generation'. (*On Aggression*) Edmund Leach, ever vigilant against the infection of biologism, has called this notion of maladaptation 'a dead duck'. *New York Review of Books*, vii. 10 (15 Dec. 1966). Leach may eventually be vindicated, but as of now the 'duck' is kicking more vigorously than for several decades.

fostered psychological strain. A spectator watching the appearance of 'herd suggestion', Trotter reflected,

> had he been interested in the destiny of the race, might have felt a pang of apprehension when he realised how momentous was the divorce which had been accomplished between instinct and the individual desire. . . . Duty has first appeared in the world, and with it the age-old conflict.[58]

As a physician, Trotter looked at social psychology from the standpoint of individual psychopathology. He found the origins of individual psychological breakdown in the conflict between social norms, internalized through 'herd suggestion' and the purely individual instincts. These ideas, though independently arrived at by Trotter, strikingly resembled those of his contemporary, Sigmund Freud, the greatest representative of the 'biological' approach to psychology.[59] Freud's psychology was pre-eminently concerned with the relations between 'nature' and 'society', between inherited impulse and environmental conditions. Though Wallas read nothing of Freudian psychology until after his own ideas had been developed, his own psychology had many points of contact with it.[60]

For both, social psychology was wholly explicable by individual psychology, which in turn was based on an instinctual concept of human nature. Freud and Wallas shared a vivid sense of the difficulties, tensions, and unhappiness underlying social life. Acutely aware of the biological limitations this viewpoint imposed on hopes for human happiness and social progress, both men felt themselves representing 'science' and 'realism' against ignorant and superficial 'Utopians'.

Wallas, however, as an educator and social reformer, balked at pessimism. Whereas Freud saw the human predicament as tragedy, Wallas saw it as a challenge to thought and effort. The instincts in Freud's conception were powerful and demanding, at root incompatible with civilized life, indeed, with any sort of social life. In modern life they could be appeased or compromised, but never satisfied. Similarly, the social environment, as Freud saw it, necessarily made impossible demands upon human nature. The resulting psychological strain could be ameliorated, Freud felt, but never eliminated. The instincts for Wallas were milder and less frightening; social demands less unreasonable. Interested less in the eternal problems

---

[58] 'The Sociological Application of the Psychology of Herd Instinct', *Sociological Review*, ii (1909), 40.

[59] Freud, like Trotter, came to psychology by way of medicine; McDougall came by way of physiology. All shared a Darwinian frame of thought.

[60] For Freud's thought assessed in terms of intellectual history, see Philip Rieff, *Freud: The Mind of the Moralist* (Garden City, New York, 1961).

of social life than in the specific problems of the Great Society, Wallas tended to see these problems as susceptible to immediate remedies. Though he saw that 'nature' and 'society' could never be completely harmonized with civilized life, Wallas felt that the proper 'social engineering' could vastly improve matters.

Wallas's version of instinct psychology was in this closer to that of his American friend Jane Addams than to Freud's. He had been familiar with her work as early as 1899, and they corresponded from at least 1908 onwards. Wallas sent her a copy of *Human Nature in Politics*, and she in turn invited him to lecture in Chicago.[61] A social reformer rather than a social scientist, Jane Addams attempted, like Wallas, to develop a 'realistic' approach to reform, based on an accurate view of human nature in place of empty moralism and idealism.[62] In the course of this attempt, she drew on the same sort of psychology, and perceived the same sort of problems.

Too little notice, she argued, had been taken of the radical novelty of the contemporary urban environment and its effects upon human behaviour. Though the age might be triumphant in the matter of inventions and technology, she warned that it would be a hollow triumph if 'it lost its head over the achievements and forgot the men'.[63] The theme of her best-known book, *The Spirit of Youth and the City Streets* (1909), was the unresponsiveness of the modern social environment to the needs of its inhabitants. Natural impulses, she had found in her settlement work, could not be denied without psychic damage; refused a healthy, life-enhancing expression, they would find other outlets, most likely anti-social and personally harmful. The modern city, for example, had failed, as she saw it, to provide for the insatiable desire for play. She commented,

This stupid experiment of organizing work and failing to organize play has, of course, brought about a fine revenge. The love of pleasure will not be denied, and when it has turned into all sorts of malignant and vicious appetites, then we, the middle aged, grow quite distracted and resort to all sorts of restrictive measures. We even try to dam up the sweet fountain itself because we are affrighted by these neglected streams.[64]

Jane Addam's message was that society and human nature, as a result of rapid technological change, had fallen out of harmony. Many of the social problems of modern life, she felt, were traceable to this maladjustment. Where natural impulses had lost their original outlet, new outlets

[61] See notes for 'Prolegomenon to Politics', and correspondence (WP).
[62] See *Democracy and Social Ethics* (New York, 1902).
[63] Ibid., 206-7.
[64] *The Spirit of Youth and the City Streets* (New York, 1909), 6.

had to be created, and the impulses redirected. Where modern society made new demands upon men, they had to be helped to meet them without having to sacrifice basic needs. Men had to learn how to live in a new environment, and how to make that environment liveable.

Observing the Great Society in the light of Darwinism and the 'new psychology', stimulated by the insights of Jane Addams and others, Wallas came to the conclusion that 'Rousseau, Ruskin, Morris, etc., had something very real to say when they talked about a "natural" life'.[65] The 'old life', now passing away, was more 'natural' than that of the Great Society because it was more harmonious with the facts of human nature. After a visit to a 'backwater of civilization', Wallas noted that the faces of people in modern society showed 'strangely few signs of that harmony of the whole being which constitutes happiness'.[66] A 'half-conscious' dissatisfaction with the 'unnatural' conditions of the Great Society seemed to be increasingly widespread—a dissatisfaction, Wallas put it, with those conditions in men's lives as part of a large organization 'which one may call monotony, unreality, want of freedom, but which is perhaps best described as want of relation to the nature which we have inherited'.[67]

In order to uncover the significance of this dissatisfaction, Wallas set out to apply the findings of experimental psychology to society as a whole. Social psychology as a science was, he decided, in its earliest stages; as in political science, he found himself a pioneer. He read M. M. Davis's *Psychological Interpretations of Society* (1909), an examination of recent attempts to establish a scientific social psychology, 'with a real sense of relief'. He wrote to the author, a professor at Columbia University,

> I had been through perhaps a tenth part of the books which you quote and had feared that my ignorance represented a much greater loss than it now appears to be. Anyone working at social psychology must now read the new books which appear on the subject, but it seems probable that he may safely neglect nearly all the old books. For the moment I believe students would be best advised mainly to read pure psychology and to apply it themselves to social and political conditions.[68]

This was the path Wallas himself took, working out his own social psychology from a personal application of 'pure psychology'. There was, of course, a serious weakness inherent in such an approach—the neglect of the specifically *social* dimension of social psychology which at least had

[65] Letter to Zimmern, 16 Mar. 1909 (WP).
[66] *The Great Society*, 7.
[67] Letter to Zimmern, 16 Mar. 1909 (WP).
[68] Letter, 3 Sept. 1909 (WP).

been seen by some of the writers he and Davis were rejecting. Yet these writers had by and large run into a dead end of excessive abstraction, and a fresh approach had much to promise. In attempting this new approach, Wallas became, as a recent historian of psychology has noted, 'the first considerable British social psychologist'.[69] Adopting a 'scientific' terminology from the psychologists (whose works he began to read extensively),[70] Wallas took as his central concept that of 'dispositions'. Dispositions—divided into 'elementary' and 'complex' (and the 'complex' further divided into 'instinctive' and 'intelligent')—were inherited tendencies, hereditary causes of human behaviour. 'Human nature' was the sum total of these dispositions. The conjunction of dispositions with their appropriate stimuli, usually facts in the environment, produced behaviour. From this viewpoint, essentially the psychology James had set out in his *Principles* brought up to date, Wallas sketched a psychological portrait of modern society, a portrait in dark colours.

He argued that the relation between disposition and stimulus, simple enough in the animal world and even in primitive man, had become highly complex in civilized man. He explained,

Man is born with a set of dispositions related, clumsily enough but still intelligibly, to the world of tropical or subtropical wood and cave which he inhabited during millions of years of slow evolution, and whose main characteristics changed little over vast periods of time. The story of civilization begins when he was driven by hunger or by insect-born disease to go North and South into new climates. There his comparatively plastic intelligence enabled him to sustain life under new conditions, not in the main by evolving new dispositions, but by acquiring new habits, and by making clothes, houses, and other modifications of his material surroundings.[71]

At no period, he continued, either in the old environment or the new, was man apparently very successful in creating a harmony between himself and his world. This problem had greatly increased with technological development, culminating in the present psychic crisis: 'In our time the coming of the Great Society has created an environment, in which, for most of us, neither our instinctive nor our intelligent dispositions find it easy to discover their most useful stimuli.'[72]

[69] L. S. Hearnshaw, *A Short History of British Psychology 1840–1940* (London, 1964), 116.
[70] *The Great Society* quotes or cites technical psychological works by E. B. Titchener C. S. Myers, E. L. Thorndike, W. B. Pillsbury, and many others.
[71] *The Great Society*, 61.
[72] Ibid., 62.

Wallas drew upon thirty years of social observations in London to paint a picture of the misdirection and perversion of natural impulses in modern life. He bade his readers visit a London slum, such as he had represented on the London School Board and County Council for thirteen years, and see 'what it is that here stimulates the instincts which one by one appear in the growth of a human being'.[73] In this environment the failure of modern civilization was most evident:

The babies are tugging at dirty india-rubber teats. The sweetshops are selling hundred-weights of bright-coloured stuff, which excites the appetite of the children without nourishing their bodies. That pale-faced boy first knew love, not when he looked at a girl whom later he might marry, but when a dirty picture post-card caught his eye or he watched a suggestive film. His dreams of heroism are satisfied by halfpenny romances, half criminal and half absurd. Loyalty and comradeship mean sticking to his street gang; and the joy of constructive work means the money which he can get for riding behind a van or running messages.

The men are never far removed from the two great social forces of gambling and alcohol. If the desire of change, of risk, of achievement comes on, then the bookmaker is always around the corner; and the publican will give at any moment, for a few pence, that dreaming reverie, that sense of the tremendous significance of the world, which led their ancestors, sitting at the tent door or among the mountain sheep, to the beginnings of philosophy and science. And because the new facts by which our dispositions are now stimulated are only inexact substitutes for the old facts by which they were stimulated during the long process of evolution, the stimulus itself is weak and capricious. Even the enthusiasm of the group at the public-house door, who are discussing a glove-fight, seems, as you watch them, to be thin and half-hearted.[74]

As Wallas pondered this situation, even more than the happiness of the members of the Great Society seemed to be at stake. The stability, the very survival of the Great Society itself, was called into question. Why, he asked himself, 'should we expect a social organization to endure, which has been formed in a moment of time by human beings, whose bodies and minds are the result of age-old selection under far different conditions?'[75] Modern civilization, in the form of the Great Society, appeared to Wallas as even more fragile than it had to Bagehot.

Technological advance, in its lack of relation to the unchanging needs of human nature, was as much a force for disruption as for cohesion. The ancient empires of Assyria, Persia, and Rome, Wallas noted, must have seemed permanent to their contemporaries. Each possessed not only

[73] *The Great Society*, 62.   [74] Ibid., 62-3.   [75] Ibid., 9.

HUMAN NATURE IN MODERN SOCIETY

irresistable military power, but a monopoly of all means of rapid communication. Yet, as ancient empires became larger,

they became too distant and too unreal to stimulate the affection or pride of their subjects. The methods of their agents became more mechanical and inhuman, and passions which grouped themselves round smaller units, local or racial or religious, produced ever-increasing inner strain.[76]

Social cohesion ultimately depended on psychic factors. When, Wallas asked, one looks behind the 'mechanical' arrangements of railways and telegraphs, or of laws, treaties, and elections, 'what are the real forces on which our hopes of national or international solidarity depend?'[77] He recalled his days spent canvassing the streets of London, in which he had seen 'how weak are the feelings which attach the citizen to a society whose power he dimly recognizes, but which he often seems to think of merely with distrust and dislike'.[78]

The Edwardian 'illusion of security', if indeed it existed among intellectuals, did not extend to Wallas. The rising domestic and international tensions in the years before the First World War seemed to him signs of grave social crisis.[79] He traced throughout the politics and 'realistic' literature of the Edwardian era a

fear, conscious or half-conscious, lest the civilization which we have adopted so rapidly and with so little forethought may prove unable to secure either a harmonious life for its members or even its own stability. The old delight in the 'manifest finger of destiny' and 'the tide of progress', even the newer belief in the effortless 'evolution' of social institutions are gone. We are afraid of the blind forces to which we used so willingly to surrender ourselves. We feel that we must reconsider the basis of our organised life because, without reconsideration, we have no chance of controlling it. And so behind the momentary ingenuities and party phrases of our statesmen we can detect the straining effort to comprehend while there is yet time. Our philosophers are toiling to refashion for the purposes of social life the systems which used so confidently to offer guidance for individual conduct. Our poets and playwrights and novelists are revolutionising their art in the attempt to bring the essential facts of the Great Society within its range.[80]

IV

From the very beginning of civilized life, Wallas realized, men had felt not quite at home in their self-created environment. Until the Greeks, this

[76] *The Great Society*, 9.
[78] Ibid., 11.
[80] Ibid., 14.
[77] Ibid., 11.
[79] See ibid., 10–11.

discontent had been projected backwards, in sterile longings for a return to a 'Golden Age'. It was the 'supreme achievement' of the Greek intellect, he reflected, 'to substitute for this vain longing a new conception of nature'.[81] Aristotle, in Wallas's estimation the greatest Greek thinker, had seen that man's nature and his environment were at war, but he also had seen that 'the remedy was not to go back to the forests of the past, but to invent the city of the future, the material and social organisation which should contrive a new harmony, higher because it was deliberate'.[82] Aristotle's famous statement that 'man is an animal adapted for living in a city-state' meant for Wallas 'not that man was living in such a state when Zeus was born, but that the city-state stimulated his nature to its noblest expression'.[83]

In Greek thought and in Greek life Wallas found the hope that the psychological problems of civilization, now so much intensified in the Great Society, could be resolved. The Great Society could become the 'good society'. To accomplish this was, in Wallas's judgement, 'the master-task of civilised mankind'. Men, he knew,

will fail in it again and again, partly from lack of inventive power, partly from sheer ignorance of the less obvious facts of their material surroundings and mental structure. But it is hardly possible for any one to endure life who does not believe that they will succeed in producing a harmony between themselves and their environment far deeper and wider than anything which we can see today.[84]

The way to attain this harmony, he felt sure, was not the purely negative 'Salvation Army' approach of repressing the troublesome natural impulses.[85] Attempts to 'mortify' the dispositions were self-defeating. If the dispositions men inherited were not stimulated they did not, he insisted, therefore die. Nor was the human being what he would have been if they had never existed. 'If we leave unstimulated', he explained, 'or, to use a shorter term, if we "baulk" any one of our main dispositions, Curiosity, Property, Trial and Error, Sex, and the rest, we produce in ourselves a state of nervous strain.'[86] Darwinism had shown that these 'dispositions' were rooted in the process of human evolution, and in that sense 'legitimate'. They represented the old instinctive way of maintaining life, which had had its role, but was no longer adequate to the demands of modern life. Reason had now to step in, not to try to replace impulse, but to supplement and guide it, to rechannel it back into constructive paths.

[81] *The Great Society*, 67. [82] Ibid., 67.
[83] Ibid., 67. [84] Ibid., 68.
[85] Ibid., 64. [86] Ibid., 64-5.

This new task required greater knowledge of human psychology and the social environment, of what was original and what was acquired, what fixed and what modifiable, in human nature. It was exactly this sort of question that Darwinism, as Wallas and many of his contemporaries interpreted it, clarified and proposed to answer.

For centuries past, Wallas pointed out (recalling his own experience),

the young men of each generation have been told by their elders that every proposed reform in social organisation is 'against human nature'. They have generally, and rightly, ignored this warning, because no one knew what human nature was, and there were no means of distinguishing between those things in human character which the reformer could hope to change and those which he must assume to be unchangeable.[87]

Human traits as apparently permanent as the belief in magic or the sentiment of monarchy, he observed, had proved changeable, while apparently superficial characteristics, like the sense of the ridiculous or the need of recreation, had turned out to be unexpectedly stubborn.

Darwin had revealed the traditional approaches to human improvement to be dogmatic and one-sided. This was particularly clear in the field with which Wallas was most familiar—education. Reading a book on education written one hundred or even fifty years earlier, he remarked to a convention of educators, he found himself 'in a new world of ideas'.

Those of our grandfathers [he explained] who thought about education were apt either to believe, with James Mill, that the human child was a lump of sculptor's clay, which could be changed by the schoolmaster into any type desired, or with Rousseau, that it was a flower which would reach perfection by its own laws of growth if it were only left undisturbed. We distinguish nowadays, in a way which would have been unintelligible both to James Mill and to Rousseau, between the native qualities which we must take for granted in each individual instance, and the acquired characteristics which we can hope to change.[88]

Social reformers, both 'environmental' and 'moral', had to come to terms with their biological inheritance. Nature, Wallas insisted, imposed severe limits on what men could do by moral striving or social reform alone. Though 'in our moral conflicts we can seek the strong allies of deeper knowledge and nobler ideals', he concluded that Darwinism had given 'a new and rather sad meaning' to the Biblical observation that 'we cannot *by taking thought* add one cubit to our stature'.[89] Reformers 'build

---

[87] 'Darwinism and Social Motive', (1906) *Men & Ideas*, 90.
[88] Ibid., 92.   [89] Ibid., 92.

with sand' when they rely on the 'deus ex machina of improved human nature'.[90] Instead of attempting to work with men as they were, fixed as well as plastic, men like the Oxford Idealists and high-minded Liberals confused wish and reality.[91]

This realism, however, had its dangerous side for a reformer. Both Ostrogorski and Wallas's good friend G. Lowes Dickinson were quick to point out after reading *Human Nature in Politics* that 'bio-psychological realism' played into the hands of Conservatives.[92] Biological thinking, Ostrogorski warned, made one 'too apt to consider that which exists if not as a *ne plus ultra* at least as something not liable to a large development'. 'The man who is thinking in that way', he continued, 'may sometimes profess very advanced views. That does not make, however, much difference in practice; his method of thinking colours his conceptions on social subjects, unconsciously for himself.'[93]

Wallas, though, was aware of the dangers and limitations of the purely biological approach to social questions. His version of Social Darwinism was more sophisticated, but not in practice fundamentally different from his Socialist interpretation of the 1880s. While giving a new importance to biological inheritance, Darwinism did not, as he saw it, down-grade the practical importance of environment. Inheritance set out the limits and the possibilities, but environment was the active principle of development. Within the long tradition of 'biological' social thinking, Darwinism represented a new recognition of environment. Wallas observed that Darwin had 'transferred the cause of development from within to without':

> Darwin demonstrated that, while it is true that there is a tendency in each living thing towards variation, yet the variation is in itself indifferent; and that the formative cause which *selects* variations and produces those permanent changes which we call the development of species must be looked for in the environment of the individual, and not in any inner tendency.[94]

A scientific view of human nature, in Wallas's opinion, offered no reason for fatalism, either optimistic or pessimistic. Men could, and indeed *had* to, learn to work *with* nature, creating an environment, intel-

---

[90] Notes for 'Prolegomenon to Politics', 1899 (WP).
[91] See *Human Nature in Politics*, 68–72, 196, for perceptive illustrations of this point. Wallas argued this position in correspondence with Ostrogorski, who completely denied the relevance of biology to 'moral' questions. Letter from Ostrogorski, 15 Aug. 1909 (WP).
[92] Letter from Dickinson, 7 Jan. 1909, and letter from Ostrogorski, 15 Aug. 1909 (WP).
[93] Letter from Ostrogorski, 15 Aug. 1909 (WP).
[94] 'A Criticism of Froebelian Pedagogy' (1901), *Men & Ideas*, 137.

lectual and moral as well as physical, which would on the one hand be more suited to human nature as it was and on the other select desirable and inhibit undesirable inherited potentialities. In short, men had to learn how to reconcile their nature with their environment, and both with their ideals, by creating new relationships between them. Social thinkers and social leaders had to become 'social-psychological engineers'. Human *nature* as inherited was in truth relatively fixed, but human *behaviour*, shaped by environment as well, was open to much alteration, as events like the French Revolution or the transformation of Japanese society since the mid-nineteenth century illustrated.[95]

For all his strictures against 'idealistic' and naïve reformers, Wallas himself remained firmly in the camp of reform. His peculiar approach, however, laid him open to persistent misunderstanding by both reformers and Conservatives. Too idealistic for the 'realists', too realistic for the 'idealists', his work was not as immediately influential as it ought to have been. Conservatives seized upon his criticism of 'intellectualism' and ignored the rest of his thought, while Liberals like Lowes Dickinson and Ostrogorski feared he had undermined his own hopes for reform by his 'biologism'. His work seemed to be flawed by a fundamental inconsistency; G. P. Gooch pointed out to Wallas after reading *Human Nature in Politics*:

In the first part, you appear to hold that [reasoning] has exceedingly little influence in the formation of opinion or the determination of action, and in your comments on Bryce's 'ideal' (a comment I think not quite fair) you seem to regard any considerable change or improvement as being as unlikely as changes in habits and needs of the human body. In the second part, however, you try to show the enormous importance of educating opinion, using of course the necessary psychological methods, but at the same time working up towards the old 'intellectualist' ideals of judgment, responsibility, etc.[96]

Gooch had a point. Wallas was trying to have his cake and eat it too— to be realistic without giving up his liberal ideal of the rational, responsible individual, to be 'tough-minded' yet satisfy his 'Evangelical' propensity to preach and exhort; to be, in short, both a social scientist and a reformer. In this he again showed his academic tendency to straddle an issue, seeing something in both sides of an argument, that had exasperated H. G. Wells. This avoidance of any 'one-sided' position, so different from Wells's style, dulled Wallas's impact upon his contemporaries.

Yet Gooch's criticism was not really fair, and reflected a failing typical

[95] Notes for a lecture at the South Place Ethical Society, spring 1905, in which he first developed this line of thought.
[96] Letter to Wallas, 28 Dec. 1908 (WP).

of English Liberals of the time. Determined not to let reality take precedence over their moral principles, they too often regarded attempts to subject man and society to scientific analysis as a betrayal of the cause of reform. Men like Gooch and Lowes Dickinson were, like Wallas, under the sway of the Evangelical tradition, soldiers in the struggle to impose morality in the form of Liberal principles upon the unregenerate world. But this moralistic tradition was not counterbalanced in their case by the fervour for science that possessed Wallas.

Wallas's 'realistic' probings had not been prompted by an abandonment of 'intellectualist' ideals, but by a recognition of their practical weakness. His aim was to make it possible for these ideals to be translated from empty rhetoric to actuality. Wallas saw himself as a social engineer working to correct the shortcomings of men and their institutions. As he remarked in *Human Nature in Politics*:

The engineer, when he wishes to increase the margin of safety in his plans, treats as factors in the same quantitative problem both the chemical expedients by which he can strengthen his materials and the structural changes by which the strain on those materials can be diminished. So those who would increase the margin of safety in our democracy must estimate, with no desire except to arrive at truth, both the degree to which the political strength of the individual citizen can, in any given time, be actually increased by moral and educational changes, and the possibility of preserving or extending or inventing such elements in the structure of democracy as may prevent the demand upon him from being too great for his strength.[97]

Wallas henceforth turned from the descriptive to the prescriptive, from social science to social reform, as he strove to help transform the Great Society into the Good Society.

[97] *Human Nature in Politics*, 253-4.

CHAPTER VI

TOWARDS A 'GREAT COMMUNITY'

I

'WE have changed our environment', wrote Wallas's American student, Walter Lippmann, echoing his teacher, in 1914, 'more quickly than we know how to change ourselves.'[1] As a result, men and their self-created environment were out of harmony. The solution, for Wallas, was still more change—deliberate, thought-out change in men's behaviour and institutions to cope with the problems created by unplanned change.

Freed by defeat in the London County Council elections of 1907 of the day-to-day demands of politics and administration, Wallas began to work on a new book.[2] He hoped to extend the psychological approach of *Human Nature in Politics* to society in general, and to provide an example of the kind of 'constructive' social thinking he had called for in his criticism of Ostrogorski.[3] Social psychology could be used, he believed, to diagnose the psychic diseases of existing social and political relations and to suggest remedies.[4] The new book was to be, as Ernest Barker later called it, 'a treatise on . . . social psychotherapeutics'.[5]

Wallas's constructive programme was shaped by two English reform traditions—Benthamism and Evangelicalism. The Benthamite tradition we might call a 'hard' one, claiming the mantle of science and looking to institutional change, to what Wallas called 'social invention'. Wallas's Benthamism was partly second-hand, through English radicalism and particularly through Sidney Webb's form of Socialism. It was also, and increasingly, direct, for in his historical work Wallas had rediscovered Bentham and had begun to read and ponder his writings. He became an

---

[1] *Drift and Mastery* (New York, 1914), 153.
[2] Wallas found it difficult to remain out of politics, even to work out these ideas. He confessed himself 'very much torn' between writing this new book and attempting a return to the L.C.C. Letter to Alfred Zimmern, 16 Mar. 1909 (WP).
[3] See his letter to his niece, 22 Mar. 1909 (WP).
[4] *Human Nature in Politics* had caused William James to reflect, as he wrote to Wallas, that a book ought to be written on 'the diseases of society and their prevention'. Letter to Wallas, 9 Dec. 1908 (WP).
[5] *Political Thought in England 1848–1914*, 204.

authority on Bentham, and in the 1920s gave several lectures on the relevance of Bentham to current problems.[6]

The Evangelical tradition was so much a part of Wallas's upbringing and *milieu* that he had no need to rediscover it. In him it complemented rather than contradicted Benthamism—'soft' where the latter was 'hard', looking to human, 'spiritual' change, resting on the authority of morality. This tradition stimulated Wallas to speculation over a possible new 'world-philosophy' or religion suited to twentieth-century life. These two traditions came together in what was the leitmotive of Wallas's work—the psychological approach to social questions.

Standing in two traditions, it was natural for Wallas to have two aims. On the one hand, he sought efficiency—not in the narrow economic sense, but in the broadest meaning. The unprecedented pace of change in modern society demanded, as he saw it, the greatest possible efficiency of thought and action to keep men in control of their environment. All institutions, traditions, habits, and values had continually to submit to the test of efficiency—Bentham's test of utility in a more dynamic form.

Wallas's second aim was at least partly at variance with the first: greater 'satisfaction', participation, and social cohesion. To Wallas it seemed that the same social developments that made efficiency imperative had undermined the emotional bases of society—harmony between the individual and his surroundings and the sense of solidarity between individuals. The scale, complexity and instability of life in the Great Society, as it made it harder for men to assert rational control over their lives, also made it harder to find psychic satisfaction and a sense of belonging.

'Efficiency' and 'satisfaction' have since emerged as the two leading questions of social thought in the advanced industrial countries, and though they can be traced back to the early nineteenth century, it is only in the opening years of this century that they begin to take on their modern form. Both elicited a great deal of concern from the Edwardians, but few persons were concerned about both. Each became the preoccupation of a different type of thinker. Efficiency and satisfaction appeared to most not complementary but alternative aims. Efficiency seemed to call for further centralization and rationalization, while satisfaction pointed in the opposite direction, towards decentralization and greater attention to emotional needs. Those concerned with efficiency tended to be most at home with 'progress', priding themselves on being scientific, and looking forward to the future. Those concerned about 'satisfaction' tended to be sceptical of 'progress'

---

[6] See 'Bentham' and 'Bentham as Political Inventor', in *Men & Ideas*, 19-32, 33-48.

and science, acutely aware of the good that had been lost by modern society, and more anxious than expectant about the future. Almost alone, Wallas tried to keep a foot in both camps, insisting on the compatibility and necessity of both aims.

II

'Efficiency' as a watchword of social thought had its origins in the loss of national self-confidence and self-satisfaction which began in the 1880s with the rise of new economic and military challengers abroad and the discovery of unjustifiable mass poverty at home. These anxieties came to a head in the aftermath of the Boer War. A mismanaged, unexpectedly prolonged war fought for dubious reasons served as a catalyst for a change in national outlook from expansiveness to self-examination. In every political camp the question was asked, what had gone wrong with England? Though answers varied, one answer that found wide support crossing party lines was 'inefficiency'.[7]

In its narrowest form, this meant military inefficiency. However, even for Conservatives the term came to mean more. The Boer War, with its mass enlistments and mass rejections, revealed the poor physical condition of the bulk of the English population. The recognition of physical inefficiency led in many directions—to the eugenics movement, to the founding of the Boy Scouts—but the most important was to an increased appreciation of the need for social reform.

One of the first to connect publicly the issue of efficiency with the change of scale of modern life was Wallas's old associate, Sidney Webb. Webb argued (extending the basic idea behind Fabianism) that the vast growth of society and shrinking of distances had made collective national efficiency an ever more widely recognized necessity. He asserted,

We have become aware ... that we are not merely individuals, but members of a community, nay, citizens of the world. ... The labourer in the slum tenement, competing for employment at the factory gate, has become conscious that his comfort and his progress depend, not wholly or mainly on himself, or on any other individual, but upon the proper organisation of his Trade Union and the activity of the factory inspector. The shopkeeper or the manufacturer sees his prosperity wax or wane, his own industry and sagacity remaining the same, according to the good government of his city, the efficiency with which his

[7] See Bentley Gilbert, *The Evolution of British National Insurance* (London, 1966), ch. 2; Samuel Hynes, op. cit., ch. 2; Bernard Semmel, *Imperialism and Social Reform* (London, 1960), ch. 3.

nation is organised, and the influence which his Empire is able to exercise in the councils, and consequently in the commerce, of the world.[8]

Webb broadened the concept of efficiency to include health, welfare, and education, the bases of what he called 'social' efficiency. He stressed the importance of enabling every member of society to make the maximum contribution to the strength, wealth, and well-being of the society.

An even broader meaning was given to 'efficiency' by Wallas's friend, H. G. Wells, who shared his dissatisfaction at Webb's preoccupation with 'social machinery'. Wells saw the inefficiency of Edwardian England as a lack of purpose, as intellectual, psychological, and moral disorder. In his panoramic novel of Edwardian life, *Tono-Bungay* (1908) (which, his narrator confessed, would have been more aptly titled 'Waste'), Wells found 'no plan . . . no intention, no comprehensive desire'.[9] Order had to be brought out of 'muddle', and this could only be done by thought.

Here Wallas made his contribution to the quest for efficiency. Thinking along similar lines to Wells, he was specifically concerned about the inefficiency of thought in society. This inefficiency was twofold: in the thought-processes themselves, where reason had to contend with the limitations of human nature, and in the application of thought, where institutions and traditions too often were obstructive. To deal with the first, Wallas turned to psychology. Like his contemporary, Freud, Wallas looked to self-knowledge as the beginning of self-mastery: 'It is when reason has brought most clearly into her view', he insisted, 'the unreasoning impulses, the weaknesses and the limitations of human nature, that the Kingdom of Reason of which Plato dreamed becomes most nearly possible.'[10]

Almost at once, Wallas was confronted with a dilemma: most current social psychology denied his own activist, rationalist outlook. Contemporary writers, influenced in part, he felt, by a misconceived Darwinism, ignored the rational, intelligent side of human nature, attributing 'ultimate reality' only to irrational, unconscious, usually instinctive impulses.

Anti-intellectual social psychology, emphasizing as a consequence of man's irrationality his fixity and lack of freedom to determine his destiny, was in Wallas's eyes a 'scientific' bastion of conservatism. As a liberal, as well as a scientist, Wallas felt impelled to attack this sort of psychology. Before it could be turned to 'constructive' use, social psychology had to be freed from its conservative and anti-intellectual bias.

[8] 'Lord Rosebery's Escape from Houndsditch', *Ninteeenth Century*, (Sept. 1901), 369.
[9] *Tono-Bungay* (New York, 1961), 349.
[10] 'Darwinism and Social Motive', *Men & Ideas*, 94.

This involved a shift from the approach that had guided the writing of *Human Nature in Politics*. In that work Wallas had attacked the errors of the liberal tradition of political thought—its abstract idealism and false intellectualism. In concentrating his fire upon them, however, Wallas had appeared to be more anti-liberal and anti-intellectual than he really was. Wanting to reconstruct liberalism, Wallas found that he had given unintentional comfort to its enemies. *Human Nature in Politics* had been introduced into a climate of opinion beginning to be deluged by a general wave of revolt against rationalism, and was thus received as part of this wave.[11] Conservatives had greeted the book as a vindication of their criticisms of democracy, while at the same time Ernest Barker pointed out to Wallas, it had 'encouraged . . . my advanced Syndicalist pupils in their contempt for politics, for representation, for the rational state'.[12]

This sort of one-sidedness was just what Wallas had thought he was getting away from; the problem of social action was not to be solved by substituting one myth for another. He wrote to M. M. Davis,

If one approaches the stimulus of social action as an art one is brought up to what seems to me the essential point in the problem, the part played in social action by 'reasoning'—by the conscious effort of the mind when forecasting results. Most writers seem to become either pure anti-intellectualists, like Ribot, or pure intellectualists, like Ostrogorski. We have to realize that the whole process of bringing the facts of instinct and passion within the sphere of conscious prediction represents a very definite and difficult effort of reason. Reason does not act in vacuo, and when we think of the whole man with his thoughts and feelings going on simultaneously, his feelings being often the subject matter of his thoughts, and his thoughts the stimuli of his feelings, we are certain to become one-sided. . . . [13]

As a rationalist to whom the traditional 'idealist' justifications subscribed to by Ostrogorski, Barker, and Lowes Dickinson were unacceptable, Wallas sought in psychology (as his friend, Leonard Hobhouse, was seeking in biology) a naturalistic justification for rationalism. With

---

[11] Even a student of Wallas's like Walter Lippmann, sharing much of his 'liberal' and reformist outlook, carried Wallas's criticism of intellectualism to lengths that distressed his teacher. His *Preface to Politics* (1913) fused Wallas's thought with all the voguish anti-intellectualist currents of thought of the time—Sorel, Freud, Bergson, and such. Wallas dedicated *The Great Society* to Lippmann in the hope that it would correct this excess of irrationalism.

[12] For a typical conservative reaction, see William Barry in the *National Review*, Mar. 1909. See letter from Barker to Wallas, 15 July 1914 (WP). See also G. D. H. Cole, *Studies in World Economics*, 'Loyalties', for the influence of *Human Nature in Politics* on him.

[13] 3 Sept. 1909 (WP).

'idealism' in the study of human behaviour in retreat, Wallas launched an even more determined (but less successful) attack on the 'false naturalism' that was succeeding it.

In his review of *Human Nature in Politics*, J. A. Hobson had warned of the danger that lay in studying human instincts, 'lest their purely irrational character be overemphasised, by treating reason as a merely regulative force'. 'Surely', he had argued, 'the desire for order which evolves into a fine sense of intellectual consistency must also be allowed to have its roots in animal instinct and to have its appropriate impulses and satisfactions.'[14] In contemplating the role of reasoning in social action, Wallas began to take up this line of thought. The error of anti-intellectualism arose, he agreed with Hobson, from seeing reason as no more than a regulative force, less fundamental or powerful than the non-rational impulses.

Wallas sought to counter anti-intellectualism first by taking for his units of study 'dispositions' rather than 'impulses' or 'instincts'. 'Dispositions'—inherited 'bundles' of associated impulses—varied in complexity. And social life, so tremendously complicated, Wallas insisted, could be explained fruitfully only by studying complex dispositions like acquisitiveness and curiosity, rather than simple ones like hunger or fear. Simple dispositions were generally below the rational level, and to exaggerate their importance led one to dismiss the rational faculty.

Among the complex dispositions, Wallas further distinguished between 'instinctive' and 'intelligent' dispositions, generally corresponding to the less and the more complex. Again, he argued that the 'intelligent' dispositions ought not to be disregarded in favour of the 'instinctive'. No clear demarcation could be drawn between them. One could not say with any certainty whether a certain complex pattern of behaviour was completely or 'really' 'unintellectual'—the 'intelligent' and 'instinctive' dispositions so interpenetrated as to invalidate any oversimplified reductionism, whether 'intellectualist' or 'anti-intellectualist'.

Wallas claimed, as a second method of attack upon anti-intellectualism, that thought was itself a disposition, or at any rate a natural tendency which conditioned other dispositions. Reason and instinct, he asserted, ought to be analysed on the same conceptual plane, for there was no scientific justification for arbitrarily assuming the primacy of one over the other. He himself had fallen into this error in *Human Nature in Politics*, and now hastened to correct himself. He particularly criticized William MacDougall for this fault. MacDougall's *Introduction to Social Psychology* (1908), as the leading scientific work on the subject, was the most impressive

[14] *Sociological Review*, ii, 293.

formulation of anti-intellectualism. As Wallas put it, 'Mr. MacDougall does not hold, as I hold, that we are born with a tendency, under appropriate conditions, to think, which is as original and independent as our tendency, under appropriate conditions, to run away'.[15] Wallas asserted,

This independent action of Intelligence is, I believe, in its simplest forms as 'natural' to us, as much due to inherited disposition, as is the working of any number of the usual list of instincts. The traditional terminology, however, of the moral sciences makes it extraordinarily difficult either to recognise this fact or even to state it clearly.[16]

The chasm between 'thought' and 'instinct' was, he now saw, a fact of language rather than of psychology. The whole subject-matter of 'crowd psychology', Wallas correctly insisted, required 're-statement and re-examination'. 'We must first', he urged, 'get rid of the verbal ambiguities which are due merely to the employment of collective terms.'[17]

Citing the recent work of experimental psychologists, Wallas argued that the supposedly scientific concepts of Tarde, Le Bon, and others—'imitation', 'sympathy', and 'suggestion'—were largely imaginary. Le Bon's identification of 'the crowd' with 'the masses' of a modern nation or the voters in a modern democratic election was, to Wallas, particularly unjustifiable. Nor were the psychological problems of modern social life due, as Le Bon would say, to an increase in unconscious motivation. On the contrary, Wallas argued:

The inhabitant of a modern city is more fully conscious, 'has his wits about him', for a larger proportion of the twenty-four hours than the peasant, and acts much less under the subconscious influence of routine. What the Crowd-Psychologists see is that the defects and the limitations of all human consciousness are much better understood and more cleverly exploited in the city.[18]

'Crowd psychology' was currently in vogue—it 'now enjoys', he observed, 'in the social philosophy of the newspapers some of the old authority of the Laws of Political Economy'—and for this reason its fallacies were

[15] *The Great Society*, 40.   [16] Ibid., 36.
[17] Ibid., 133. However, though Wallas was right in attacking 'crowd psychology', his reasoning had flaws of its own. Anti-intellectual conservatism and 'collectivist' social psychology, usually closely related in Wallas's time, became inseparable in his mind. Consequently, Wallas's liberal zeal led him astray. Partly because of writers like Le Bon, who joined collective psychology (the concept of the 'Group Mind') to instinctivism, irrationalism, and contempt for 'the masses', Wallas was unable to appreciate the pioneering work of Durkheim, who rejected all biological approaches to human behaviour, and sought instead purely *social* explanations.
[18] Ibid., 132–3.

at least as socially pernicious as those of the old Political Economy had been.[19] As a rationalization of conservative prejudices—anti-intellectual, anti-libertarian, anti-democratic, anti-urban—it was a powerful negative force in modern life. As Wallas remarked in reviewing a typical example of this literature in 1915, men may be irrationally motivated much of the time, social life may be permeated with irrationality, emotion, and prejudice—'nevertheless, men have to live and act in societies, and it is the business of social psychology to ascertain the conditions under which they are likely to live and act more wisely or less wisely'.[20]

The inhabitants of a modern state [Wallas concluded], whether they are officials or journalists or working men, are indeed ignorant of much which it would be well for them to know, and unmoved by much which it would be well for them to feel. That they are so is due not to the fact that 'individually' they are thoughtful and temperate, and 'collectively' blind and ferocious, but to the fact that they are human beings, whose intellectual and emotional nature was evolved in contact with the restricted environment of the primitive world, and who have not yet learnt, if ever they will, either to educate in each generation their faculties to fit their environment, or to change their environment so as to fit their faculties.[21]

This 'evolutionary gap' between man's modern environment and his inherited nature meant that both the non-intelligent dispositions—fear, combativeness, and such—and a more or less non-intelligent process like habit—were becoming less and less useful as guides to life. The rigid inflexibility of what Wallas called 'instinctive inference' was an increasingly dangerous factor in modern life, when the greatest need was for the adaptability and autonomy of conscious rational thought. 'The mere growth', he observed, 'of the scale of our social organisation has destroyed, in the case of popular decisions on national policy, the main advantage which Instinctive Inference could claim, that it was stimulated, not by abstract generalisations, but by a direct perception of our concrete environment.'[22] The sorts of instinct stimuli employed during a modern election or war fever, the carefully constructed stereotypes of 'foreigner', 'landlord', and 'agitator', for example, were at least as far removed from concrete reality as the abstract ideas in the minds of the French revolutionaries.[23]

Habit, too, was becoming more and more inadequate without the guidance of conscious thought. While the enlarged scale of modern society made habit increasingly necessary for social order, this very complexity

[19] *The Great Society*, 121.
[20] Review of Christensen, *Politics and Crowd Morality*, *Hibbert Journal*, Oct. 1915.
[21] *The Great Society*, 137–8.   [22] Ibid., 225–6.   [23] Ibid.

of the environment and its rapid pace of change demanded that it be supplemented by thought. As always, Wallas returned to the Greeks, who, he felt, had understood these problems more deeply than modern writers. Men like Plato and Aristotle, who lived in times of profound social change, knew the inadequacy of habit and the need for 'philosophy', if men were to attain to 'virtue'.[24] 'Thought', Wallas conceded, 'may be late in evolution, it may be deplorably weak in driving power, but without its guidance no man or organisation can find a safe path amid the vast impersonal complexities of the universe as we have learnt to see it.'[25]

Could there be, he wondered, 'an art by which the efficiency of Thought can be improved?' Ultimately he foresaw the rapidly developing science of psychology yielding such an art. Until then certain conditions surrounding the thought-process could be brought under conscious control, indirectly improving the thought-process itself.

There were, of course, the material conditions, which could be improved by such obvious reforms as adequate financial support for those engaged or capable of being engaged in creative thought. The psychological conditions were more subtle, matters of 'mental attitudes' and emotions, as well as the reasoning tools available to work with. Attitudes and emotions could be affected, Wallas was sure, by conscious effort, and he examined ways of promoting the self-consciousness of thinkers. Thought and emotion, he had already concluded, did not exist in separate compartments in the mind, but freely interacted, and could thus be deliberately used to influence each other. Even instincts could be harnessed to motivate thought.[26] Wallas foresaw this sort of psychological 'engineering' becoming increasingly important as the science of psychology developed.

The chief realm of 'psychological engineering' was the educational system. To this lifelong teacher and educational administrator, it quite naturally appeared to be the most important set of social institutions. Education at every level, Wallas was convinced, needed a thorough overhauling aimed at the greatest possible stimulation of thought, in quality and in quantity. This overriding concern for intellectual efficiency led Wallas to take issue with traditional educational principles such as the emphasis on discipline and 'character-building', the central role of religion, the classical curriculum, and the reservation of all education beyond the elementary level for a small minority. It also, however, led him into conflict with many 'modern' ideas, particularly the philosophy that came to be known, loosely, as 'progressive education'.

[24] *The Great Society*, 76–7.   [25] Ibid., 45.   [26] Ibid., 230.

Nineteenth-century education had ignored biological reality in aiming to 'conquer' nature in the child, and to impose a given pattern of behaviour and body of knowledge—the same error of 'idealism' and 'abstraction' that Wallas had criticized in political and social thinking. However, like the developments in these wider realms of thought, the reaction against 'Victorianism' in education was, it seemed to him, falling into the opposite error of extreme 'naturalism', indiscriminately accepting and even glorifying whatever 'nature' one found in the child. As he complained to a meeting of the Froebelian Association, the foremost English representative of this trend, in 1901, it was false and harmful to oppose the natural impulses of the child to the 'artificial' demands of adult society. Rather than allowing an unfolding of pre-existing potentialities, the function of education in Wallas's conception was precisely to provide an 'artificial' environment that would select and stimulate those particular capacities most necessary in the special conditions of the Great Society.[27]

It was true, he agreed with the Froebelians, that the child was born with a great number of tendencies and instincts already formed by the slow selection and adaptation of many preceding ages. But, he pointed out, 'they are formed by adaptation to those ages, and therefore not necessarily to our own'.[28]

We cannot, therefore [he continued], now say 'Let us follow Nature' with the old feeling that we thereby free ourselves from the 'intolerable disease' of responsible thought. If 'Nature' means anything, and it is difficult to find a use for that word which is not misleading, then we ourselves and our anxieties are part of Nature. The child will not of itself 'grow' into perfect harmony with its surroundings; it must, in part, be 'made' during its own life, and we must bear our conscious share in the making.[29]

Education was to be centred on the whole life, not 'child-centred'; difficult, not hedonistic. Natural impulses, when they opposed the long-term interests of the child, were to be controlled and redirected. Wallas sharply criticized the new worship of spontaneity and 'concreteness', and the attempt to make education 'fun', as irresponsible. This educational philosophy seemed to him anti-intellectual, for in exalting the most immediate impulses it down-graded the importance of deliberate thought, and in emphasizing the concrete and the immediate experience over the more abstract and difficult intellectual processes it weakened the capacity for mental effort. Froebelian education, he complained, was decidedly

[27] See 'A Criticism of Froebelian Pedagogy', *Men & Ideas*, 137.
[28] Ibid., 138.   [29] Ibid.

harmful to those children who had the capacity to become brain-workers, and most especially and tragically to those children of poor parents 'who have to fight their way, in spite of difficulties, up into the intellectual life, because those children can only do so through *books*'.[30]

This 'intellectual' philosophy of education shaped Wallas's position as a member of the School Board for London and its successor, the London County Council Education Committee. In particular, it provided a rationale for a struggle against clericalism. The most formidable obstruction to the free cultivation of thought was for Wallas the extensive educational influence of the Church of England. His own intellectual career had begun with a break from the religious orthodoxy of his father, and he tended to generalize from his personal experience. Chided by Shaw for wasting his talents in 'futile anti-clericalism', Wallas defended himself vigorously:

For the past two years [he wrote in 1908] I have lectured each year for the Gilchrist people in half a dozen manufacturing towns, and have always spent a day with a couple of young working-men going round the town and learning about it. In every case it has seemed to me that the intellectual and political life of the place has depended on the existence of a few young men who have got a conception of the universe which starts with a break from orthodoxy. The 'well organised parish' ... kills out the possibility of thought.[31]

His persistent struggle against Church influence in education brought him, as we have already seen, into continual conflict with the Webbs. Sidney Webb's position seemed self-contradictory to Wallas. Webb looked without concern, at least in talking with Wallas, at the gradual decline of denominational schools yet he asserted the principle that 'every child shall be brought up in the religion of its parents'. 'This principle would', Wallas objected, 'if it had been consistently adopted, have kept England in the condition of A.D. 1500 and, if adopted now, would soon reduce it to the condition of Spain.' He continued,

I can't help feeling that your first statement represents your habit of thought of ten or fifteen years ago which still comes easily to you when you fall into the old train of ideas, and the second represents your new sympathy with and understanding of the religious position, your conviction that 'all truth is relative', and your anger at the attitude of the ordinary Liberal on the education question.[32]

---

[30] Ibid., 148. He was especially critical of the anti-intellectualism pervading American education. See *Our Social Heritage* (New Haven, Conn., 1921), 49–53.
[31] Letter, 13 Dec. 1908 (BM).
[32] Letter to Sidney Webb, 5 Mar. 1905 (PP).

The Webbs, for their part, regarded Wallas as obstinate and unreasonable, more interested in fighting the Church than in building a public educational system.³³ Wallas, on the other hand, was most upset about the Webbs' relativism, which, to his mind, played into the hands of obscurantists. He remained throughout his life a late Victorian rationalist, and indeed became more zealously anticlerical with age.

Where the question of religion did not arise, however, Wallas could collaborate enthusiastically with Webb. Webb's programme for a 'scholarship ladder' fitted in perfectly with his own ideas, and he worked together with Webb in pushing it through. Through this innovation, intellectually gifted children of working-class and lower middle-class families were given the chance to receive grammar school and university education. Wallas's interest in developing the intellectual resources of society went beyond this, however, and led him into differences with Webb. The new conditions of the Great Society, he felt, required of *all* its members, not just the gifted, a great ability to deal with abstract intellectual material. 'Practical' education was having less and less to do with the 'concrete'.

Wallas consequently objected to the organization of two separate systems of post-primary education—an 'intellectual' and a 'vocational' system—supported by Webb. This, he feared, would condemn the vast majority of working-class children to a narrow illiberal 'handicrafts' sort of education, leaving them utterly unequipped to understand and cope with the society they were to live in. A broad, humanistic general education, he was convinced, was a necessity for all in the Great Society. For years Wallas fought unsuccessfully for this sort of education, against efforts to make working-class education chiefly vocational.³⁴ As far back as 1886 he had criticized middle-class enthusiasm for the establishment of a programme of vocational education in the elementary schools, to keep up with the Germans. 'The workmen themselves', he had observed, ' steadily oppose any such plan. They feel'—and Wallas agreed—'that the only hope for the working-class lies in their future *intellectual* education'.³⁵ He wrote to Alfred Zimmern, justifying his struggle to preserve 'academic' subjects like history and geography in the 'Higher Elementary' curriculum,

---

³³ See *Our Partnership*, 301–2. Wallas worked energetically against the Education Bill of 1908, chiefly because of its provisions favourable to religion. He wrote articles, sent letters to newspapers, and corresponded with M.P.s, Civil Servants, and publicists. The Bill was withdrawn. See 'A Revolution in Education', and 'The Future of Cowper-Templeism', *Nation*, v (10 and 24 July 1909), 520–1, 597–8, and WP.

³⁴ For the general background of the issue, see Brian Simon, *Education and the Labour Movement 1870–1918* (London, 1965) and Andreas M. Kazamias, *Politics, Society and Secondary Education in England* (Philadelphia, 1966). ³⁵ *Today*, x. 127.

TOWARDS A 'GREAT COMMUNITY'

Undoubtedly in the years from ten to fourteen, handicrafts possess a pungent reality for the boy which books do not, but I fancy that after about twenty-five years of age, the pure handicraftsman who has no book learning and who has to work under the conditions of a great city, is liable to a deeper sense of unreality.[36]

In opposing Webb's plan to give the new 'Higher Elementary' schools in London a strong 'industrial bias' by making them largely technical schools to train skilled labour, Wallas drew on 'meritocratic' as well as democratic arguments. The need for trained intellect, he pointed out, was so urgent that no potential source ought to be overlooked; working-class children prematurely condemned to working-class occupations represented an irreplaceable loss to the nation.[37]

The difference between Webb's and Wallas's view of the function of secondary education came out clearly in their correspondence. Webb wrote,

I cannot help thinking that your abhorrence comes ... from the fear that you will find the Higher Elementary Schools as now devised, *leading educationally nowhere*.... I should think this an advantage. It is not their business to lead up to any higher *school*, but to the counting house, the factory or the kitchen. If the terms of the Minute prevent them for ever from preparing for London Matriculation or the Oxford Local, I should unfeignedly rejoice. They have another work to do—a more important work I suspect you would say—that of educating the *mass* of ordinary average children for the ordinary average life. Let us make both this life, and the preparation for it, as good and as elevating as we can— but do not let us mix up, to their common detriment, the other function, that of preparing the exceptionally clever boy or girl for exceptional work.[38]

Wallas wanted to see the emerging double system give way to an extension of the single primary system for several years more. He was fighting, however, against the trend of the time towards a rigidly stratified national education system. Only in recent years has that trend been reversed as comprehensive schools have begun to replace the dual system. Though he lost the immediate battle to Webb, the position Wallas supported has come back into favour. Wallas's educational views now seem more relevant and less time-bound than Webb's.

Yet Wallas's priorities were not those of most recent supporters of comprehensive schools. His chief aim was not equality but the fullest

---

[36] Letter to Zimmern, 16 Mar. 1909 (WP). Although defeated for re-election to the L.C.C. in 1907, Wallas served on the Education Committee from 1908 to 1910 as a 'co-opted', advisory member.
[37] See letter from Webb, 6 Sept. 1909; letter from Wallas to L. Hobhouse, 20 Sept. 1906; and letter from Wallas to Zimmern, 16 Mar. 1909 (WP). Also see Wallas's article, 'The Local Authority for Secondary Education', *Speaker*, 16 Mar. 1901.
[38] Letter to Wallas, 6 Sept. 1900 (WP).

development of everyone's intellectual potential, so that society should not be deprived of any possible intellectual resource. Wallas, like Webb, expected an *élite* to emerge from the system, but his *élite* was to be as large as possible, and backed by as 'intellectual' a populace as could be had. Efficiency, not equality, was the overriding need for Wallas almost as much as for Webb, though he differed sharply with Webb's programme for attaining it.

This concern with intellectual efficiency made Wallas highly critical, not only of popular education, but even more of the education offered to the *élite*. The curricula of the 'public schools' and the ancient universities seemed to him hopelessly out of touch with the needs of the modern world. Even worse, these institutions provided no intellectual or emotional stimulation. These schools, supposedly providing the 'thought and leadership-capacity' for English society, were steadily decaying intellectually and emotionally, and, as a result, 'the English governing class is every year growing politically weaker'.[39]

This state of affairs, though 'perfectly satisfactory' to those 'to whom the whole social question simplifies itself into a "class-war" between the haves and the have-nots', disturbed Wallas. The progressive incapacity of the traditional *élite* was a blow to the general intellectual state of society, with everyone the worse for it.[40] The traditional instruments for the education of the English governing class were, in Wallas's eyes, potentially invaluable for the training of a new *élite*. For this purpose, however, they had to be thoroughly modernized.

Noting that 'it is not simply a change of curriculum that is wanted but a change of stimulus', Wallas urged a sweeping reform of endowed education: to break the stranglehold of the well-to-do upon admissions, of the classics upon the curriculum, of official religion upon spiritual life, and of the 'gentleman' ideal upon social life.[41] An extension of state supervision would be necessary to carry out these reforms. He vigorously supported the suggestion raised in the Liberal press after 1906 for a Royal Commission to examine endowed education on both the secondary and university levels—a suggestion unheeded by the Government until after the First World War.[42]

[39] Review of 'Let Youth But Know', *Men & Ideas*, 152 (1906).   [40] Ibid., 153.
[41] Ibid., 153-4, 156-61 ('Oxford and the Nation') (1908).
[42] Ibid., 153, 161. Between 1907 and 1909, when the 'condition of Oxford' was being widely discussed, Wallas worked diligently for reform. Many letters in the Wallas Papers deal with this subject. The pace of change was, however, slow, particularly for the public schools. A Royal Commission was not appointed until 1919, and then only for Oxford and Cambridge.

If there was one constant theme in Wallas's thinking from Oxford to the end of his life, it was the insistence that thought and public life must be joined, that the ablest thinkers must become actively involved with the problems of society. 'Ivory-tower' intellectuality and 'pure' social science seemed to him betrayals of the responsibility of the intellectual. The vague impulses of a modern nation could only result in corporate action on lines which someone, wise or foolish, had deliberately laid down. He warned,

If in America today the ablest men should take Seeley's implied advice and stand by to watch passively the results of the 'half-instinctive' political efforts of a population of one hundred million souls, those efforts would express themselves in the creation of new political machinery deliberately invented by less able men.[43]

All collective action in the Great Society, as Wallas viewed it, rested on thought. The very existence of the Great Society stemmed from 'the discovery, handed down by tradition and instruction, that Thought can be fed by deliberately collected material, and stimulated, sustained, and, to a certain extent, controlled by an effort of the will'.[44] The task Wallas foresaw was to find ways of better feeding, stimulating, sustaining, and controlling the process of thought, thought both *on* and *in* the Great Society.[45]

The need for what he liked to call the 'organization of thought' was clearest in politics, where 'public thought' was chiefly—and so inadequately—developed and expressed. In spite of this inadequacy, Wallas refused to turn against democracy. Abandoning some of the elitist ideas he had briefly entertained with Wells, he cautioned Shaw, whose elitism was becoming even more pronounced: 'I know of no other way than democracy of securing that the "end" of the State shall be the good of all and not the good of some.'[46]

Pondering the experience of British rule in India, 'an experiment in government without consent larger than any other that has ever been tried under the conditions of modern civilisation',[47] he further saw that no *élite* existed, or was likely to exist, which based its conduct and policy on reason alone. The distorting effects of human psychology upon judgement operated for the Anglo-Indian ruling class as for working-class electors in London—in some ways no doubt less, but in others even more. Wallas took issue with his former intellectual comrade, who in *A Modern Utopia*

---

[43] *The Great Society*, 226–7. [44] Ibid., 50–1.
[45] See letter from Wells, 15 Oct. 1906 (WP), and letter from Wallas to Wells, 6 Dec. 1906 (Wells).
[46] Letter to Shaw, probably 1903 (WP). [47] *Human Nature in Politics*, 217.

(1905) had envisaged a 'Platonic' world-order resulting from the overthrow of representative government by a new aristocracy of trained men of science. The Indian experience demonstrated for Wallas that 'the problem of the relation between reason and opinion is . . . one that would exist at least equally in Plato's corporate despotism as in the most complete democracy'.[48]

To make representative democracy more intellectually effective, 'rights' alone, as he had pointed out in criticizing Ostrogorski, were useless. 'The continued existence of modern democracy', he told his students at the University of London, 'depends upon the fact that the citizen has not only the "right" to vote, but the means of obtaining some actual knowledge of the questions on which political decisions have to be taken.'[49] Ever since his American visit in 1897, he had argued the need to make politics and government more comprehensible to the average man. 'I want', he told Shaw, 'to simplify the machine so that all men can understand it.'[50] To this end, he called for fewer elections, for fewer positions and on fewer issues, and greater regulation of the electoral process.

Wallas saw the means of communication being increasingly abused by private interests. Growing knowledge of psychology was being applied to worsen rather than to improve the 'conditions of public thought'. The question of how 'to diminish the number and money-power of the "interests" who find it worthwhile to pay for the professional manufacture of political motive' was now 'the central problem of Democracy'.[51] Surveying electoral legislation enacted since the coming of democracy in 1867, Wallas found that

government now tends to regulate, not only the process of ascertaining the decision of the electors, but also the more complex process by which that decision is formed; and that this is done not in the interest of any particular body of opinion, but from a belief in the general utility of right methods of thought, and the possibility of securing them by regulation.[52]

Wallas drew an analogy between this change and the earlier and more complete change in the conditions under which the decision of a jury was reached. Trial by jury was in its origins simply a method of determining the opinions of a group of average men, without any concern for how those

---

[48] *Human Nature in Politics*, 219.
[49] Syllabus, London University Extension Lectures, 1907: 'Evolution of Modern English Government'.
[50] Letter to Shaw, probably 1903 (WP).
[51] 'The Money-Power at War', *Nation* (11 Dec. 1909), 454.
[52] *Human Nature in Politics*, 222-3.

opinions had been formed. Yet, over a long period of time, it had come to be assumed that the opinions of the jurors, rather than being formed before the trial began, ought to be formed in court. 'The process, therefore', Wallas noted, 'by which that opinion is produced has been more and more completely controlled and developed, until it, and not the mere registration of the verdict, has become the essential feature of the trial.'[53]

The whole organization of a trial was now directed towards fostering a new mental climate that would aid the jurors in reaching a rational, carefully considered decision, free from preconceived influences and from non-rational suggestion. Wallas went so far as to characterize an English law court during a well-governed jury trial as 'a laboratory in which psychological rules of valid reasoning are illustrated by experiment'.[54] Here was a model towards which reforms of the electoral process should aim.

Sidney Webb took issue with Wallas on his concern for the intellectual quality of politics, complaining that

> you . . . rather miss the point of the Consent argument. It is necessary (or convenient) to get popular consent, i.e. popular consciousness that they consent. Representative assemblies are a device for doing this. Juries do *not* secure it (they give something else). That expedient is an old one. . . . Moreover, it is only consent that is needed, not understanding or intellectual appreciation, i.e. feeling not thought. All the defects of elections and the stupidities of voters . . . do not detract from the feeling of consent.[55]

Their disagreement on politics paralleled their differences on education. In both cases, Webb drew a sharp line between the *élite* who would run society and the masses, for whom neither intellectual education nor understanding of government were necessary. To Wallas, on the other hand, the intellectual demands of the Great Society were so great that a highly trained *élite* was not enough: the intellectual resources of the entire populace had to be tapped. Beyond this, Wallas had an idealistic commitment to democracy that Webb lacked. For Wallas, democracy was not merely necessary or convenient, but desirable in itself. Social efficiency, rather, was the means; it had to be increased to enable democracy to master the Great Society.

Yet, for all his commitment to democracy, Wallas saw that improving the thought-processes of the elector was not enough. Equally important was the quality of the leadership and expertise offered. Wallas cautioned against exaggerating the task that each voter could properly perform. Politicians had to realize that 'they are not servants of an eager public

[53] *Human Nature in Politics*, 224.   [54] Ibid., 226.   [55] Letter, 23 July 1908 (WP).

but a small and responsible minority who has to force an absorbed and indifferent public to realise its own opportunities'.[56] To accomplish this, they needed the expertise that only a strengthened and invigorated bureaucracy could supply.

As early as the 1890s, Wallas had hoped the weaknesses of popular thought could be counteracted by stressing the responsibility of the representatives to think for themselves. This hope had remained strong after the turn of the century,[57] but as he began to examine the conditions of representative thought he became aware of the intellectual limitations they imposed.

Collective thought seemed at its best when the product of a face-to-face interaction. 'Oral dialectic', Wallas observed, provided an emotional climate supporting and encouraging thought.[58] But representative assemblies like Parliament or the L.C.C. were too large and too partisan for oral discussion to be psychologically effective.[59] Further, the knowledge and the intellectual ability of representatives, selected by the very imperfect method of popular election, was falling increasingly behind the difficulty of the problems confronting them. As a consequence of the intellectual inadequacy of representative assemblies, the work of 'systematically organising national thought', he felt, would probably fall to the Civil Service.[60]

Modern society required some reliable intellectual authority to replace the discredited authorities of the old, relatively static order. Democratic politics provided no such authority, but a permanent, expert bureaucracy could. This high opinion of the Civil Service was no doubt partly shaped by Wallas's Fabianism, and by his early experiences: having missed the chance for a good appointment in the Service by failing to take a first at Oxford, he seems to have envied his friends Olivier and Webb in the Colonial Office.

Just because the Civil Service did not exercise sovereign power, Wallas argued, it could remain free from the 'art of manipulating opinion' and cultivate instead objective expertise. English Civil Servants, he remarked, mixing shrewd insight with Fabian *naïveté* concerning the freedom from 'politics' of the bureaucrat, 'have the right and duty of making their voices heard, without the necessity of making their will, by fair means or foul, prevail'.[61]

---

[56] Letter to Shaw, probably 1903 (WP). This was the theme of an American political novel, *Peter Stirling* (1894), which Wallas had praised.
[57] See 'The American Analogy', *Independent Review*, i (1903).
[58] See *The Great Society*, 248.   [59] See ibid., 248–60.
[60] Ibid., 268.   [61] *Human Nature*, 262.

TOWARDS A 'GREAT COMMUNITY'

The creation of a competitive Civil Service had been 'the one great political invention of the nineteenth century';[62] but, Wallas noted, it had now fallen behind the times. The work of the early and mid-Victorian reformers had to be done again. Wallas was himself an authority on this subject, teaching the history of British government since 1832 at L.S.E., and his views commanded some attention. A member of the Royal Commission on the Civil Service from 1912 to 1914, he was asked by Methuen to write a book on public administration.[63]

He discovered in the Civil Service tendencies to narrowness, rigidity, and political irresponsibility resulting from the self-enclosed and undisturbed official life.[64] Further, a body of well-paid officials, largely recruited from the well-to-do, tended, he felt, to develop a sense of a corporate interest opposed to that of the majority of the people. The general confidence in their disinterestedness, essential to the effectiveness of officials, was being eroded by their unconscious sympathy with the upper classes.[65]

In his lectures at the London School of Economics, in his books and articles, and especially as a member of the Royal Commission on the Civil Service between 1912 and 1914, Wallas stated and restated these criticisms of British administration as arbitrary, inflexible, and inefficient. Wallas devoted a great amount of time to the work of the Commission: his attendance record was the best of any member's with the exception of the chairman, Lord Macdonnell. More far-seeing than most of his colleagues, Wallas marked out several paths of change which were eventually taken by the Civil Service.

Wallas's psychological approach to Civil Service reform stood in contrast to that of most of his contemporaries. Shortly before the Commission was created, he had objected to a proposal for setting up a Parliamentary Committee to exert central financial control over the Civil Service. 'The vice of the Public Service', he wrote to Murray Macdonald, who had drafted it, 'is that on one dares take any risk', and the existence of that committee would only worsen this vice. The real sources of waste, he argued, were 'the woodenness, the red tape, the refusal to go through the mental labour of invention or the moral effort of disturbing one's own and other people's comfort—the waste that does not show itself in rising

---

[62] Ibid., 263. See his notes from the early 1890s for lectures on the history of English government, and notes for *Human Nature*.
[63] See letter from J. Spencer Hill, 12 Dec. 1913 (WP).
[64] See *Human Nature*, pt. ii, ch. 3, and *The Great Society*, 269.
[65] See *Human Nature*, 278, and *Second Report of the Royal Commission on the Civil Service 1912–14* (London, H.M.S.O., 1912), 101 (exchange no. 4541).

Estimates, but in the fact that the wrong thing instead of the right thing is constantly done'.[66]

One problem particularly close to Wallas's experience was the lack of relation between the higher educational system and the administrative system, between knowledge pure and knowledge applied. The work carried out at the London School of Economics, where many of the students were Civil Servants, had shown to his satisfaction the great value of co-ordinating the intellectual work of a university with that of the bureaucracy.[67] In Germany, he remarked to the Permanent Secretary of the Board of Education during the hearings of the Royal Commission, there existed between the vast body of collected and distributed knowledge in the educational system and the administrative application of it an intimate relation extremely beneficial to government. But in Britain, the opposite was true: 'the two things, the organisation of the pursuit of knowledge and the application of knowledge, are kept, although carried on in each case by the State, in two entirely water-tight compartments'.[68]

Any relation that did exist in Britain between the educational and administrative systems—the educational qualifications for admission to the Civil Service—Wallas found largely harmful. He urged the revision of the requirements for admission to take account of new subjects and eliminate the gross over-emphasis upon the classics. This over-emphasis, he felt, virtually excluded men with vitally needed 'modern' or technical education, while greatly favouring 'Oxbridge' against the other universities and the well-to-do against the rest of the population.

Provision, he further argued, ought to be made for admitting men after graduate or professional study, and for making graduate or professional degrees earned while employed one criterion for promotion. This would help meet the ever-growing need for specialized knowledge in administration, while at the same time widening the horizons of Civil Servants through contact with men of different skills and specialties. The Civil Service as a whole, he was convinced, was far too ingrown.

The organization of the Civil Service, with the division of managerial work into two classes, he found quite arbitrary, owing more to class

---

[66] Letter, 14 Nov. 1911 (WP).

[67] See *Men & Ideas*, 128-9 ('The British Civil Service', 1928). For several years he taught a class in administration for army officers, and the practical success of this innovation encouraged him to urge its extension to the rest of the Civil Service. See *Third Report* (1913), 248 (nos. 21, 298). Sir Josiah Stamp, a prominent Civil Servant, testified to the stimulating effect Wallas's classes had on the practical administrators who took them. *Economica*, xxxviii (Nov. 1932), 401.

[68] *Second Report*, 286-7 (nos. 9722, 9732). See also *Third Report*, 208 (nos. 21, 298).

prejudice than to reasons of intellectual efficiency. Promotion from Class II, recruited from boys of sixteen and eighteen years, to the much smaller Class I, recruited from university graduates of twenty-two to twenty-four, was very difficult and rare. In practice, the 'Administrative Class'—Class I —was the virtual province of Oxbridge graduates from the upper-middle and upper classes. After questioning many officials, Wallas could find no sharp division in the nature of the administrative work that would justify such a sharp division in organization, and called for the replacement of this two-class system with one Administrative Class. Wallas wanted a Civil Service whose general rule was meritocratic, and from which any deviations would have to be thoroughly justified.

Wallas's 'intellectual' approach, unorthodox in his time, has now become the 'conventional wisdom'. The Fulton Report on the Civil Service, issued in 1968 to widespread approval, was in many respects the fruition of Wallas's labours. It saw the central problem of the bureaucracy as that of intellectual effectiveness in a rapidly changing world. It carried forward Wallas's criticisms of the over-emphasis upon classics and arts in the education of its recruits; a majority of the Committee wished to discriminate in favour of 'modern' subjects like the social sciences. Many of Wallas's arguments for specialized knowledge and professionalism in government were restated by the Fulton Committee in its attack upon 'amateurism'.[69] Fulton recommended the unification of the upper Civil Service and the flexibility of staffing that Wallas had advocated in 1914. The Fulton Committee's proposals for a Civil Service College and long-term planning units in every department recall Wallas's concern for raising the quality of administrative thought. The establishment in place of Treasury control of a new Civil Service department, particularly charged with promoting improvements and flexibility, represents a fulfilment of Wallas's hopes. He had suggested in 1914 the establishment of a special department to encourage innovation, and had been anxious lest Treasury control mean the sacrifice of intellectual to financial efficiency.

Wallas's aims eventually have been realized, but the path has been slow and uneven; only a beginning was made in 1914.[70] Many of his

[69] *Report of the Committee on the Civil Service 1966-68* (Cmnd. 3638, London, H.M.S.O., 1968). Lord Fulton himself is a striking example of the 'new man' Wallas wanted, bridging universities and government. A Fellow of Balliol, he spent the war in Whitehall, and has since worked on the reform of both higher education and the Civil Service. See the 'Profile', in the *New Statesman*, lxxvii (7 Feb. 1969), 183.

[70] Upon completion of the work of the Commission, Wallas summed up his criticisms in an anonymous article for the *New Statesman* of 25 Apr. 1914, 'Parliament and the Report on the Civil Service'.

suggestions failed to win the support of other members. On the question of educational requirements the Commission merely proposed the appointment of a committee of inquiry to decide whether over-emphasis on classics and favouritism for Oxbridge existed. It refused to call for the opening-up of all higher-level positions to women as Wallas urged. Finally, the Commission supported the basic two-class division in the higher Civil Service, citing the need to maintain high standards, and saw no benefit in making promotion easier.

Even those proposals concurred in by the Macdonnell Commission were often presented in an indecisive way; many, further, were never given real effect by the Government. The Commission asked for greater co-ordination of the national educational system and the Civil Service examination system, and declared the importance for administration of other educational backgrounds as well as classical. It made, however, no specific recommendations for change in this sphere. The Commission adopted Wallas's proposal for the creation of a special department to oversee operations and methods, and encourage intellectual efficiency, but nothing was done about this until the Second World War.[71]

The outbreak of the First World War soon after the Commission's report prevented any general reform of the Civil Service, and in the post-war climate interest in, and enthusiasm for, administrative reform was weak.[72] As in education, the pace of change was slow until the Second World War. As also in education, Wallas's pleas for efficiency through flexibility, fluidity, and openness were insufficiently heeded in his time. The improvement of 'thought-organization', it came to appear, would be a long and arduous process.

III

As a 'Benthamite', Wallas saw the Great Society threatened by insufficient thought; as an 'Evangelical', he also saw it imperilled by insufficient emotional satisfaction and solidarity. Like the question of intellectual inefficiency, this issue must be seen in its Edwardian context. A general concern about the seeming lack of personal satisfaction, participation, and sense of solidarity provided by modern society existed in Edwardian England, and, as with the concern about inefficiency—to which it provided a counterpoint—it crossed traditional political lines.

---

[71] See *Fourth Report of the Royal Commission on the Civil Service 1912–14* (London, H.M.S.O., 1914).

[72] For the history of the Civil Service in the twentieth century, see H. Finer, *The British Civil Service* (London, 1927), G. A. Campbell, *The Civil Service in Britain* (London, 1955), and Fabian Tract 355, *The Administrators* (London, 1964).

This genre of social thought paralleled Fabianism in linking its complaints to the appearance of a new society, vast and complex. But whereas Webb looked upon this 'Great Society' as an opportunity, G. K. Chesterton, Hilaire Belloc, the early Guild Socialists, religious pluralists like J. N. Figgis, and even the Liberal Minister C. F. G. Masterman saw it more as a threat.[73] Consequently, they, and others of similar spirit, looked backwards in time for a solution: they wished to reverse rather than accommodate to the trend of modern history. A. J. Penty wrote

> To Medieval social arrangements we shall return not only because we shall never be able to regain complete control over the economic forces in society except through the agency of restored Guilds, but because it is imperative to return to a simpler state of society. . . . When any society develops beyond a certain point, the human mind is unable to get a grip of all the details necessary to its proper ordering.[74]

Fabian collectivism was from this perspective no cure at all, but only a symptom of the disease of inhuman bigness. It was true after all, as *laissez-faire* Conservatives had claimed, that this sort of Socialism 'left human nature out of account'.[75] Fabianism was 'far too intellectual and too little human ever to get to grips with the realities of life'.[76] It led only to what Hilaire Belloc called 'the Servile State'—the mastering of the problems of an inhuman society through dehumanization of its members.

These writers proposed an alternative route—decentralization and the restoration of emotional and spiritual ties between men. The specific paths this route would take varied from writer to writer—from peasant proprietorship to guilds to localism. All had in common the restoration of a society on a human scale, a society that ordinary men could understand, feel a part of, and control. This concern was given fictional expression by G. K. Chesterton. In his novel, *The Napoleon of Notting Hill* (1902), he

---

[73] Guild Socialism had really two sides: It contained an early 'reactionary' discontent with modern society in general, and a wish to return to simpler times, usually the Middle Ages. It also came to have a 'radical' side which was critical only of certain aspects of modern society, chiefly the vastly unequal distribution of power, in work and everyday life even more than in politics. The former is best represented by A. J. Penty, the latter by G. D. H. Cole. It is chiefly the 'reactionary' aspect of Guild Socialism that is relevant here, though to some degree it permeated the entire movement. See S. T. Glass, *The Responsible Society* (London, 1966), and L. P. Carpenter, 'G. D. H. Cole: The Guild Socialist Period', Ph.D. dissertation, Harvard University, 1966.

[74] *Guilds and the Social Crisis* (London, 1919), 46–7. Though written after the war, this general line of thought was characteristic of Penty from his first 'Guild' book in 1906.

[75] A. J. Penty, *Old Worlds for New* (London, 1917), 29.

[76] Ibid., 33.

attacked modern society for 'starving the soul'. Men needed 'a thing to love', and they could not love what was beyond their comprehension. His novel provided this 'thing to love' in the rise of a suburban London patriotism, a solution that could hardly be taken seriously.

Wallas felt these writers were dealing with real problems that current politics ignored, and Fabianism dismissed—problems stemming from the disharmony between the Great Society and human nature. Their proposals, however, he could not accept. Like Chesterton's suburban patriotism, they all seemed hopelessly impractical and, in their backward-looking stance, not even really desirable. The Great Society could not be wished away. It *could* be reformed to allow greater scope to smaller units within it, and to provide greater satisfaction to human nature. More than this, men themselves could be 'reformed' to live more happily and freely in the Great Society. These paths of social and psychological 'engineering' offered to Wallas realistic solutions to the quest for satisfaction and solidarity in the Great Society.

Industrial psychology, for example, just emerging as a separate field in Wallas's time, promised a guide to modifying modern organization to 'fit' human nature. However, Wallas was at pains to distinguish its creative possibilities from its exploitative use, then coming into vogue, solely to raise productivity. This sort of applied psychology was the economic parallel to the manipulative use of psychology in politics that he had warned against; both were intensifying the psychic *malaise* of the Great Society. 'Human good', he agreed with his friend J. A. Hobson, 'may be opposed to industrial "efficiency"'.[77] Properly applied, industrial psychology could find ways of increasing the element of intelligent variation in work, and encouraging social integration in work-groups and the development of sustaining work-culture.[78]

Wallas was very much interested in the rapidly growing town planning movement. However, to accomplish what he was looking for, urban planning had to be *social* planning, 'planning for people', in our current phraseology. The wrong kind of urban planning was exemplified for Wallas by Chicago, whose grandiose redevelopment plan, the forerunner of much twentieth-century American 'urban renewal', was, he felt, 'suited to giants and not men, or at least only to the gigantic qualities of mankind':

... ten parks [he went on], which the inhabitants of ten quarters can reach in a

---

[77] 'Economics of Human Welfare', *Nation*, xv (27 June 1914), 495 (a review of Hobson by Wallas).
[78] See *The Great Society*, 323–6.

twenty minutes' walk, are better than one park ten times as large which few can reach without losing a day's work; and if a workingman's wife is to buy the family supplies in comfort shopping streets must be neither too distant for her feet nor too broad for her eyes.[79]

Wallas was in sympathy, though not complete agreement, with the 'Garden City' writers and propagandists, who were seeking to revitalize local life and restore 'human scale'.[80] One field of 'social engineering' in which Wallas had long been involved was the settlement house movement. Associated with Toynbee Hall from its founding, Wallas was particularly impressed with the writings of Jane Addams and the possibilities for 'social invention' they opened up.[81] 'No more fruitful field of social invention now exists', he remarked, 'than that which concerns the customs of average family life in the new industrial districts.'[82] This sort of activity might seem trivial to those bent on immediately transforming society, but Wallas looked for social progress to a multitude of just such small efforts and small changes.

'Social engineering', however, was by no means a complete programme. Piecemeal changes had to be part of a general social philosophy. The Great Society needed to be organized as a whole, on the basis of some consistent set of principles. 'Almost the whole of what we call "the social question"', it seemed to Wallas, could be reduced to the 'controversy as to what Organised Will should direct the enormous industrial units of our time.'[83] Three systems of what he called 'will-organisation' were competing to direct society: 'Private Property, the State (organised at present on the basis of locality) and non-Local Associations (mainly on the basis of common occupations)'.[84] Each of them he examined for their basis in human nature, the adequacy of their social motives, and the efficacy of their material organization.

The will-organization of Private Property, or Individualism (or Capitalism), had the advantage that its chief institution was based, he believed, upon a true human instinct. However, this instinct, like most primeval instincts, was becoming increasingly maladapted to the new conditions of the Great Society. The instinct of property had less and less relation to the actual capitalist organization of society, as individual ownership

---

[79] See *The Great Society*, 356–7.
[80] Wallas wrote to Joseph Wicksteed expressing interest in his 'garden city' article written in 1908 (WP).
[81] Testimonial to Wallas on his marriage, 1897 (WP). Wallas praised Jane Addams's writings in *The Great Society*, 353–4.
[82] Ibid., 353.   [83] Ibid., 290.   [84] Ibid.

gave way to the joint-stock system. Further, the substitution of concentration for competition had destroyed the old presumption ('never very sound', he added) of an identity of interest between producer and consumer; while the large-scale nature of modern industrial organization provided no motive for the workman to maintain or increase his output. 'The institution of Private Property', he concluded, 'only now works tolerably as the main organising force of the Great Industry because it gives scope for other impulses besides that of personal or family accumulation, and because it is constantly checked and modified by other forms of Will-Organisation.'[85]

Chief among these other forms of will-organization was Collectivism, or Socialism, the control of economic life by the State. Firmly convinced of the necessity for a large degree of collectivism, democratically controlled, in the organization of the Great Society, Wallas saw the reaction during the nineteenth century from individualism towards Collectivism as inevitable:

Given [he explained] that the choice was between a Will-Organisation based solely upon Property and one based solely upon Representative Government, the argument in favour of Collectivism in the Great Industry seemed irresistible. Collectivism substituted a direct aiming at the public good for a very hypothetical calculation that the public good might indirectly result from individual and family accumulation. It encouraged and depended on conscious public spirit, instead of a blind property-instinct distorted by the disappearance of its original environment. Above all it seemed that a democratic government would necessarily use the enormous wealth-producing power of the Great Industry so as to lessen instead of increasing economic inequality.[86]

However, he pointed out that the growth of collectivism rested on 'the continued efficiency and acceptability of the machinery by which the collective Will is ascertained and enforced'.[87] In so far as territorial, representative democracy was inadequate to the governing of the Great Society, to that degree collectivism failed also. The rising wave of dissatisfaction with representative democracy that Wallas had noted in *Human Nature in Politics*, and, indeed, unwittingly contributed to with that book, was also a challenge to collectivism. In Syndicalism and its variants, many young radicals claimed to find a better psychological basis

---

[85] *The Great Society*, 295.
[86] Ibid., 296. 'If our civilisation is to survive', he insisted in *Human Nature*, 'greater social equality must indeed come', though by itself it would not be enough. (p. 245).
[87] Ibid., 297.

for social life than that provided by representative collectivism. Taking over, as Wallas observed, from the current individualist criticism of Socialism nearly all the reasons advanced against collectivist democracy, they aimed at creating a will-organization which, as Wallas put it, 'has behind it some stronger emotion than that produced by the accidental residence in a few score of adjoining streets of a few thousand men who have adopted a common party name for their opinions'.[88] This will-organization they found in the fact of common industrial employment.

Wallas's experience had led him to partial agreement with the Syndicalists. 'Representative government', he had discovered, 'is not strong enough to bear the weight of managing the whole organised life of a modern nation.'[89] Moreover, in the vast and impersonal organizations of the Great Society Wallas too had found that the individual was becoming lost, satisfaction in work was becoming more difficult to find, and, in general, social institutions were becoming more remote from human nature. The Syndicalists proposed to do away with this 'alienation' by basing social life upon the immediate work-group. Here Wallas refused to follow them; they saw only one side of what was, to him, a two-sided problem. Social institutions ought, he agreed, to be based as far as possible upon immediate human experience. This experience, however, needed to be altered and enriched to enable men to cope with their new environment. Wallas sought a mutual adjustment of human nature and the Great Society, of immediate satisfaction and social efficiency, and opposed any sacrifice of one to the other. 'I want', he explained to Shaw, 'to decentralise . . . to the point where the curve of increasing units of government meets the curve of decreasing governmental efficiency per unit.'[90] What was needed was an 'art of adjusting the need of organisation as a basis for efficiency, with the facts of human nature'.[91]

The organizational programme of English Syndicalism was not new— the early Fabians had encountered similar views in the labour movement, and Wallas's attitude to it had formed then.[92] He traced its principle back

[88] Ibid., 305. See also Wallas's lecture to the Sociological Society on 'Syndicalism', *Sociological Review*, v, 248 (July 1912).
[89] 'English Teachers' Organisations', *New Statesman*, v (25 Sept. 1915) 586. 'My experience on the L.S.B.', he had observed in 1903, 'goes to show that the public machine has enormous advantages in providing for the universal consumption of an article generally though vaguely desired. But the public organisation for such purposes is no good unless it is surrounded by a crowd of voluntary organisations, political societies, scientific societies, staffs of newspapers . . . Trade Unions . . . etc.' Letter to Shaw, probably 1903 (WP).
[90] Ibid.   [91] Letter to Zimmern, 16 Mar. 1909 (WP).
[92] See McBriar, *Fabian Socialism and English Politics*, 100–7.

to the medieval guilds, in whose history he saw the claims of vocational organization tested and found wanting. The guilds, though providing in many ways a satisfying life for their members, had become barriers to both innovation and social harmony. The result of vesting public powers in private groups was, just as in an Individualist social organization, the use of this public power for private benefit, and the subordination of public spirit to private loyalties. In the end, Wallas concluded, the unchecked power of the guilds sealed the doom of their societies. He noted,

Cities which could enter into no binding agreement that did not bear the seals of twenty jealous gilds, and which could not keep order in their own streets during a trade dispute, proved too weak to stand against the more highly organised national states which began to appear during the sixteenth and seventeenth centuries.[93]

'It proved to be more important', warned Wallas, 'that under Syndicalism men loved each other less as citizens than that they loved each other more as Gild-brothers.'

Wallas came to favour no '-ism' in its entirety, but instead sought a coherent 'mix' of the valuable elements of each system. The central place in this amalgam was to be given to Collectivism. Its faults were less serious, its virtues more necessary than those of its rivals. Modified by the contributions of Individualism and Syndicalism, non-doctrinaire Collectivism offered the best chance of a system that could order the Great Society.

However, even changing social institutions and organization was not enough. To reconcile men and society, *both* needed change. Institutional reform had to be combined with direct psychological reform. Besides bringing the Great Society closer to human scale, Wallas envisaged 'expanding' human nature to the new scale of society. One way was, as we have seen, the training of the intellect through a greatly improved educational system. The product of the 'educational revolution' would be minds capable of dealing with the new social environment. Yet the author of *Human Nature in Politics* was acutely aware of the limitations of intellect. This awareness turned him to explore the constructive possibilities of the non-rational. Were the emotions also capable of being 'expanded'? Could thought and emotion be joined to support instead of threaten the Great Society?

Did 'philanthropy' (in its original sense of love of one's fellows), he asked, have a basis in human nature? This was a more difficult question

[93] *The Great Society*, 309.

TOWARDS A 'GREAT COMMUNITY'

than that regarding thought. Nonetheless, Wallas ventured a qualified affirmative, identifying a 'disposition of Philanthropy' which, however, varied widely among individuals. He admitted,

Its weakness and uncertainty suggest that it is a late and half-finished product of evolution, and those who have to use the dispositions of man for their own purposes constantly tend to rely, as a substitute for, or aid to it, on the stronger and earlier instincts of Loyalty (Following the Lead) for a party or a chief, or the still earlier affections of sex or parenthood.[94]

Weak though this disposition might be, it was indispensable to the very existence of the Great Society. Its stimulation and cultivation were as important as that of the disposition of thought. One means of stimulating it, perhaps, was by knowledge itself. Thought and emotion, as he had already seen, did not exist in separate compartments in the mind, but freely interacted. They could therefore be deliberately used to influence each other. Psychological knowledge had helped to stimulate the feelings of 'love' and 'public spirit' in him; it could do so for others as well:

If, after a period of psychological reading one stands on a railway platform or at a window, looking at that unknown crowd which makes the solitude of London, the faces which one will never see again seem less indifferent than they did before. Those men who are innocent of psychology, but have an exceptional gift of reading physiognomy, may see more than the less gifted in spite of their book-learning. But book-learning and the habit of attention which it produces does seem to make it easier to interpret the less obvious signs of psychological states, and more probable that those states will stimulate a certain degree of love. The tired mother snapping at her tired child, the weak smile of the dreamy youth, the intense self-consciousness of the two talkers who are 'showing off' to the other inmates of the omnibus, all seem intelligible and kindly. And if formal psychology lends a measure of reality to those whom one sees only for a moment, it can also sharpen and make more poignant the mental picture, which every member of the Great Society forms, of that larger multitude of his contemporaries whom he will never see, but whose lives he must necessarily influence.[95]

Wallas—the 'Evangelical' in him now overshadowing the 'Benthamite' —looked beyond the stimulation of emotions of love to the ultimate joining of thought and emotion in a new 'world-outlook'. 'A change in the conditions of human life', he had felt as early as 1901, 'so great as that which is involved in making the world one place ... cannot be effected without a far-reaching influence upon human imagination.'[96] In the course of social development, 'political entities' had been successively created—moral

[94] *The Great Society*, 145.   [95] Ibid., 154-5.
[96] 'Religion and Empire', *Inquirer*, 29 June 1901.

ideals which had the power of focusing feeling and motivating action. Now the new relations of men to men and to their environment demanded new entities. The future would see 'the deliberate adoption and inculcation of new moral and intellectual conceptions—new ideal entities to which our affections and desires may attach themselves'.[97]

He found one such entity in science. Built up over many generations by a few students, the conception of 'Science' had by his time spread to the whole world. He pointed out,

In every classroom and laboratory in Europe and America the conscious idea of Science forms the minds and wills of thousands of men and women who could never have helped to create it. It has penetrated, as the political conceptions of Liberty or of Natural Right never penetrated, to non-European races. Arab engineers in Khartoum, doctors and nurses and generals in the Japanese army, Hindoo and Chinese students make of their whole lives an intense activity inspired by absolute submission to Science, and not only English or American or German town working men but villagers in Italy or Argentina are learning to respect the authority and sympathise with the methods of that organised study which may double at any moment the produce of their crops or check a plague among their cattle.[98]

The strength of the idea of Science, in contrast to the weakness of appeals to 'thought' or 'reason', had been, in Wallas's view, 'that it does touch men's feelings, and draws motive power for thought from the passions of reference, of curiosity, and of limitless hope'.[99]

So far, however, 'Science' was associated only with the external world; Wallas wanted to show that, through the science of the mind, it could lead to the Greek ideal of conduct—'the co-ordination of reason and passion as a moral ideal'.[100] Exactly how this was to be brought about, was still unclear, but he was convinced that it would come. Japan, for instance, seemed to him to be moving in that direction. Reflecting the great impression made in Europe by the Japanese victory over Russia, Wallas described that nation as having joined the scientific conception of life with a 'religious' devotion and enthusiasm, acquiring by this a mental outlook 'which was determinist without being fatalist, and which combined the most absolute submission to nature with untiring energy in thought and action'.[101] 'That the Japanese outlook on life'—joining a scientific attitude and ancient moral teaching—'is a real religion', Wallas concluded, 'credible, lasting,

---

[97] *Human Nature in Politics*, 202.   [98] Ibid., 202–3.
[99] Ibid., 204.   [100] Ibid., 206.
[101] Ibid., 212. Beatrice Webb, also seeking a 'social motive' that would fuse 'Science' and 'Religion', was similarly impressed. See *Our Partnership*, 299 (22 Dec. 1904).

TOWARDS A 'GREAT COMMUNITY'   157

capable of rising to the utmost heights of human emotion, has been proved by the sternest of all tests.' In France, too, he thought he saw 'the slow birth of a new religion' in the secular civic creed—'morality tinged with emotion', he described it, using a phrase of Matthew Arnold's—taught to schoolchildren.[102] A new religion—secular, 'scientific', and humanistic —was what Wallas began consciously to look and hope for: a new ethic, a new imaginative conception of life for the new social world.

Here he shed the garb of a pragmatic social engineer and revealed himself as fundamentally a visionary. His family's Evangelicalism had left an indelible impression on Wallas's mind, leading him to seek throughout his life for a sweeping psychological change in men—'conversion' of a sort. A friend recalled after his death: 'You felt that, while he was young, he had lost something that mattered, and had spent his life trying to find a working substitute....'[103] The classics studied in his youth had seemed to provide such a 'working substitute' for religion in Greek philosophy and civic *ethos*. Wallas had found in the *polis* an ideal towards which to strive. The *polis*, as conceived by Aristotle, represented a form of social life that gave full satisfaction to both reason and passion, that bound man to man in understanding and sympathy, and in which man and his institutions, without coercion, were in harmony. In it, human beings could attain the fullest possible life.[104]

The world to which the *polis* belonged, however, had vanished forever with the coming of the Great Society. For a while Wallas had hoped for the re-creation of the *polis* through Socialism, but eventually he decided it was too narrow a movement for that end. The struggle for economic and political equality, he had become aware, was 'a part only, however important it may be, of some larger conception of life'.[105]

The new 'world-society' demanded a 'world-*ethos*' to match the civic *ethos* of the Greeks.[106] The limits of modern political consciousness were

---

[102] 'Impressions of Paris', *Daily Chronicle*, 13 Feb. 1906.
[103] Sir Michael Sadler, *The Times*, 13 Aug. 1932.
[104] 'No modern thinker has expressed, for the purposes of modern national democracy, a conception of Liberty approaching in psychological insight the ideal which Pericles offered to the ancient City-state.' *Our Social Heritage*, 168.
[105] 'Socialism and the Fabian Society', (1916) *Men & Ideas*, 107.
[106] Alfred Zimmern, writing to Wallas on his work in progress on the Greeks (which became *The Greek Commonwealth*), was struck by 'How very much more politics meant to a Greek than they can ever mean to us, now that they are divorced from both morality and religion'. Wallas wished to restore the connection, this time on a world scale. See 'Religion and Empire', op. cit. This aim placed Wallas within the tradition of cultural criticism traced by Raymond Williams. See his *Culture and Society 1780–1950* (London, 1958).

set not by the rigid range of the senses, but by men's powers of imagination and sympathy, which had no permanent limit. If 'the old affection for place and home' had disappeared, Wallas looked forward to 'a new affection': he noted,

now that men lived in the larger world of knowledge and inference, rather than in the narrower world of sight and hearing, a patriotism of books and maps might ... appear which should be a better guide to life than the patriotism of the village street.[107]

The modern era had seen nationalism replace localism, but Wallas questioned whether nationalism was not already dangerously outdated by social development. From the standpoint of the entire human race, national and imperial rivalries seemed merely a new form of the guild particularism that had undermined the late medieval town. To men of the future, these modern rivalries would appear no more relevant than the theological controversies of the late Roman world did today. Wallas recalled the armed conflict of those who had held the 'Homoousian' view of the Trinity against the 'Homoiousians'. He observed,

We can now see that the practical interests of Europe were very little concerned with the question whether 'we' or 'they' won, but very seriously concerned with the question whether the division itself into 'we' or 'they' could not be obliterated by the discovery either of a less clumsy metaphysic, or of a way of thinking about humanity which made the continued existence of those who disagreed with one in theology no longer intolerable. May the Germans and ourselves be now marching towards the horrors of a world-war merely because 'nation' and 'empire' like 'Homoousia' and 'Homoiousia' are the best that we can do in making entities of the mind to stand between us and an unintelligible universe, and because having made such entities our sympathies are shut up within them?[108]

The revolution in communication and transport in the Great Society was helping to create a new world-consciousness. As a result, Wallas noted, 'an idea of the whole existence of our species is at last a possible background to our individual experience'.[109] Even the outbreak of world war, with its rekindling of national hatreds, did not dampen his hopes. In a way, he felt, it might even accelerate the trend towards a 'world consciousness'. He remarked to Walter Lippmann,

Now that mankind have been forced to think in terms of alliances of two or three hundred million people and empires of four hundred million the final effort when they will come to think in terms of all the human race cannot be very far off.[110]

[107] *Human Nature in Politics*, 284.   [108] Ibid., 297.
[109] Ibid., 307.   [110] Letter, 30 Dec. 1916 (Lippmann).

TOWARDS A 'GREAT COMMUNITY'

Since Darwin, he observed,

we have . . . been able to represent the human race to our imagination, neither as a chaos of arbitrarily varying individuals, nor as a mosaic of homogeneous nations, but as a biological group every individual in which differs from every other not arbitrarily but according to an intelligible process of organic evolution.[111]

As 'that which exists for the imagination can exist also for the emotions', evolutionary biology might have made it possible for a new 'world-ethic' to arise directly.[112] However, that was not to be: 'It was', Wallas felt, 'the intellectual tragedy of the nineteenth century that this discovery of organic evolution, instead of stimulating such a general love of humanity, seemed at first to show that it was for ever impossible.'[113] The 'struggle for life' misinterpretation of Darwin had become a powerful rationalization for national hatreds and world conflict. To destroy this pernicious habit of mind, more than a new argument was required; it would take a new 'conception of man's relation to the universe which creates emotional force as well as intellectual conviction'.[114] Wallas did not know what form this 'conception' would take, nor where it would begin—possibly from Japan or France; perhaps, he ventured, it might develop out of Buddhism, or he later suggested, out of Chinese philosophy.[115] There was no way, though, to be at all sure; all that he was sure of was that such a secular 'world-religion' had to come, if the Great Society were ever to become a Great Community.

Having perceived by 1897 that men were living 'in new and untried circumstances', Wallas had begun to study the character of these circumstances. From this study he had immediately proceeded to the search for solutions to the new problems they posed. Unlike other Edwardians, his quest was twofold: for efficiency and at the same time for emotional satisfaction, social cohesion, and a sense of 'meaningfulness' for the individual. Both concerns were part of the Edwardian intellectual climate, but Wallas was almost unique in attempting to combine them and to reconcile their conflicting demands. The first aim placed him in the collectivist tradition; the second made him sensitive to the objections of anti-collectivists of all political hues. Wallas remained a collectivist, but a chastened and 'enlightened' one. He saw collectivist organization of society as only the base of the edifice that would arise in coming years. Existing collectivism left untouched the crucial area of psychology. In this realm new approaches were needed to decentralize as anti-collectivists wished, wherever this

[111] *Human Nature in Politics*, 298.   [112] Ibid., 298.
[113] Ibid., 299.   [114] Ibid., 304.
[115] 'Religion and Empire'. See unfinished MS. for *Social Judgment*, pt. ii (WP).

would not cripple social efficiency, but, even more important, to 'expand' the thought and feeling of men to match the scale of their new circumstances.

Wallas's insight into the fundamental problems of modern society was ahead of his time, and many of his particular proposals in education, politics, administration, and other areas were most valuable. However, much of his 'constructive' work was flawed by the attempt to be all-embracing, to see all sides, and to balance and reconcile. The result of this admirable intention was the loss of intellectual clarity and impact. The incapacity of his specific proposals for reform to add up to a complete social philosophy, and his emphasis, valuable but excessive, upon psychology led him into the misty realms where the outlines of a new 'world-philosophy' might be glimpsed. As he entered these regions, exhortation, always present, began to replace invention and the Evangelical side of his character gained predominance over the Benthamite. The preacher's son was returning to the spirit, if not the faith, of his youth.

CHAPTER VII

FROM THE OLD WORLD TO THE NEW

A FEW weeks after *The Great Society* appeared, Europe was plunged into the first general war in a century. What Wallas had feared, and warned against, had happened. The war did not challenge Wallas's ideas, as it did those of so many others. Indeed, it seemed to confirm his wisdom and prescience in criticizing pre-war optimism. He pointed out in 1915,

> Our whole assumptions as to the growth of 'public opinion', 'nobler ideals' and the rest in modern Europe prove, indeed, to depend on the free use of railways and cables and post-offices from which a corporal with a bayonet can drive, at any moment, the prophet who might have founded a new religion.[1]

The fragility of modern civilization and the imminent danger of war, dwelt upon in both *Human Nature in Politics* and *The Great Society* had generally been dismissed not only by the public, but by the 'thoughtful minorities seriously concerned in politics' as well.[2] Thus, ironically, the 'awful disaster for all civilisation' that plunged Wallas into the deepest gloom,[3] at the same time gave him new recognition and an increased sense of importance. Bertrand Russell, in writing *Principles of Social Reconstruction* (1916), acknowledged his debt to *The Great Society*, whose ideas he found 'more readily applicable to the present situation than those of most pre-war reformers'.[4] Similarly, Wallas rose in Beatrice Webb's estimation. His books, which she reread, seemed 'extraordinarily vivid and apt in the present state of things'. 'Indeed', she wrote him, 'your *Great Society* might have been written after the war—which is a great testimony to your foresight.'[5]

Beatrice Webb noted in her diary that 'Wallas has a greater consciousness of success than we have'.

---

[1] 'Ante-War Ideals', *Nation*, xviii (2 Oct. 1915), 23.
[2] Hobson, *Confessions*, 94.
[3] Letter to Dr. Larsson, 11 Nov. 1914 (WP).
[4] Letter to Wallas, 16 Jan. 1916 (WP), in which he asked Wallas to meet him to talk over the book, whose aim was 'to suggest a philosophy of politics based upon the belief that impulse has more effect than conscious purpose in moulding men's lives' (Preface to book, p. 5 of 1927 edn.).
[5] Letter to Wallas, 27 Dec. 1917 (WP).

He does not feel [she continued], as I certainly do, beaten by events. The war is a world catastrophe beyond the control of my philosophy. Such social philosophy as I possess does not provide any remedies for racial wars. To-day I feel like the fly, not on but under the wheel. Graham Wallas is working at a new book with the enthusiasm of a man in his prime: he feels he is doing his bit, and that it is a good deal bigger than some of his old friends think.[6]

The war years marked the peak of Wallas's career. Holding now the Chair of Political Science in the University of London, heading the department at the L.S.E., he enjoyed much influence at home and across the Atlantic. Beatrice Webb reflected,

The oddly slovenly young man of a quarter of a century ago... with his incapacity for steady work, his large appetite and delightful but alarming disinterested devotion to unpaying and unpopular causes, is now a leader of thought, with a settled and sufficient livelihood and a body of devoted disciples. He is an encouraging example of the markedly good man who is also, according to his own desires, a markedly successful man, with a fully satisfied conscience combined with a pleasant consciousness of public appreciation. His books are widely read in the U.S.A., his lectures are well attended, he sits on Royal Commissions, and is often referred to and consulted. He has many friends among leading publicists and minor Cabinet ministers.[7]

This public recognition, however, worked together with increasing age to make self-criticism and intellectual creativity more difficult for Wallas, His mind now began to turn in upon itself, rephrasing and elaborating, but not advancing much beyond his earlier work.

The war merely emphasized for Wallas what he had concluded before its outbreak: that the greatest need was for a rethinking of the social, political and psychological foundations of modern civilization. To surrender oneself to the 'peace of mind' that came with war, he warned, 'would be to abandon... any attempt to control by reasoned thought the policy of [the] nation', at a time when this attempt was more urgent than ever before.[8] He urged his fellow countrymen to

begin again the 'mental fight' of which Blake spoke, and to undertake again the weary and controversial task of building up a civilization in which some measure of harmonious satisfaction for the human spirit can be found in time of peace.

Turning in exasperation from the 'escapism' of Oxbridge, Wallas found the sort of 'naturalistic' thinking he was looking for in America. He

---

[6] *Beatrice Webb's Diaries 1912–24*, ed. M. Cole (1952), pp. 66–7.
[7] Ibid., 66.
[8] Comment on Dr. Jack's article, 'The Peacefulness of Being at War', *Men & Ideas*, 97.

particularly praised the work of Thorstein Veblen in exploring 'the general relation between the modern industrial system and the needs and tendencies of human nature'.[9] Though differing with him on details, he saw Veblen's work as the kind of psychological social science that held the key to the future. He urged Veblen to go on from critical to constructive work, to take up Bentham's role as a social inventor.[10]

For his part, Wallas hoped to provide guidance for post-war reconstruction by means of a new book, which would continue the path charted in *Human Nature in Politics* and *The Great Society*. Plagued by attacks of bronchitis and pneumonia, distracted by administrative duties (he was a member of the Academic Senate of London University in addition to his other tasks), he devoted all his free time to this project, 'desperately anxious' to complete it.[11]

Written works, however, were not his only means of influence. Wallas had a special gift for teaching. Harold Laski later recalled,

His lecture room at the L.S.E. was an amazing sight. Half the nationalities of the world had their representatives there; and one had only to scan their faces to realise that what he said opened new and attractive horizons to them.[12]

Wallas's private counsel, Laski remembered, was even more stimulating than his public lectures:

He had always something original to suggest. He always left you with a new and vivid sense that to think seriously was to fulfil a great social obligation. He never sought to impose himself in these talks. He made the young recruit feel that here was not the professor lecturing the disciple, but the fellow-hunter in the greatest game in the world.[13]

His students and friends, even where they differed on the value of his writing, agreed on his extraordinary talent as a teacher.[14] He had, according to the sociologist Morris Ginsberg, 'the power of creating in his listeners a sense of great urgency and a feeling, perhaps illusory, that they, together

---

[9] Review of Veblen's *Imperial Germany*, *Quarterly Journal of Economics*, xxx (November 1915), 179.
[10] Ibid., 186–7.
[11] Letter to Walter Lippmann, 19 Jan. 1919 (Lippmann).
[12] *Economica*, xxxviii (Nov. 1932), 404.
[13] Ibid. Sir Josiah Stamp, a leading Civil Servant, had much the same happy experience of Wallas's personal counsel. *Economica*, 395–6.
[14] See H. G. Wells, in *Literary Guide and Rationalist Review*, Sept. 1932. 'In his living self', Sir Michael Sadler noted, 'he taught us more than we have learned from his books'. Quoted by Sir Josiah Stamp, *Economica*, xxxviii, 401. See also *The Times*, 11 Aug. 1932 and *Manchester Guardian*, 11 Aug. 1932.

with him, were engaged in a co-operative effort of great importance'.[15] The later Prime Minister, Clement Attlee, came to the L.S.E. as a young lecturer and found Wallas 'the most interesting of the dons I knew'.[16] At Cambridge, when he lectured for a term in 1920, Wallas made a deep impression. As Kingsley Martin, an undergraduate at the time, remembered, he 'made young men and women aware of new worlds of knowledge; they discovered political science as a way of thinking disinterestedly about current events and a way of reading the newspapers that made sense'.[17]

Many of Wallas's students at the L.S.E. were young Civil Servants, fired by his enthusiasm for administrative reform and his 'power to make a naturally unattractive subject, such as the study of administrative detail and machinery, really fascinating'.[18] His efforts at infusing a new 'scientific' spirit into the Civil Service were rewarded in 1922 by the founding of the Institute of Public Administration; his former students acknowledged their debt by making him the first Fellow of the Institute.[19]

His influence upon the academic study of politics and society in Britain was, however, limited. Wallas's relative lack of influence in his own country is part of a larger problem, that of the weak development (until very recently) of social science in modern Britain.[20]

One source of this failure lies in the structure of English higher education in Wallas's time. The academic world was very small, numbering only a handful of institutions, and growing rather slowly. Within this world was a sharp class division, with Oxford and Cambridge on a separate, and much higher, level from the other universities. Oxford and Cambridge had long traditions, and more important, a mystique of tradition and the powers of self-government to protect it. Within both universities, the entrenched position of history, philosophy, and economics made it difficult to introduce studies infringing upon their jurisdictions.[21]

---

[15] Quoted by Janet Beveridge, *Epic of Clare Market* (London, 1960), 80. [16] Ibid., 86.
[17] *Harold Laski*, op. cit., 48. These lectures, Martin recalled, 'were very important to me'. *Father Figures* (London, 1966), 94.
[18] Sir Josiah Stamp, in *Economica*, 401.
[19] WP. 'He had a considerable following', Beatrice Webb later recalled, 'among the intellectuals of the Civil Service, and all who followed him intellectually loved him as a man.' Diary, 9 Aug. 1932 (PP).
[20] H. Stuart Hughes, in his study of the 'founding fathers' of modern social science, *Consciousness and Society*, typically—and justifiably—dismisses England.
[21] See A. Flexner, *Universities—American, English, German* (New York, 1930), and H. E. Barnes, 'British Sociology', in Barnes & Becker (eds.), *Social Thought from Lore to Science*, ii (New York, 1938). As late as 1948, G. D. H. Cole was arguing for a separate department of Politics, and an end to its division between History (for facts) and Philosophy (for theory). 'The Teaching of Social Studies in British Universities', *Essays in Social Theory* (London, 1950), 35–6.

All these characteristics of a 'closed' system placed obstacles in the path of innovation. The English situation was in sharp contrast to that of American higher education. In America, as Abraham Flexner noted in 1928, the multiplicity of universities, the rapid increase in their number, the diffusion of prestige, and the lack of attachment to tradition made change far easier—for both good and ill.[22] Though Flexner paid more attention to the ill effects of American 'lack of standards', this characteristic was valuable as far as the new social sciences were concerned. The firmness of English 'standards', by contrast, chilled intellectual vitality and left work such as Wallas's on the fringes of approved scholarship.

Beyond the obstacles placed by academic structure, the prevailing intellectual climate was largely hostile to Wallas's kind of work. The Idealism Wallas had scorned at Oxford had grown in influence. English Idealism had arisen as a way of accommodating religion and modern science.[23] If it disquieted High Churchmen and Low Church fundamentalists by 'rationalizing' religious faith, it also 'domesticated' rationalism to be compatible with religion. Such a metaphysical rationalism was ill-suited to nurture the development of behavioural science, for it turned the existing study of man away from behaviour and towards 'essences'. T. H. Green had insisted that man was a free, self-determining agent who could not be explained in biological or physiological terms. A natural science of psychology was philosophically impossible: 'The consciousness through which alone nature exists for us is neither natural nor a result of nature.'[24]

By the end of the nineteenth century, this anti-naturalist frame of mind was prevalent in the leading universities. In social and political thought, as Wallas had complained, abstractions like 'the State' were kept carefully shielded from contamination by the actual behaviour of states and men. In psychology, too, the study of behaviour was at a discount. James Ward, perhaps the most influential British psychologist of the late nineteenth and early twentieth century, declared that psychology as a science was totally distinct from both the biological and the social sciences. Mental life formed a realm of its own, governed by its own principles and to be studied by its own methods. These methods were introspective and philosophical.[25] A recent historian of the discipline has concluded that 'if British psychologists were for long almost wholly unsympathetic to behaviourism in any of its forms . . . if the educated British public came to regard psychology . . . as merely a rather odd sub-species of philosophy,

[22] Op. cit., especially pp. 221–2.
[24] Quoted in L. S. Hearnshaw, op. cit., 129.
[23] See Melvin Richter, op. cit.
[25] See ibid., 136–9.

the responsibility lies to a considerable extent with Ward' and, indirectly, with Idealism.[26]

The innovative behavioural approach of *Human Nature in Politics* consequently failed to make much headway behind the ancient walls of Oxbridge. Wallas himself was rejected for a professorship at Oxford in 1911; the position was given to a 'safer', if less creative, candidate. In the study of politics, the traditional classicist and idealist viewpoint espoused by Wallas's friend Ernest Barker remained dominant for years to come.

The universities were not alone in resisting the development of the behavioural sciences. Attitudes inimical to their nurture were pervasive throughout English culture.[27] English thinkers—including Wallas himself—carried on the moralistic legacy of nineteenth-century Evangelicalism. Thought about society rarely was separated—even momentarily—from moral judgements, whether in the lofty form of political philosophy or in the everyday form of 'practical' political opinion. Even friends like Lowes Dickinson, Hobson, and Gooch expressed uneasiness at Wallas's scientism. His efforts at realism appeared to them chiefly as a threat to Liberal ideals, and they complained that he was playing into the hands of Conservatives.[28]

The new sciences also had to struggle against a powerful nominalism—again, shared to an extent by Wallas. The search for general laws and uniformities in human affairs was widely disdained as arid speculation. A common reaction to *Human Nature in Politics* had been scepticism about its hopes for a science of politics.[29]

Wallas found greater recognition, ironically, in the nation whose politics had provoked him to re-examine his belief in democracy. The climate of opinion in America was more favourable to Wallas's ideas than in England. The turn of the century had seen the beginning of an era of great intellectual ferment, particularly in political and social thinking. Nearly all of the new generation of thinkers shared the assumption that the traditional approaches to the study of man and society had to be swept away, and this study built up afresh.[30] Wallas's call for intellectual re-

---

[26] Quoted in L. S. Hearnshaw, op. cit., 136.
[27] See Noel Annan, 'Curious Strength of Positivism', op. cit., 26.
[28] See Chapter V.
[29] See the reviews of *Human Nature in Politics* by Wallas's friends: J. A. Hobson, 'The Qualitative Method', *Sociological Review*, ii (1909), 293-4; [G. Lowes Dickinson], 'Can There Be A Science of Politics?', *Nation*, iv (12 Dec. 1908), 439-40.
[30] See Morton White, *Social Thought in America*, Richard Hofstadter, *Social Darwinism in American Thought*, ch. 8, and Bernard Crick, *The American Science of Politics*.

construction appealed more strongly to these men than to his compatriots, who were either dwelling in the realm of pure theory and ideals or preoccupied with this or that particular reform.

The new American thinkers were rebelling against what Morton White has called 'formalism'—idealism and abstract deduction as the bases of social study. A. Lawrence Lowell of Harvard had as early as 1889 objected that 'anyone who attempts to study a carpet loom, or even an ordinary steam engine, when at rest, will find its mechanism hard to understand. . . . The same principle applies to the study of politics, for the real mechanism of government can be understood only by examining it in action'.[31]

In place of 'formalism', the Americans proposed to make the core of their social science the study of behaviour. Their aim was, as Lowell put it in his *Public Opinion and Popular Government* (1913), 'to look through the forms to observe the vital forces behind them'.[32] These 'vital forces' were usually seen as psychological. The most important change in sociological method in these years, Richard Hofstadter has noted, was 'the tendency to place social studies on a psychological foundation'.[33] From the 1890s, America began to develop rapidly into the world's leading centre of psychological research. Traditional psychology was condemned as a bulwark of formalism, and a 'new psychology' espoused. The new 'functional' psychology, developed from the work of William James, John Dewey, and others, claimed to be both 'dynamic' and 'concrete', piercing behind the façades of intellectualism and associationism.[34]

Alongside a new interest in psychology went a budding enthusiasm for quantitative methods that would ensure scientific accuracy and objectivity. Lester Ward, in 1897, arguing that statistics were 'to the legislator what the results of observation and experiment are to the man of science', called for their use as the basis of a new political science.[35] Lowell did pioneering work in applying not merely statistics, but statistical techniques to politics.[36] Both were surpassed in quantitative zeal by Arthur Bentley, whose highly influential *Process of Government* was published the same year as *Human Nature in Politics*. 'It is impossible', Bentley argued, 'to attain scientific treatment of material that will not submit itself to measurement in some form. Measure conquers chaos.'[37]

---

[31] *Essays on Government* (Boston, 1889), 1.   [32] p. 4.   [33] *Social Darwinism*, 157.
[34] See F. B. Karpf, *American Social Psychology* (New York, 1932).
[35] *The Psychic Factors of Civilization* (Boston, 1897), 316.
[36] See his 'Oscillations in Politics', *Annals of the American Academy of Political and Social Science*, xii (July 1898), 69–97, and Crick, op. cit., 101–6.
[37] *The Process of Government* (New York, 1908), 200.

In these preoccupations with psychology and with quantification, as in their general mood of revolt against the study of forms and ideals, the new generation of Americans were thinking along remarkably similar lines to Wallas. Not surprisingly, they formed a receptive audience for *Human Nature in Politics*. Here, it seemed, was an Englishman 'speaking their language'. The sociologist Edward Ross confessed,

Hitherto I have regarded the English as several laps behind the Americans in the development of political science. I saw in them too much Plato and too little attention to the mind of Demos. Your book has not only redeemed the backwardness of political science in England but has put us all in your debt.

Ross accurately predicted that

your book may be more keenly appreciated in this country than in England seeing that English political thinkers seem to be less psychological, and more rooted in the intellectualist assumption than are the younger political thinkers on this side of the water.[38]

Wallas's importance for Americans went beyond his direct intellectual contributions. His work was also a 'ratification' from the Old World of the new directions they were already marking out. To Arthur Holcombe, a teacher of Government at Harvard whom Wallas met in 1910, both *Human Nature in Politics* and *The Great Society* were 'thoroughly American rather than English'.[39] Wallas was in a sense 'adopted' as an 'honorary American'; he came to be esteemed as an 'elder statesman' of the new political science.

The new generation of Americans was confronted with the same basic problem that concerned Wallas—the revolution wrought by the coming of the Great Society. Urbanization, industrialization, the explosive growth of population and technology—all these had occurred with even greater rapidity in America than in England. In the space of one generation, a new environment had appeared, and the speed of the change forced it more strongly upon the American imagination than upon the Edwardian English mind.[40] Wallas's insistence upon relating everything to this overall transformation, his refusal to deal with specific problems in isolation, as many Edwardian social critics did, made his work (and H. G. Wells's, for the same reason) especially attractive to Americans.

[38] Letter, 9 April 1909 (WP).
[39] Letter, 28 June 1914 (WP).
[40] See, for example, Morton and Lucia White, *The Intellectual Versus the City* (Cambridge, Mass., 1962), chs. 8–10.

The swift coming of the Great Society with all its new problems had brought about a rapid change in American social thinking. The anti-intellectualism and the individualism that had distressed Wallas on his first visit in 1896 were giving way to a new respect for intellect and an awareness of the need for purposive, collective action. Richard Hofstadter, in his history of American anti-intellectualism, has seen in this period 'the rise of the expert',[41] and Wallas himself was struck, on his third visit in 1914, as a Lowell lecturer in Boston, by 'an apparent growth... of the authority of methodical and specially instructed thought on social and political questions, as against average unspecialized opinion'.[42]

This change of outlook was part of a broader movement away from a traditional 'optimistic fatalism'—a belief in an automatic national 'destiny' to be fulfilled by the uncoordinated self-seeking of individuals—to a new activism. This activism was the theme of perhaps the most influential book of the era, Herbert Croly's *Promise of American Life* (1909). Croly contrasted, in a phrase borrowed from H. G. Wells, the old belief in national 'destiny' with the new conception he advocated of national 'purpose', to be achieved by deliberate, organized effort, using the best knowledge and talent available. To those taking up this conception, the work of Wallas, as well as that of Wells, the Webbs, and others in the Fabian tradition, provided inspiration and example.

The new American reformers, beginning with Jane Addams, attacked the 'moralism' and 'legalism' of older reformers, and proposed to replace them by a realistic understanding of human nature and its relation to society.[43] Social problems were to be resolved, not by moral injunctions or the passing of restrictive laws, but by human 'engineering' and education, based on the development of the social sciences. Wallas's criticisms of English Liberalism, and his constructive efforts to open up a new field of study were perfectly attuned to this mood. To Jane Addams, *Human Nature in Politics* 'explore[d] and formulate[d] whole regions of experience which I have never seen dealt with before'.[44] She wished Wallas could carry on a series of such studies in Chicago, and did succeed in bringing him there to lecture for a few days in 1910.[45]

The most important person in spreading Wallas's ideas in America was

---

[41] *Anti-Intellectualism in American Life* (New York, 1963), ch. 8.
[42] 'Universities and the Nation in America and England', in *Men & Ideas*, 175.
[43] See Morton White, *Social Thought in America*, ch. 2, and, especially, Christopher Lasch, *The New Radicalism in America 1889–1963* (New York, 1965), ch. 5, 'Politics as Social Control'.
[44] Letter to Wallas, 21 Dec. 1908 (WP).
[45] Ibid., and letter to Wallas, 7 May 1910 (WP).

undoubtedly Walter Lippmann.⁴⁶ At Harvard in 1910 (at Lowell's invitation), Wallas gave a seminar in the application of psychology to political and social thought in which Lippmann, then an undergraduate, quickly stood out. The psychological method advanced by Wallas seemed to Lippmann the key to politics he was seeking, and one of the aims of his precocious *Preface to Politics* (1912) was to popularize *Human Nature in Politics*.⁴⁷ Wallas, he wrote enthusiastically,

has described what political science must be like, and anyone who has absorbed his insight has an intellectual groundwork for political observation. . . . he has deliberately brought the study of politics to the only focus which has any rational interest for mankind. He has made a plea, and sketched a plan which hundreds of investigations the world over must help to realize.⁴⁸

Wallas's psychological approach, Lippmann declared, provided a basis for a new 'realistic' and 'creative' politics to replace the sterile 'machine conception of government' inherited from the eighteenth century and still dominant.⁴⁹ 'If political science could travel' in the direction suggested by Wallas, he argued, 'its criticisms would be relevant, its proposals practical.'

There would [he continued], for the first time, be a concerted effort to build a civilization around mankind, to use its talent and to satisfy its needs. There would be no more empty taboos, no erecting of institutions upon abstract and mechanical analogies. Politics would be like education—an effort to develop, train and nurture men's impulses.⁵⁰

This 'politics of human engineering' had been foreshadowed by William James, in his speculations on a 'moral equivalent' for war. Lippmann portrayed Wallas as the heir of James. Like James, Wallas was trying, he wrote, 'to found statesmanship on human need'. Like James, Wallas saw that 'there are good and bad satisfactions of the same impulse'.

The routineer [Lippmann continued] with his taboo does not see this, so he attempts the impossible task of obliterating the impulse. He differs fundamentally from the creative politician who devotes himself to inventing fine expressions for human needs, who recognizes that the work of statesmanship is in large measure the finding of good substitutes for the bad things we want.⁵¹

As did many others exposed to *Human Nature in Politics*, however, Lippmann saw only anti-intellectualism, not its more subtle 'higher

⁴⁶ 'I've always regarded myself', Lippmann has remarked, 'as a disciple of Wallas's.' 'Reminiscences' (Oral History Research Office, Columbia University, 1950), 35.
⁴⁷ See ibid., 32–3, 35.   ⁴⁸ *Preface to Politics*, 79–80.
⁴⁹ Ibid., 13, 80.   ⁵⁰ Ibid., 80.   ⁵¹ Ibid., 83.

FROM THE OLD WORLD TO THE NEW 171

intellectualism'. Simultaneously reading Bergson, Sorel, and Freud, Lippmann was swept with youthful enthusiasm into an exaltation of irrationalism. To Wallas's dismay, he not only recognized but approved the power of slogan and symbol in political life. Wallas took the unusual step, so much respect had he for his student's intellect, of prefacing his next book, *The Great Society*, with a letter to Lippmann, urging him to take its warning against anti-intellectualism into account when writing the sequel to *Preface to Politics*.[52] Having read *The Great Society* in manuscript, Lippmann produced *Drift and Mastery*, which bears a similar relation to that book as *Preface to Politics* does to *Human Nature in Politics*. Rejecting his former irrationalism, Lippmann set forth a mature and influential assessment of the coming shape of politics in the Great Society. The existing alternatives, as he saw them, were either further 'drift'—the 'fatalism' Croly condemned—or 'mastery'—the deliberate, scientific control of life, the substitution 'of purpose for tradition'. 'We can no longer', he urged, 'treat life as something that has trickled down to us. We have to deal with it deliberately, devise its social organization, alter its tools, formulate its method, educate and control it.'[53]

Lippmann's two widely-read 'manifestoes' certainly made Wallas better known in America and promoted the assimilation of his ideas into the main stream of American progressive thought. Through his editorship of the *New Republic*, starting in 1914, Lippmann introduced Wallas to leading progressive intellectuals like Herbert Croly, Walter Weyl, and Justice Brandeis, and helped draw Wallas even closer to Felix Frankfurter, whom he had met in America before the war. Entertained by Wallas on visits to England, many of them became his personal friends.[54] Wallas served as unofficial 'contact man' for Frankfurter, in England on a mission for the Secretary of War. He returned full of praise for Wallas's 'general sanity and foresight'. In fact, during the Peace Conference, Frankfurter, a member of the American delegation, sent for a copy of *Human Nature in Politics* to read once more in the light of current events.[55]

Urged along by Lippmann and Croly, Wallas contributed a number of

---

[52] His high opinion of Lippmann rose even higher over the years. A few years later he wrote: 'You are the only man working at this problem whom I believe to be abler than myself.' 19 Jan. 1919 (Lippmann).
[53] *Drift and Mastery* (New York, 1914), 267.
[54] See letter from Weyl, 17 Sept. 1915 (WP). Also see Kenneth McNaught, 'American Progressives and the Great Society', *Journal of American History*, lii (1967), 504–20.
[55] *Holmes-Laski Letters*, 141 (Laski to Holmes, 11 Mar. 1918); letter to Wallas from Ella Winter, 13 May 1919 (WP). There are quite a number of letters to Wallas from Frankfurter, and some from Brandeis, in the personal possession of Miss May Wallas.

articles to the *New Republic* during the war years.⁵⁶ Clifford Sharp, editor of the *New Statesman*, was also eager to have contributions from him, but not surprisingly, he found the tone of the American journal, whose editors clearly admired him, more congenial than the familiar atmosphere of the English Fabian review. The guiding spirits of the *New Republic*, moreover, were younger and less fixed in their ideas than the Webbs and their circle, and more open to Wallas's influence. Wallas increasingly preferred to leave behind the relatively unreceptive and 'unimaginative' English public and come across the ocean to bask in the admiration and enjoy the lively interest in the 'big questions' of American students and thinkers.

In the two decades since his first visit, Wallas's impression of America had changed significantly. America had always been to him a 'laboratory of the future', but in 1896 it was the dangers in this future that had struck him. He had returned home with new anxiety over the problems created by mass democracy and by the rapid appearance of the Great Society. What most fascinated him about the country was the combination of extreme 'modernity' in so many fields of life with 'archaic' political and social attitudes. He envied Wells his trip there in 1906 (from which came *The Future in America*), wishing he could join him to see 'whether the American young men are getting anything in the nature of a religion or philosophy to take the place of the eighteenth-century corpse'.⁵⁷

On his visits in 1910 and 1914, he began to feel that they indeed were: the new Progressivism of social engineering was daily gaining wider acceptance, while both the quantity and quality of social research, and the popular appreciation of such research, were soaring.⁵⁸ After all, it had been the work of an American, William James, that had given Wallas the insight to work out his 'new view of politics', and it was now the rapidly growing body of American psychological research that made the writing of *The Great Society* possible.

By the war years, Wallas's feelings towards America had made, in one sense, an about-face. Though behind England in practical matters of legislation, America now appeared to him the more hopeful place intellectually. Having always, unlike the Webbs, placed more faith in attitudes than in institutions, he now became something of a partisan of America.⁵⁹

---

⁵⁶ Letters from S. K. Ratcliffe, 12 July 1915 and 14 Dec. 1915 (WP).
⁵⁷ Letters to Wells, 25 Mar. 1906 and 13 June 1906 (Wells).
⁵⁸ On the latter, see 'Universities and the Nation', *Men & Ideas*.
⁵⁹ See letter from Ella Winter, 13 May 1919, on Wallas's high opinion of Americans

In this new view he took on some of the naïve optimism of his *New Republic* friends, for, after all, he knew little of the America that lay beyond the intellectual and professional circles he frequented. Led by a man of 'real humanitarian outlook and real imagination', he wrote,

America as a whole is striving to attain a new world vision of world problems. One recognises in the modern leaders of American finance a real desire to make their tremendous powers to serve the needs of humanity. American universities are turning out a fresh and vigorous crop of geographers, and transport engineers and historians and international lawyers.[60]

He urged that this great potential be applied to the 'formation of a conscious world policy' for organizing peace, something the European powers seemed incapable of doing. Though deeply worried by the post-war triumph of reaction and isolationism, Wallas never lost faith in America's potential. With every year that passed, America became more the home of the new human sciences, and with knowledge came, as he saw it, an increasing readiness on the part of young scientists and intellectuals to apply it to social problems. Wallas returned there as often as he could after the war, to lecture and to observe. The University of Chicago (then the leading centre of social research), he wrote to an American friend in the 1920s, was 'the most interesting place in the world just now—except, perhaps, New York.'[61]

The plans for a 'research university' in New York—'an attempt', Herbert Croly explained, 'to do something, in a more elaborate way, similar to what you started to do in England many years ago when you started the Fabian Society and which is now being carried on, in a somewhat different way, by the London School of Economics',—evoked Wallas's enthusiasm.[62] The object of the 'New School of Social Research' was to 'work out a technique of social progress and to turn out people who are capable of carrying on a work of that kind in a scientific spirit and from a psychological point of view'.[63] With an aim so close to Wallas's heart, the New School was irresistible, so that he could hardly refuse Croly's

---

and the 'American spirit'. Seeing the new importance of America, Wallas wrote to his friend Gilbert Murray and other Oxford acquaintances, to press for the establishment of a permanent lectureship in American history (WP).

[60] 'The Eastern Question', *New Republic*, ix (27 Jan. 1917), 349.
[61] Letter to C. W. Everett, 26 Nov. 1928 (WP).
[62] Letter from Croly, 29 Mar. 1919 (WP).
[63] Ibid.

offer of a visiting lectureship, to give 'the star course of the year', for its opening semester.[64]

[64] Letter from Croly, 16 May 1919, and letter from S. K. Ratcliffe, 13 Apr. 1919 (WP). In addition to the New School lectures, he gave the Dodge Lectures at Yale, and was invited by Frankfurter to speak at Harvard, and by Jane Addams to speak at Chicago. He was eager, not only to speak at the New School, but to give its organizers the benefit of his administrative experience at the L.S.E. His advice, aimed at ensuring the school's research character, was unfortunately not followed, and the New School never fulfilled its original promise. A friend, S. K. Ratcliffe, reported in 1921 that it was 'going just the way you predicted—good audiences for the star events, but very little or no research'. (Letter, 21 Apr. 1921 (WP)). Harry E. Barnes returned in disappointment to Clark University. 'I wish', he wrote, 'that the New School might have taken some of your advice about future organization.' (Letter, 10 Feb. 1922 (WP)).

CHAPTER VIII

RECONSTRUCTION (1919-1932)

WALLAS took the opportunity of the New School lectures in the autumn of 1919 to put together the book he had been writing on social reconstruction. The problem, he remarked to Walter Lippmann, was how to organize co-operation:

Men can't exist with their present numbers in the 'temperate' parts of the globe, and enjoy the material wealth, and beauty, and knowledge which they want, unless they cooperate on a much larger scale and with more exactness and continuity than is natural to them. What ought we to do about it?[1]

Christianity had certainly failed as a stimulus to co-operation: in each country the churches had become the willing, even eager adjuncts to the war effort. The zest with which Wallas belaboured the churches betrayed a certain satisfaction in finding his prejudices confirmed. He remarked to Lippmann,

Conventional Christian orthodoxy has made such a mess of things that in the rest of Christendom as well as in France those who do not in fact believe will find themselves compelled to recognise that fact, with important results all around.[2]

More saddening to Wallas was the failure of Socialism, which had 'no more influence than Christianity on either [the war's] origin or its course'.[3] The war, he saw in 1916, was going to leave 'the condition of international relations as dangerous as a mined trench, and we shall all be forced to treat the prevention of a new explosion as the main purpose of our political lives'.[4] Would Socialism be a sufficient guide for that purpose? Wallas thought not. The struggle for economic equality would have to be seen as 'a part only, however important it may be, of some larger conception of life'.[5] The word 'Socialism', he predicted, 'may go the way of "natural rights" and the "greatest happiness principle" and in our new need we may find a new name for our hopes'.[6] As always, Wallas was looking at

[1] Letter, 19 Jan. 1919 (Lippmann).
[2] Letter, 30 Dec 1916 (Lippmann).
[3] 'Socialism and the Fabian Society', (1916), *Men & Ideas*, 107.
[4] Ibid.   [5] Ibid.   [6] Ibid.

things from a psychological point of view. What he sought was a new ideal, a 'world-view', not a mere economic or political rearrangement.

More and more, psychologism and the 'Evangelical' impulse were dominating his views, at the cost of a growing insensitivity to concrete issues of economic and political power. 'His sympathies lie', Beatrice Webb perceived, 'more with the young men of the *Round Table* [a journal devoted to promoting Imperial co-operation] than with any of the Socialist and radical groups who are in revolt against the existing governing class.'[7]

This was true enough: like Wallas, the 'new Imperialists' of the *Round Table* saw the chief problem of the age as psychological rather than economic, a question of finding new ideals and propagating new attitudes. Their appeal, like Wallas's, was addressed not to the general public, but to those governors and opinion-leaders of society about whom Beatrice Webb was then despairing. Seeking a 'higher' form of politics than either class conflict or 'Prussianism', they argued for the ideal, taken from the Greeks, of a 'commonwealth' blending authority and liberty, responsibility and justice, taking account of man's spiritual as well as material nature. To match the scale of modern life, this commonwealth was to embrace the whole Empire, and, perhaps, ultimately the world.[8]

Among this group was Wallas's good friend and former student, Alfred Zimmern, whose writings show the classical Greek roots of the political idealism Wallas shared with the members of the *Round Table*. Zimmern, professor of international relations at Oxford, had learned his Thucydides and his Greek grammar as a preparatory school pupil of Wallas's. Their relationship continued after Zimmern went on to Winchester, and he remarked in 1916, 'I have been learning steadily from him ever since'.[9] His well-known book on *The Greek Commonwealth* (1912), discussed with Wallas before and during its writing, attempted to answer for the *polis* many of the questions Wallas had raised in *Human Nature in Politics*. Zimmern tried in this work 'to analyse the different strands of feeling which attached the Greek citizen to his state'.[10] 'Of course', he commented to Wallas, 'I want most of all to make people think about the nature of the twentieth-century polis.'[11] This underlying aim found expression in the rest of his life-work, devoted to furthering international co-operation, and extending the principles of the Greek *polis* to the whole of the modern world.

---

[7] *Beatrice Webb's Diaries 1912–24*, 66.
[8] See J. R. M. Butler, *Lord Lothian* (London, 1960), ch. 3.
[9] *Nationality and Government* (London, 1919), 87.
[10] Letter to Wallas, 5 Jan. 1910 (WP).   [11] Ibid.

The methods Wallas chose to reach his new *polis*, however, were not only those of the Round Tablers, but also those of the Benthamites. His 'Evangelical' idealism was tempered, as always, by his zeal for science. He had earlier called for applying the science of social psychology to social policy; this became the central theme of his latest book.

Our Social Heritage, published in 1921, reflected even more strikingly than his earlier books, Wallas's dual outlook. He hard-headedly canvassed the possibilities of applying scientific knowledge through 'social invention', while preaching the vague but fervent gospel of a new 'world-philosophy'. The first approach apparently predominated in his American lectures, while the second developed in importance during the final writing in London in 1920.

By the time of these American lectures, Wallas's psychology had undergone changes, reflecting American influence. There had always been in his thinking a tension between the 'social' and the 'biological' viewpoint; against environmentalist reformers, he had emphasized biological factors, while against conservatives and eugenicists he had insisted upon the importance of environment. At bottom, however, the instinct psychology he had adopted assumed that the essentials of human nature were inherited. This assumption was being questioned by the development of a sociology and anthropology in Europe and America based on the social origin of human behaviour. The new approach quickly caught on in America, where it seemed to provide a scientific basis for optimism concerning the possibilities of social progress.[12]

Soon after the publication of *The Great Society*, Wallas was criticized by Wesley Mitchell, an American acquaintance, and a prominent economist and social thinker, for overestimating the importance of the instincts. Relying on the 'environmentalist' psychology developed by another American, E. L. Thorndike, Mitchell argued for the extreme plasticity of human nature, pointing out its encouragement to social reformers. What belonged to 'nature' could not be greatly altered, but what belonged to 'nurture' was open to human control.

Nurture indeed [Mitchell wrote] cannot eradicate unlearned capacities, it cannot supplant them; but it can select certain among them for development and others for repression; it can make the most various combinations among them as well as modify their forms.... Most important of all, the influence of nurture may be cumulative. Every increase of social widsom may be applied in bettering the

---

[12] See Nisbet, *Durkheim*, and Hofstadter, *Social Darwinism*, chs. 4-8, especially 159-60.

nurture given to the generation that follows, so that this generation in turn may give its successor training better than it received.¹³

Wallas took this view, increasingly popular in America and really quite close to his own aims, to heart in his new book. As the title indicated, he now stressed the importance of 'social heritage', or, as he called it in his New School lectures, 'social inheritance'. Our social heritage was that part of our 'nurture' handed down from one generation to another by the social process of teaching and learning, a second kind of inheritance whose importance relative to biological inheritance was growing with the development of civilization. This 'second inheritance' had to make up for the inadequacies of the first.

With this concept of 'social heritage', Wallas was moving away from 'individualism', but not far enough away. His view of 'social heritage' remained relatively superficial—he saw it as a collection of techniques—'knowledge, expedients and habits'—usable by conscious purpose to modify the effects of biology.¹⁴ The sense, emerging among his younger contemporaries, of society as above and behind the individual, shaping men without their choice or consciousness, passed Wallas by. He lived long enough to begin to move in this direction, but by this time was too old to discard his former way of thinking.

Consequently, this change in emphasis did not affect Wallas's ideas as much as it should have, for he proceeded to use the new terminology to restate the thesis of *The Great Society*. He argued that with social development men had become ever more dependent upon their social heritage, which, however, was failing to keep pace with social change. The result was a growing gap between the capacities of men and the social demands placed upon them. 'Each generation', he observed, 'must adapt to its present needs the social heritage which it received from the preceding generation.'¹⁵ Some periods of history—the 'golden age' of Athens, the early-middle nineteenth century among others—had seen unusual bursts of adaptation and invention. Such a creative surge, which he had called for in 1914, had become in the aftermath of world war a desperate necessity. In its absence, he warned, prophetically, in the most pessimistic mood of his life, 'the nations of the earth, confused and embittered by the events of 1914-20, may soon be compelled to witness—this time without hope or

---

¹³ 'Human Behavior and Economics', *Quarterly Journal of Economics*, xxix (Nov. 1914), 11.
¹⁴ *Our Social Heritage* (New Haven, 1921), 14.
¹⁵ Ibid., 20.

illusion—another and more destructive stage in the suicide of civilization'.[16]

Wallas took his stand for the 'middle way' between blind conservatism and violent revolution. As he wrote, the Bolsheviks in Russia were

attempting to make such an adjustment [between social heritage and present needs] by wholly ignoring the past, and are doing so at the cost of destroying the wealth, the organization, the traditions, and to an appalling extent the lives of the trained functionaries of the old dispensation. In Britain, America and France it is still possible to hope that, if time is allowed us, we may make an approach towards a more complete adjustment at an infinitely less cost of suffering and waste.[17]

Adjustment could be facilitated by the application of psychological knowledge. The sustained muscular and mental efforts required by the Great Society were, unfortunately, 'unnatural'. Psychological knowledge, he had learned through his work on the Committee for Psychological War Research, could help in the invention of means to increase mental and physical efficiency while compensating for the strain involved.[18]

Improving the processes of group co-operation by the application of psychology particularly interested Wallas. He had always enjoyed taking part in administration through committees, from the London School Board to the Senate of London University; for 'these allowed him', the Director of the L.S.E. remembered, 'to watch the play of human nature'.[19] A colleague on university examination committees had observed his attention 'divided between the merits and substance of the subject under discussion and the modes of thought by which we were all approaching a decision'.[20]

The many years of personal observation of 'the modes of thought' of committees enabled Wallas to make good use of the experiences of the war. Drawing on the Reports of the British Dardanelles and Mesopotamia Commissions of 1917, he discussed, in one of the most illuminating chapters of the book, the pitfalls inherent in thinking and planning by groups. He used the botched planning that had led to the disastrous Dardanelles landings, and to the equally disastrous advance on Baghdad to illustrate his theme, that

[16] Ibid., 23. This pessimism was present in his New School lectures in 1919. See letter from Abraham Flexner, 5 Dec. 1920 (WP).
[17] Ibid., 94.
[18] See Wallas's article, 'Instinct and the Unconscious', *British Journal of Psychology*, x (Nov. 1919), 24–6.
[19] Sir William Beveridge, *Economica*, xxxviii, 408.
[20] Sir Josiah Stamp, ibid., 397.

our socially inherited expedients of group-cooperation by discipline and discussion are still imperfectly worked out, and are apt at any moment to break down, and their place to be taken by the primitive instinctive process.[21]

The only alternative to dangerously inefficient planning, dominated by unconscious attitudes and emotions, was to realize the need for psychological self-consciousness. Yet, though mental efficiency was needed, it was not enough. Unlike the British War Council, the German General Staff had been rigorously trained in clear thinking and efficient procedures, yet had still miscalculated. Their error in July 1914 was due, he felt, not to technical military inefficiency, but chiefly to the fact that

> the narrowing of human sympathy which was consciously involved in much of the training of individual Prussian civil or military Realpolitiker involved also a narrowing of their thoughts, and a lessening of the ultimate efficiency of any cooperative group of which they formed part.[22]

Returning to a question he had touched on before the war, he asked what sort of over-all 'will-organization' the Great Society required. During the nineteenth century, the industrial nations had directed their large-scale co-operative activities by means of the territorial state. This 'expedient' had come under widespread attack in the second decade of the twentieth century. Pluralist thinking, spearheaded by the most brilliant of the new generation of social thinkers—men like G. D. H. Cole and Harold Laski—had captured much of progressive opinion. Cole wrote, and many agreed,

> There can be only one escape from the futility of our present methods of parliamentary government; and that is to find an association and method of representation for each function, and a function for each association and body of representatives. In other words, real democracy is to be found, not in a single omnicompetent representative assembly, but in a system of coordinated functional representative bodies.[23]

Wallas's own views had changed since his Fabian days; he had learned that vocational organization could supply something that representative government lacked. His own work had, by its realistic method and its psychological criticism of representative government and modern society, stimulated Cole, Laski, and others to think about these problems and to develop pluralist solutions.

Human Nature in Politics 'helped' the young G. D. H. Cole 'enormously' in his search for the roots of social behaviour. There Wallas made

---

[21] *Our Social Heritage*, 8. [22] Ibid., 76.
[23] *Social Theory* (London, 1920; rev. edn., 1921), 108

just the approach to the study of sociality that I needed. MacDougall and the so-called Social Psychologists I had found exceedingly unhelpful. The more I read them, the more they seemed merely to revive the older abstraction of 'Faculty Psychology' in new forms. Their classifications of instincts led me nowhere. But Wallas did set out ... to look at human behaviour, and especially social behaviour, with the eyes of a keen observer, attempting a real measurement of social phenomena as the starting point for a practical valuation.[24]

Harold Laski, a student at Oxford just after Cole, was also deeply impressed by *Human Nature in Politics*.[25] Wallas was forging, he felt, 'new weapons of sociological investigation'—'quantitative and psychological'.[26] 'In arrangement, in illustration, in selection of material, in method of enquiry', he remarked during the war, 'no one has made more fundamental contributions, than Mr. Wallas.'[27]

Laski's first book, *Studies in the Problem of Sovereignty*, published in 1917, while he was a tutor at Harvard, reflected the influence of Wallas's methods and ideas. In this work Laski examined, in the legal terminology of 'sovereignty', the various possibilities of 'will-organization' in modern society. His effort to base theory on psychological facts instead of on *a priori* 'rights' and 'obligations' impressed Wallas so much that he wrote to the young author offering praise and suggestions.[28] He urged that Laski, having brilliantly criticized the traditional justifications of state-sovereignty, go on to work out more satisfactory administrative and 'spiritual' areas of state organization—a task Laski attempted in his *Grammar of Politics* (1925). This initiative on Wallas's part was the beginning of a long friendship, during which Wallas was instrumental in bringing Laski back to England by obtaining a position for him at the L.S.E.[29]

Laski agreed with Wallas that 'something has got to be deduced from the breakdown of parliamentary government' that began before the war and which became more obvious during it.[30] 'The complexity of social

[24] G. D. H. Cole, *Studies in World Economics* (London, 1934), 271.
[25] Letter to Wallas, 21 Dec. 1919 (WP).
[26] Review of Hugh Elliot, *Herbert Spencer*, in *New Republic*, xi (23 June 1917) 224; *Holmes-Laski Letters*, 15 (Laski to Holmes, 13 Sept. 1916).
[27] Review of R. M. MacIver, *Community*, in *New Republic*, xi (7 July 1917), 284.
[28] 'Your books', Laski replied, 'and a happy year I worked with Karl Pearson before I went to Oxford, has [*sic*] made me distrust the elaborate analyses of Sidgwick or Bluntschli.' 17 May 1917 (WP). Laski described Wallas to Holmes as 'one of the best stimulants I know' (*Holmes-Laski Letters*, 230; 4 Jan. 1920) and wrote to Wallas in 1919 expressing appreciation for his friendship and advice, classing him with Holmes and Roscoe Pound as having 'made real landmarks in my life'. 21 Dec. 1919 (WP).
[29] Lord Beveridge, *The London School of Economics and its Problems 1919–1937* (London, 1960), 53. See letter from Laski thanking Wallas (WP).
[30] Letter, 17 May 1917 (WP).

problems', he worried, 'seems to have outrun rather woefully the possibilities of the parliamentary system.'³¹ These difficulties Wallas himself had pointed out before the war had brought them to general attention, yet he found unacceptable [the deductions Laski, like Cole, drew from them.

He continued to believe, more strongly than ever after the 'Coupon election' of 1918, that the existing political system was 'a clumsy and stupid arrangement'. Yet, at the same time, he felt 'almost sure that G. H. Cole, H. J. Laski and the other pluralists are on the wrong lines'.³² The new complexity of society could be met in either of two ways: by 'devolution', that is, by breaking down social and political functions and distributing them over a wide area of groups, or by finding new means of reasserting the unity of the community as a whole. The first way was that of the pluralists, who wanted to re-form the Great Society around strong and 'sovereign' groups, vocational and otherwise. In the process, however, Wallas feared, the *polis*-ideal that meant so much to him would move further than ever away from realization. To him, the Great Society was already far too pluralistic; modern life, compared to that of the classical Greeks, was fragmented and confused, without unity or coherence. Seen from this angle, pluralism merely confirmed the malady.

Wallas's vision of the good life, derived from his classical studies, involved a unified, integrated society, where the political relation embraced all aspects of life and all members of society. Only the political relation was general enough to fulfil this function; other relations could never supplant it. Though pluralism was as logical a deduction from Wallas's own psychological analysis of society as the ideal of 'the Great Community', for Wallas himself it was unacceptable.

His influence, however, was evident on both sides of the issue. When Walter Lippmann showed a highly sympathetic appreciation of Laski's work, Alfred Zimmern, equally close to Wallas intellectually and personally, sharply criticized Lippmann. Accepting Laski's assertion that allegiance in the modern world was necessarily experimental and federal, Lippmann wrote:

The problem before us is to invent the machinery, methods of thought and educational practice by which such federal citizenship can be made workable. Without it there is no decent solution possible of the issues raised by class, nationality, religion and imperial expansion. How, for example, shall a man

---

³¹ *Holmes-Laski Letters*, 19 (Laski to Holmes, 13 Sept. 1916). See also 40-2, 45, 53, 57, 76, 89.
³² Letter to Lippmann, 19 Jan. 1919 (Lippmann).

distribute his available energy between a league of nations, the government at Washington, his state government, his city, his neighborhood, his family, his church, his vocation?[33]

One might well have imagined this passage to have been written by the author of *The Great Society*, so similar is it in phraseology and spirit. And yet Zimmern was speaking with Wallas's approval when he protested the lowering of 'the claims of the political state' to the level of other social groups. 'The main stream of the world's thought', Zimmern argued, 'has ... held fast to what Mr. Lippmann calls the "archaic" view that political allegiance takes precedence of all others because it embraces the common concerns of the whole community.'[34]

Against the new pluralist ideas, Wallas took his stand with what he saw as 'the main stream of the world's thought', beginning with the Greeks. He did not, however, justify his position on philosophic grounds only, but brought in practical arguments. He pointed out danger after danger in pluralist organization, particularly in its leading proposed form, vocationalism.

In doing so, Wallas did not feel himself to be, nor was he, as Cole and the Webbs claimed, an unreasonable hater of trade unions. His own experience with the National Union of Teachers when on the School Board for London had shown him how unions could improve the lives of their members.[35] On a more general level, he readily agreed with the Guild Socialists on the psychological value of occupational organization:

> The feeling of human solidarity is so difficult to create under modern conditions that we cannot afford to leave unused for the purposes of social co-operation the unforced knowledge of each other, and the direct good-will, which may arise as an incident of common occupation.[36]

Yet to those who upheld vocationalism as a complete system, Wallas was ruthless. Though his ultimate purpose was constructive, he felt he had first to clear the ground of this fashionable but misleading panacea. In carrying out this demolition work, his tone shifted from the 'scientific' to the polemical, betraying an emotional commitment made long before this particular controversy arose.

To those disillusioned with existing politics, he pointed out that once vocational organization attained a national scale, it would be at least as

---

[33] 'A Clue', *New Republic*, x (14 Apr. 1917), 316–17.
[34] Letter to *New Republic*, xii (15 Sept. 1917), 191.
[35] See 'English Teachers' Organisations', *New Statesman*, v (25 Sept. 1915), 586–87.
[36] *Our Social Heritage*, 108.

subject to the difficulties and dangers of electioneering as the present system.[37] In addition, it was liable to peculiar weaknesses of its own.

Not only industrial vocationalism, but all 'professionalism', whether legal, medical, military, or educational, drew his fire. The chief weakness, as he saw it, was psychological—the tendency to shrink from change, common enough in all men, but given greatly increased strength by professional organization. 'Like the fear instinct', Wallas noted, the shrinking from any change in one's habits 'is increased in force when it is experienced by a body of human beings assembled in one place, or otherwise made aware of a common impulse'.[38] Resistance to change in a vocation was further increased by the tendency to attach aesthetic feeling, 'and indeed something like personal affection', to any traditional art. Gothic architecture, classical education, canon law, navigation by sails—all of these and other arts he had seen 'become personalities loved for themselves and defended with passionate loyalty'.[39]

Wallas was not arguing theoretically, but drawing on the varied experiences of his own life. His observant mind never forgot

an old Chelsea bricklayer to whom five and thirty years ago I described the methods of rapid construction which I had seen in use on the piers of the new Battersea Bridge. 'It isn't brick-laying', he shouted, 'it's bloody paving.'[40]

Mechanization, the pluralists failed to see, had made vocational conservatism more and not less obstructive:

In the efficiency of manual work to-day [he argued] the two main factors of productivity are the willingness of the workman to use the power of the machine to the full, and the transferability of labour from one machine or process to another in accordance with changes in demand.[41]

A workman, in other words,

who can shift from one process to another is more likely, *ceteris paribus*, to feel zest in his work . . . and also more likely to do that work which is most needed, than one who can only superintend one process.[42]

This held true also, it seemed to him for many forms of intellectual work, as he had argued on the Civil Service Commission. Wallas's whole view of the 'crisis of the Great Society', seeing new thought and invention as

---

[37] 'English Teachers' Organisations', *New Statesman*, v, loc cit.
[38] *Our Social Heritage*, 112.
[39] Ibid., 113.
[40] Ibid., 113.
[41] Ibid., 114.
[42] Ibid., 114.

the sole hope of civilization, inclined him against anything that might resist or obstruct intellectual or social innovation.

The foregoing criticisms were indeed to prove relevant not only to their moment but to British social and economic experience in the half-century since.[43] Yet Wallas knew that criticism without constructive suggestion was not enough. In the latter part of *Our Social Heritage*, and in the decade after its publication, he sought an alternative social philosophy both to that underlying the existing state of affairs and to pluralism. His efforts in this direction, unfortunately, were more tentative and less convincing than his specific psychological observations or his criticisms of pluralism.

Since the 1890s Wallas had felt that the primary psychological function of modern political institutions had to be 'clarification'—making a complex reality comprehensible to the ordinary citizen. By this criterion, he now condemned constitutional monarchy as a mentally disabling 'make-believe', deceiving instead of educating the public. His predecessor in the psychological analysis of politics, Walter Bagehot, fearful of the political participation of the ordinary unqualified citizen, had praised monarchy as a brilliant device for distracting attention and ensuring loyalty while government by the few went on undisturbed. Wallas, with precisely the opposite aim—wanting to make political participation real and meaningful—was as hostile to monarchy as Bagehot had been friendly. Wallas was, and had always been, a republican in the original classical sense of the word, wanting 'the public thing', the *polis*, to be clearly seen and personally felt. He knew what was standing in the way of this goal—pluralist diversions, monarchical confusions—but what political forms would further it, remained unsettled. On the positive side, Wallas confined himself to expressing a preference for the French method of 'personifying' the Republic over the British use of a 'symbolic person', and to making his by now standard call for invention.

Examining political ideals, he argued in *Our Social Heritage* and later, that principles like liberty and natural rights had been too much looked at in isolation. Nineteenth-century liberals and twentieth-century pluralists had both forgotten that these principles were not ends in themselves, but only means to a wider aim. In this new critique of liberalism, Wallas marshalled both 'Darwinism' and classicism. Since 'our instincts of today are not perfectly adapted either to our present environment, or, if it could be reconstructed, to our primitive environment', it followed that

---

[43] An investigation, for example, of the professions for 'restrictive practices' that Wallas urged in 1926 ('Occupational Recruiting', *Nation*, xxxix, 491–3) had to wait until the late 1960s.

No way of living... can now be so 'natural' to us as never to involve the obstruction of impulse. The principle of Liberty can never be absolute, and in the organisation of our society, we must ask, not merely how we are to prevent the occurrence of the feeling of unfreedom, but how we are to live the good life.[44]

In seeking 'the good life', Wallas felt that his contemporaries still had much to learn from the Greeks.[45] Against the shallowness of Mill and Sidney Webb, he set the psychological insight of Pericles, who saw liberty as part of a way of life, involving obligations, responsibilities, and aims—'positive' instead of 'negative'. The future of Liberalism, he warned, 'may depend on its power to apply to modern conditions the vision of Pericles'.[46] One Englishman in the nineteenth century, it seemed to Wallas, had grasped this vision. Re-reading Matthew Arnold during the war, he had been struck by the feeling that 'here was a great opportunity missed'.[47] The distinction between 'culture' and 'anarchy'—between 'the good life' and mere freedom from restraint—which pointed the way to a more fruitful Liberalism, had been ignored by Liberals and misused by Conservatives.

'It is more immediately important', Wallas told the Fabians in 1930, 'that men should desire the proper things than that they should have informed means of realising their desires.'[48] William Morris had, after all, been right to insist, many years back, on the primacy of 'ends' over 'means'. It seemed to him that the early Fabians, himself among them (though he in fact was least guilty) by taking ends too much for granted, had produced and propagated an inadequate social philosophy. Collectivism, as Arnold had remarked about liberty, was a fine horse, but one that had to be ridden somewhere. Planning and organization presupposed aims, yet in the existing intellectual and social flux of the Great Society Wallas saw no general agreement on these. Lloyd George, for example, had called in 1927 for a government scheme 'for providing useful, productive and necessary work for the unemployed'. Wallas asked in the uncompleted second part of *Social Judgment*,

What do these words, 'work', 'useful', 'productive', 'necessary' mean? Human activity can only be called useful, productive and necessary by reference to some

---

[44] *Our Social Heritage*, 165.

[45] The Greek philosophers provided a model to which Wallas perennially returned. At a dinner commemorating his seventieth birthday, the keynote of his speech 'was that in ancient Greece this was this influence of Plato and Aristotle; have I, G. W., too kept the faith?' (*Holmes-Laski Letters*, 1064 (16 June 1928)).

[46] *Our Social Heritage*, 10.

[47] Ibid., 179.

[48] Lecture on 'Ends and Means', *Fabian News*, Dec. 1930.

standard of choice and that standard can only be based on a conception of a 'good' or desirable life. We are therefore driven back to the old attempt of Plato and Aristotle to relate our plans for the organisation of human activity to our conception of the 'good life'.[49]

This age-old attempt would have to be taken up again in an atmosphere far less confident than that in which Wallas had grown up. 'During the years which have passed since I was born', he reflected in a discarded draft for the first chapter of *Social Judgment*,

the material and intellectual background of human life has changed more profoundly than in any equal period in the history of mankind. The bound volumes of Chambers Journal, and All the Year Round, and Good Words, and the Leisure Hour, which I would devour as a child, were nearly all well-pleased, both with the existing state of civilisation and with its prospects for the future. In 1928 cheerfulness has disappeared from thoughtful literature, and hardly anyone in Europe except a few fanatical Fascists or Communists, or in America except a few Rotarian boosters, pretends to feel any confidence in the future of himself or his children or grandchildren.[50]

Ironically, Wallas himself was a forerunner of the new pessimism. The attitude underlying his books had been much less optimistic than his 'progressive' admirers had at first perceived. His work had stemmed as much from anxiety as from hope, but Americans, especially, saw only the hope that harmonized with their own mood. Psychological 'realism' could lead to enthusiasm for the replanning of society; it could also cast grave doubt on the efficacy of such replanning. 'It may be', Wallas had admitted in *The Great Society*, 'that no satisfactory Will-Organisation of human beings with their present limitations, in a society on so vast a scale, is possible. . . . '[51]

One American had immediately seen the distance between Wallas's middle-aged, 'European' ambivalence and the youthful, 'American' optimism of Wallas's student and popularizer, Walter Lippmann. Harold Stearns, a friend of Lippmann's and a member of the Harvard seminar Wallas had conducted in 1910, perceptively contrasted the 'assurance' of *Drift and Mastery* with the 'despair' underlying *The Great Society*.[52] Lippmann himself was coming to see this; Wallas's ultimate influence upon him was very different from his first impression. Lippmann later recalled this influence:

[49] WP.
[50] WP. See Beatrice Webb's similar remark in her diary, 23 Oct. 1920 (PP).
[51] *The Great Society*, 309.
[52] 'Assurance and Despair', *Boston Evening Transcript*, 27 Jan. 1915. See also letter from Stearns to Wallas (WP).

... by the time of my senior year I was no longer really a socialist. The man who really diverted me more than anyone else was Graham Wallas himself. I thought he was a socialist, naturally, being one of the Fabians. But he began more and more, gradually, slowly, and patiently to explain to me his doubts as to how it would work. His doubts centered on the inability of man to administer a greater society. His book *The Great Society* was really an anti-socialist book.

That started the whole train of thought which I later developed into my book, *The Good Society*, which was consciously named to sort of correlate with *The Great Society*, and which has as its crucial idea the idea that there are limits to the power of man to conceive, plan and administer human affairs. Therefore, you must find other methods of regulating them than administration. That stems from Wallas.[53]

These doubts derived from the psychological approach, which shifted the emphasis in political reform from laws and institutions to attitudes and thoughts. 'It is puerile', Lippman had remarked in 1913, 'to say that institutions must be changed from top to bottom and then assume that their victims are prepared to make the change. No amount of charters, direct primaries, or short ballots will make a democracy out of an illiterate people.'[54] At that time he was sure that the necessary psychic changes could be brought about, but by the Harding era he had lost this faith. In his pessimistic post-war books, *Public Opinion* (1922) and *The Phantom Public* (1924), the conservative implications of *Human Nature in Politics* are fully drawn out.

Lippmann's change of outlook reflected a general change in the intellectual climate. The war and its chaotic aftermath had undermined confidence in parliamentary democracy. What had been a growing current of dissatisfaction now became a torrent of disillusion. Harold Laski reflected, writing to Justice Holmes,

Since 1848 our main political energies have gone the world over to the making of parliamentary democracies. Today, you have their abandonment in Italy, Spain, Russia, Hungary, Roumania, Bulgaria; practically they are nonexistent in France and Germany and, of course, Japan. China is anarchy tempered by civil war; India shows little aptitude for democratic institutions. Does all this mean that democracy is historically an episode, or that we want new forms?[55]

Laski inclined to the view that 'democracy is really dubious for large scale civilisations', particularly those that did not share Anglo-Saxon habits of mind. Yet though this conclusion could draw on *Human Nature in Politics* for support, Wallas himself refused to agree. As with pluralism,

---

[53] 'Reminiscences', op. cit., 40.
[54] *A Preface to Politics*, 305.
[55] *Holmes-Laski Letters*, 540-1 (16 Sept. 1923).

he staunchly resisted those who took the thread of his argument further than he deemed necessary—so much so that Laski appended the observation, 'I'm pretty sure the mind of G. Wallas would be horrified'.

The only alternatives Wallas saw to parliamentary democracy were the new movements of Fascism and Communism, and the remedies they offered for the ills of democracy were clearly worse than the disease. If 'the tactics of parliamentary majorities and parliamentary elections seem utterly inadequate to provide wide and progressive direction for the organised co-operation of great industrial societies',[56] the solution was not to dismiss these institutions. Most modern practical democrats, he argued in his unfinished manuscript for *Social Judgment*,

would agree with the Fascists and Communists that plans for the policy of a modern state must be worked out on behalf of the community by the conscious and co-ordinated intellectual efforts of a few supernormal individuals. But they feel that if the power of accepting or rejecting or modifying those plans is based, even under the highly organised economic conditions of the Great Society, on uncensored discussion and on the habit by which minorities, when they have had a fair hearing, give way to majorities; and if the majorities act with moderation in the use of their power; democracy offers the individual citizen the opportunity of a fuller and more satisfying life than he can obtain under any form of despotism. And if they look beyond the happiness of a single generation to the possibilities of ordered progress in the future the Great Society seems to require a constantly renewed energy of thought and sympathy with every section of the population, which no despotism has yet succeeded in maintaining.[57]

The first step, therefore, towards the creation of a 'good society' would have to be that reconstruction of democracy he had called for, unheeded, years before the war, so that it could compete effectively with its challengers. Here, he felt, was the crucial task confronting the post-war generation: to find a *via media* between the Scylla of 'drift' and the Charybdis of dictatorship, to secure 'mastery' without surrendering individual liberty and dignity.[58] Could democracy equip itself with new institutions and new values more relevant to its new environment; could it, as he liked to put it, become 'scientific', or would its fatal decline continue?

'Scientific democracy' was Wallas's goal—'a government', as he defined it, 'that is based upon the votes of the majority of the people but so based upon such institutions and such habits of thought that use can be made of

[56] Introduction to R. M. Dawson, *The Principle of Official Independence* (London, 1922).
[57] WP.
[58] Taking up Lippmann's phrase, Wallas described *Our Social Heritage* to Shaw as a plea for 'mastery' and against 'drift'. (Letter, probably 1921, BM). He later upbraided Shaw for praising Mussolini (Letter, 13 Feb. 1927, BM).

the accumulation of... modern knowledge'.[59] Before the war, he had had few doubts about which political party was the best vehicle for constructive, 'scientific' government, but with the decline of Liberalism and the rise of Labour the political situation had become much more confusing. 'I believe', he confessed to Gilbert Murray in 1922, 'that it is everybody's duty to take sides publicly in politics, and yet for the moment I can't do it. I am, for instance, swinging helplessly between Rivers (Lab.) and Pollard (Lib.) in the London University election.'[60] Throughout the 1920s Wallas wavered between the Liberal and Labour parties, unable to attach himself firmly to either.

Labour, he felt, was handicapped in any constructive efforts by its mental attitudes, the same attitudes that had exasperated him years before in the Socialist movement and in London government. It was true,

The Labour Party is attracting to itself a steadily increasing proportion of the idealist thought and emotion of our time. The party publishes in their 'Local Government News' the best general survey of contemporary English municipal development; and it is on the increased efficiency of local administration that the party rests most of its hopes for social progress and social equality. But it too often happens that the Labour members who secure election on our municipal bodies show less rather than more appreciation than do the members of the older parties of the essential conditions of administrative efficiency.[61]

The Labour politician—and Labour's intellectuals, too—had to learn, he insisted, to rely on expertise instead of doctrine, on free thought instead of strict party discipline, on reason and discussion instead of emotion. He rebuked his young friend Kingsley Martin (soon to become editor of the *New Statesman*) for succumbing to emotionalism himself in criticizing the emotionalism of the British public during the General Strike.[62] Even those among Labour who thought clearly, like the Webbs, were not thinking constructively enough for Wallas. Social criticism, he noted in reviewing their *Decay of Capitalist Civilisation* (1922), when separated, even in a single book, from the intellectual process of social construction, encouraged an unfortunate mental attitude among reformers. Those employing a purely critical method would, as Marx had, he argued,

almost inevitably subconsciously tend to present the existing 'system' as a consistent body of facts, assumed to be wholly evil and to contrast it with a new

---

[59] Talk on 'Scientific Democracy', delivered as part of a conference on 'Methods of Social Direction', (Williamstown, Massachusetts, 1928) (WP).
[60] Letter, 14 Apr. 1922 (WP).
[61] Preface to E. D. Simon, *A City Council from Within* (London, 1926).
[62] '"Common Sense" and the General Strike', *Nation*, xl (22 Jan. 1927), 566–7.

'system', assumed to be completely thought-out in theory, capable of being adopted by a single political decision, and wholly good.[63]

The Labour movement, in short, retained far too many of the characteristics of his *bête noire* of the 1890s, the old Independent Labour party, to win his permanent support. The policy of the current Labour party seemed to Wallas to be determined by two factors, both detrimental to constructive thought—the dogmatic systems of the intellectuals and the vested interests of the trade unions. The events of 1924–6, which discredited the dogmas, did not stimulate creative thinking. He reflected in 1925,

The Labour Party gave up under 'guild socialist' criticism their old 'nationalisation' policy, and they are now having a reaction against guild socialism, so that MacDonald Snowden etc., are now, though they won't confess it, not really convinced of any programme beyond that of an opportunist liberal democracy.[64]

The General Strike further lessened the attractiveness of Labour for Wallas by reinforcing the trade union influence. The Labour party, he felt in the aftermath,

has got itself so tied up with the special interests and prejudices and funds of the big Trade Unions that any sincerity of thought and public speech is becoming almost impossible for its leaders—And in consequence the leaders are becoming 'cynical' and intellectually uncomfortable.[65]

However unappealing Labour was to Wallas, the Liberal party, in the state to which it had been reduced, was not much more attractive. By and large it had abandoned the zeal for reform (at least until Asquith's retirement), and appeared far more afraid of Socialism than of Conservatism. A policy of anti-collectivism, however, was to Wallas only sterile negativism; in this sense, he was still a Socialist. 'Individualism', he had always held, was utterly unrealistic in the Great Society, which demanded government intervention in a multitude of fields. Further, 'individualism' meant in practice the defence of social and economic inequality. The party would never recover its position, he warned the *Westminster Gazette* group of right-wing Liberals, until it convinced the working-class majority that it was working for, and not against, their interests.[66]

Liberalism's decline, he argued, was due to more than the fortuitous rise of Labour. Wallas traced it to the intellectual stagnation that turned him as a young man to Fabianism, and which he had warned against as far back as

[63] 'The Webbs Sum Up', *New Republic*, xxxiv (11 Apr. 1923), pt. ii, 18.
[64] Letter to Lippmann, 25 May 1925 (Lippmann).
[65] Letter to Lippmann, 6 Dec. 1926 (Lippmann).
[66] Letter to *Westminster Gazette*, Jan. 1925 (WP).

1901. 'The Liberals of the eighteen-eighties', he recalled, 'were living on the intellectual capital created by the life-long toil of Locke and Adam Smith and Bentham. Their leaders ... had come to assume that no more creative intellectual work was needed.'[67] The Fabians had taken up the task that the Liberals had shirked, and now the true heirs of Liberalism were as much in the Labour as in the Liberal party. He urged Liberals to take a lesson from the Webbs or from their own heroes, Locke, Bentham, and John Stuart Mill.[68] 'Until the Liberal Party is based again on "the intolerable disease" of life-long thought', he warned, 'it must continue to decay.'[69]

'Politics here are in a dreadful mess', he told Walter Lippmann;[70] neither Liberals nor Labour had the necessary combination of qualities for progressive, 'scientific' government. What Wallas was really looking for was a party embodying the type of Fabianism he had embraced in youth and never abandoned—a 'freethinking' collectivism, gradualist and libertarian, economically egalitarian but intellectually elitist.[71] He found the closest approach to this in the Radical Liberal group around the *Nation*, unfortunately a minority in their party.[72] 'I feel myself most comfortable', he wrote to Lippmann, with men like H. D. Henderson, W. T. Layton, and J. M. Keynes. 'They are not afraid to move very far in the direction of social equality, and at the same time have what seems to me most necessary now—intellectual industry and sincerity.'[73] As their influences rose within the party after Lloyd George's accession to the leadership, Wallas's hopes rose also. 'I voted Liberal at an L.C.C. election this morning, and not Labour', he wrote Lippmann in 1928.[74] He explained,

---

[67] 'The Education of Beatrice Webb', *Nation*, xxxviii (review of *My Apprenticeship*) (6 Mar. 1926), 779.

[68] Ibid.

[69] Ibid., 780. Wallas here fell into the error that afflicted many Liberal intellectuals in the 1920s, that of 'intellectualism'. Ideas, programmes, 'continuous thought' would not revive the Liberal party by themselves, this was demonstrated by the failure of the 1929 Liberal campaign, in which they 'out-thought' both other parties put together, to no avail. See Trevor Wilson, *The Downfall of the Liberal Party 1914–1935* (London, 1966).

[70] Letter, 6 Dec. 1926 (Lippmann).

[71] 'A diminution', he wrote in his uncompleted second part of *Social Judgment*, 'of the artificial economic inequality which has resulted from the form taken by modern industrial organisation may help towards a clearer recognition of the existence and importance of innate inequality in brain and character.' (WP)

[72] Letter to Gilbert Murray, 14 Apr. 1922 (WP), and to Walter Lippmann, 6 Dec. 1926 (Lippmann).

[73] 6 Dec. 1926 (Lippmann). He was particularly impressed with Keynes, but, he confided to Lippmann, 'I wish he had not a touch of rather hard "Launigkeit" (if that is a real German word) in him'. Ibid. Keynes's droll, somewhat cynical humour grated, apparently, on Wallas's sense of moral seriousness.

[74] 8 Mar. 1928 (Lippmann).

As things are now the Liberals seem to have more intellectual stuff in them (largely owing to Keynes, Layton, H. D. Henderson etc. . . .) than the Labour people. And it seems more possible for the Liberals than for the Labour Party to provide the machinery for a progressive block in the House of Commons.

The collapse of Liberalism in 1929–31, however, left him back where he had started after the war. A decade of challenge, capped by economic crisis, had failed, in America and Europe as well as Britain, to elicit a creative response from the party system. 'Scientific democracy' seemed no closer, while the problems of the Great Society multiplied. Under this disappointment, shared by many in those dark years, even Wallas's staunch commitment to parliamentary democracy began to falter. Beatrice Webb, who had little hope left for parliamentarianism after the destruction of the second Labour government, and who was turning to Communism for a new faith, noted in February 1932 that 'he and we are much nearer in opinion than we have been for many a long year'.[75] She went on to observe, with some exaggeration, that Wallas

has dropped his liberalism as a possible creed: he thinks that American capitalism will fail to give a decent and continuous livelihood to its people; and that Soviet Russia will succeed in doing it. And though he fears the suppression of free thought in politics under Communism, the Soviet system has his sympathy in its anti-God crusade, and in its subordination of the Trade Unions to the will of the consumer-citizen.[76]

Politics, however, had never been for Wallas the only means of progress; what political parties seemed incapable of doing might yet be realized in the long run by 'education', in the broadest sense of the word. For many years he had taught the modern history and structure of British governmental institutions at the London School of Economics. Here was an area, he had come to feel, that cried out for rethinking. These institutions, the study of history had impressed upon him, 'are so heedlessly fashioned, and when once fashioned pass so easily out of the knowledge of the overwhelming majority of those who are to be affected by them'.[77] The great work that Bentham had begun had to be taken up again:

Our only hope is that political and administrative arrangements may some day be made as simple and intelligible as possible, and that understanding and criticism

---

[75] *Beatrice Webb's Diaries 1924–32*, ed. Margaret Cole (London, 1956), 299 (26 Feb. 1932).
[76] Ibid., 299–300.
[77] Review of the Webbs' *English Local Government: Statutory Authorities*, in *Economic Journal*, xxxiii (Mar. 1923), 86–90.

of those arrangements, and of the processes needed to adapt them to new conditions, may become part of the accumulated heritage of every civilised community, arranged in accessible libraries, explained in university courses, and valued, as the achievements of natural science are now valued, by the whole community.[78]

Upon Wallas's voluntary retirement in 1923, the editors of *Economica*, a journal published by the School, hoped for 'the completion of the great intellectual task to which he is devoted'.[79] The students and the staff of the London School of Economics, they observed,

> look forward to that discussion of Bentham's influence, about which Graham Wallas' knowledge is unique; they clamour for that study of the Civil Service for which no man is better equipped; above all, perhaps, they demand that book on local government which, more than any other, will enshrine for them memories of lectures which have moulded the outlook and determined the inventiveness of many officials, elective and appointed.

'Now give us the book on administration', Laski replied to the gift of a copy of *Our Social Heritage*, and so Wallas intended.[80] He gave a series of lectures on 'administration' at Cambridge in the autumn of 1920, but turned down as premature an offer to have them published by the University press. Wanting his book on 'the reconstruction of English institutions' to be definitive, he planned to spend more time on it.[81]

In the meantime, he reiterated his pre-war criticisms of the Civil Service, and repeated his earlier proposal (this time before a Royal Commission) for the creation of a municipal Civil Service to modernize local government.[82] He hailed the establishment of the Institute of Public Administration as a way of providing the same help to the community of officials 'in the way of ideas and authoritative experience which is provided by the learned Societies in other sciences'.[83] Yet he did not go on to write the book he had planned; instead, he found himself returning to psychology.

Purely institutional questions always seemed to give him a feeling of confinement. Wallas never was content with a problem until he had separated out its psychological elements. As he had remarked to Zimmern,

[78] Review of the Webbs' *English Local Government: Statutory Authorities*, in *Economic Journal*, xxxiii (Mar. 1923), 86–90.
[79] *Economica*, ix. 169–70.
[80] Letter to Wallas, 11 Apr. 1921 (WP).
[81] See correspondence between Wallas and Cambridge, 20 and 22 Mar. 1920, and letter from Graham Balfour, 22 June 1921 (WP).
[82] See 'The British Civil Service' (1928), *Men & Ideas*, 114–30, 'Government', *Public Administration*, vi (1928), 3–15, 'A Municipal Civil Service', *Nation*, v (13 Feb. 1909), 745–6, and *Minutes of Evidence*, xiii, 2414 of Royal Commission on Local Government (1929).
[83] *Men & Ideas*, 128.

he was interested in town councillors, not in town councils, and the consideration of the latter unfailingly turned into consideration of the former.[84] He wrote to Lippmann after completing *Our Social Heritage*,

> I am wondering what is the next book that I ought to start on. I could write a good book (based on my School of Economics lectures) on the part played by deliberate planning in the reconstruction of British Institutions since 1832. I should like that and ought to do it.... But I have a subconscious feeling that the best thing would be for me to put in a few months reading on the newer psychology—I have no new ideas, only an uncomfortable feeling that new ideas might come if I worked hard enough.[85]

After these months of reflection, the problem of administrative organization and invention gave way to that of improving the thought processes of administrators and potential inventors. More and better thought, he had always been convinced, was the key to social progress, and thought, he now concluded, like anything else, could be improved by the application of scientific knowledge. Drawing on recent professional psychological work, but building much more upon his experience as a teacher and upon personal accounts of their thought processes by students, friends, poets, and other 'amateurs', Wallas set out to illuminate 'the art of thought'. Here, as his former student, Sir Josiah Stamp, observed, 'Wallas most clearly struck his own perfect note—the development from *within*'.[86]

The very possibility of an 'art of thought', however, was put in doubt by the determinism of many psychologists, of both the 'instinctivist' and the newer 'behaviourist' school, who generally allowed reason no dynamic of its own. Wallas found himself playing the role of Victorian idealist in taking issue with psychological anti-intellectualism. He was not, however, at all abandoning his earlier naturalism. Against the 'mechanist' conception of the human organism Wallas took up, not a naïve intellectualism, but the 'hormic' conception advanced by some psychologists. This psychology saw the human organism 'as an imperfectly integrated combination of living elements, each of which retains some initiative of its own, while co-operating with the rest in securing the good of the whole organism'. The aim of the art of thought, Wallas felt, 'is an improved co-ordination of these elements in the process of thought'.[87]

---

[84] 'I can never remember', Zimmern remarked in 1917, 'what he is supposed to be Professor of, but if it is not Social Psychology it ought to be.' *Nationality and Government*, 88.
[85] 13 Mar. 1921 (Lippmann). [86] *Economica*, xxxviii, 399.
[87] *The Art of Thought* (London, 1926), 8.

Thought was a mixture, he argued, of conscious and unconscious, intellectual and emotional elements, and while their combination and interaction were not determined on a level beyond the reach of conscious efforts, these efforts had to be subtle and sophisticated. Thought could not be improved by simply trying—Wallas himself had attacked that sort of simple-mindedness in *Human Nature in Politics*—but it could be by conscious efforts that altered the conditions surrounding and affecting the thought process. He told an audience of teachers,

> While it is true that you cannot, by direct effort, secure great new thoughts, any more than you can write great new poetry, there are certain indirect efforts by which you can make it more likely that the great new thought will come into the world.[88]

He found four stages in the development of an idea—'preparation', 'incubation', 'illumination', and 'verification'—each open to influence:

> At the Preparation stage we can consciously accumulate knowledge, divide up by logical rules the field of inquiry, and adopt a definite 'problem attitude'. In Verification we can consciously follow out rules like those used in Preparation. At the Incubation stage we can arrange, either to think on other subjects than the proposed problem, or to rest from any form of conscious thought. . . . If we are consciously to control the Illumination stage we must include in it the 'fringe-conscious' psychological events which precede and accompany the 'flash' of Illumination, and which may be called Intimation. We can to some degree control Illumination by making ourselves conscious (as many poets are conscious) of Intimation; and by both encouraging the psychological processes which Intimation shows to be occurring, and protecting them from interruption.[89]

Part of Wallas's success as a teacher, attested to by many of his students, lay in his attention to the means and methods of thinking. He impressed upon his preparatory and public school pupils that it was their 'duty to acquire correct intellectual habits', and not merely to memorize Greek and Latin grammar, and later, he made a point of using his psychological knowledge 'as a means of helping my university students to capture and record thoughts which would otherwise never have come into full consciousness'.[90] However, as a teacher by profession, and a 'preacher' by background and inclination, Wallas was too much dedicated to the psychological approach and to the idea of self-improvement to see the problem in perspective and apportion his energies accordingly.

---

[88] 'Mental Training and the World Crisis' (1924), *Men & Ideas*, 191.
[89] *Art of Thought*, 10.
[90] See *Art of Thought*, 252, and *Our Social Heritage*, 48 n.

The Art of Thought (1926) contained many interesting suggestions, culled from years of practical experience. Given to students and acquaintances in the course of discussion, they had been valuable; formalized and elaborated into a book, their value was diminished rather than augmented. As an amateur in psychology, Wallas was on uncertain ground—a difficulty he recognized. 'I shall be glad', he confided to Elie Halévy, 'when the Thought book is finished. I am not a really trained psychologist and am continually finding new doubts and new points of view.'[91]

After *The Art of Thought*, Wallas returned to social and political problems, but still very much from a psychological point of view. General questions of philosophy increasingly absorbed his attention. 'I have felt myself impelled', he reflected at the end of 1927, 'by what I hope is not the garrulousness of old age, to spend a larger proportion of [the time given to 'young students of politics who each year ask me for advice'] in discussing certain more general aspects of the intellectual work required for the kind of social and political readjustment which is required at this crisis.'[92]

From thought he moved to 'judgment', which included and transcended thought alone. Judgement was practised, effectively or ineffectively, by everyone who made decisions, but it was most critical in those who were responsible for directing society. Even more than 'inventors' and experts, the Great Society demanded statesmen, men who could harness thought and knowledge to social purposes and human ends. Statesmanship, however, was by the very nature of the forces at work in the Great Society rare and becoming still rarer. The explosive and uncoordinated growth of specialized science had created the present social crisis, 'but', he observed, 'specialized sciences themselves are to a constantly increasing degree refusing to accept responsibility for the social results of their work or to give advice on social policy'. 'The gap between knowledge and judgment is', therefore, 'steadily widening.'[93]

In his last and unfinished book *Social Judgment*, he consequently sought to analyse this most socially vital of all psychological processes and to ask 'how far it can be improved by conscious effort, and whether it is possible by better social and political organisation to increase and direct its influence on corporate action'.[94]

What Wallas had attempted to do for thought, he now sought to do on a wider, really too wide, scale. Before the war he had aimed at a co-operation

---

[91] Letter, 7 Apr. 1925 (WP).
[92] Early, discarded version of chapter 1 of *Social Judgment* (WP).
[93] *Social Judgment* (London, 1935), 15-16.   [94] Ibid., 16.

between 'reason' and 'impulse'. Similarly, the process of judgement, he now argued, required 'a successful co-operation, which is neither inevitable nor impossible, between [the same] two imperfectly coordinated psychological factors'.[95] The problem, he observed to H. G. Wells (on friendly terms again after years of estrangement), was not banished by modern 'value-free' science; indeed, one had still to go back to the Greeks. 'Plato', he noted, 'tried to solve it by pleading for a "harmony" of thought and impulse. I am trying to work out on this basis a sort of theory of conscious social purpose including economics and politics.'[96] However, Wallas did not get beyond Plato in this effort, for, with all his exhortation, he never showed—perhaps it was not possible to show—how this harmony was to be brought about.

When he got away from strictly psychological analysis, Wallas had more to say. His search for 'judgment' and 'wisdom' was part of the larger search, begun in the 1890s and intensified after the war, for 'scientific democracy'—government that, while preserving liberty and democracy, would be able to master the ever-increasing problems of the Great Society. Such government demanded the highest possible degree of ability in its leaders. He wrote in his notes for *Social Judgment*,

For the effective direction of long-range [social] co-operation we can no longer trust either to the unintended results of short-range individual motives, however curiously dovetailed into each other, or to the unintended interaction of specialist sciences . . . effective co-operation requires now, and will increasingly require in the future . . . the production and training of persons of unusual imaginative range, and of institutions in which their powers will be so used as to influence policy.[97]

The intellectual elitism that had always been part of his thinking came to the fore in the post-war years, for the plight of the Great Society and of democracy seemed increasingly to require decisive measures. 'As the Great Society grows bigger and more complicated', he wrote to Wells, 'the difference between the few boys and girls and men who can understand Einstein and can have convictions on a managed currency, and the many who cannot becomes every decade more important.'[98]

However, 'meritocracy' was not enough, if government was to be democratic as well as 'scientific'. A new psychological relation between leaders and public had to be created. 'I am feeling', he explained to Walter Lippmann, 'after the possible development of a degree of moral and

[95] *Social Judgment* (London, 1935) 21.
[96] Letter, 9 Dec. 1931 (Wells).   [97] WP.
[98] 8 Oct. 1926 (Wells).

intellectual confidence and responsibility which has disappeared from the modern world.'[99] Whatever form of government, he wrote in an uncompleted chapter for *Social Judgment*, was adopted in the Great Society,

it must, if it is to be successful, provide that all plans for compulsory corporate action shall be invented by the organised thought of persons drawn from the limited supply of supernormal ability and sympathy. . . . [But] it must further provide that between those supernormal political persons and the rest of the community there shall be as far as possible a mutual relation of responsibility and trust, that the inventors of plans shall feel themselves responsible to the rest and that the rest shall feel that the inventors of plans have the same ultimate purposes as their own.[100]

The Greek *polis*, always Wallas's ideal, at its best had possessed this sort of relation, based on a generally accepted intellectual authority and on a shared 'civic religion'. Wallas looked towards the creation of similar conditions in the modern world. In the authority of the scientific expert he saw the model for the much-needed intellectual authority in politics. The development of the social sciences, if coupled with a realization of their social responsibility, could ultimately provide this political authority.[101]

Even more important to Wallas than the development of scientific authority in politics was the need for a new 'civic religion' similar in its role to that of the Greeks, but extending over the whole of the Great Society. This was what he had meant in remarking to Lippmann during the war that 'a good deal depends on the development of religion among the civilised peoples'.[102] He had always sought this 'new religion'. Originally he had thought that Socialism would provide it; when that proved a dream, he began to search elsewhere, seeing hopeful signs in Japan and in France. Yet all he had been able to find were hints, and the search had gone on. The war and the crises that followed upon it had turned the problem from a distant to an immediate one. Yet he still seemed unable to define with any precision the content of this new 'world-outlook'.

It was *not*, he was sure, being provided by Christianity. The Christian churches, as he had observed them, had clearly failed in guiding conduct in the modern world.[103] The post-war strengthening of High Church 'sacramentalism' in England, and the general growth of Catholic influence, developments that would no doubt have saddened his Evangelical father,

---

[99] Letter, 16 Nov. 1920 (Lippmann).   [100] WP.
[101] See 'Authority in Politics', *Nation*, xl (6 Nov. 1926), 171–2.
[102] Letter, 30 Dec. 1916 (Lippmann).
[103] See *Our Social Heritage*, ch. 12.

pushed Wallas further into anti-clericalism. As President of the Rationalist Press Association from 1925 to 1929, he spent a good deal of his time in these years warring on Christianity, particularly its High Church and Roman Catholic forms.[104] This increasing anti-clericalism was distorting his judgement: 'the Roman Catholic Church in Europe and still more, in America', he remarked to H. G. Wells in 1926, 'seems to me to be the most amazing and in some ways the most dangerous fact of our time.'[105]

Sacramentalism offended him by its explicit irrationalism, its lack of connection with ethics, and its encouragement of narrow professionalism among the clergy. By stressing sacramentalism, the English Church had, he charged, renounced its claims to the intellectual and moral leadership of society. Instead, it was degenerating into mysticism, exploiting rather than releasing men from the most elemental emotions. Confident that this degeneration was a symptom of decline, Wallas looked elsewhere for signs of the ethical and emotional organization of the future. He recalled,

On November 11, 1918, as I came back from telling the news of the armistice to a family of Belgian exiles who had wept with joy, I passed the buildings of a big endowed school. The boys were assembled in the hall, and were apparently singing all the doggerel verses of 'God Save the King'. I listened, trying to imagine the hymns that were being sung before other national flags in all the schools of the Allies; and a conviction swept through me that the special task of our generation might be so to work and think as to be able to hand on to the boys and girls who fifty years hence, at some other turning point of world history, may gather in the schools, the heritage of a world-outlook deeper and wider and more helpful than that of modern Christendom.[106]

This world-outlook would, he felt, be based in part upon science, as he had first envisaged in *Human Nature in Politics*. Science provided a universal intellectual framework and a common discipline, knowing no national or cultural boundary. His hopes for science as a 'philosophic' force led Wallas to take great interest in the Zionist experiment in Palestine. His friend, Herbert Samuel, now High Commissioner for the new British mandate, seems to have aroused his interest in it at the end of the war.[107] In 1924 he visited Palestine as Honorary Vice-President of the Friends of

---

[104] See his speeches to the Association, in *Literary Guide and Rationalist Review*, nos. 301, 361, 374, 385, 397. He was not, though, the fanatic that many anticlericals were. He left the Secular Education League in 1931 when that group pushed secularism to a point which would have meant the forbidding of state-aided secondary education to all but convinced agnostics (Letter to Gilbert Murray, 13 Feb. 1931 (WP)).
[105] Letter, 8 Oct. 1926 (Wells).   [106] *Our Social Heritage*, 290–1.
[107] See letter from Zimmern, 12 Oct. 1919 (WP).

the Hebrew University of Jerusalem,[108] and was impressed. The Jewish 'Pioneers', he wrote upon his return,

even when they think they are recreating the life of their Palestinian ancestors, represent an absolutely new impact of the Western upon the Eastern world-outlook at the most critical point of the frontier between Europe and Asia. One cannot help comparing it with the impact which took place at the same point two thousand years ago, when the conquests of Alexander and Pompey opened Syria and Palestine to the world-outlook of Hellenism.[109]

The mental force he saw them bringing to the East was modern science, 'less beautiful, but more immediately powerful for good or evil than the philosophy of Philo or Plotinus, or the poetry of Maleager'. The Pioneers were driven not only by religious and national patriotism, but even more, he felt (or hoped)

by the fact that they have been trained in Realschulen and technical colleges, to look on each half-acre of their land as a laboratory, and each crop as an experiment whose results are to be accepted and applied with scientific patience and watchfulness.... And if the colonists succeed in growing three tons of produce where their Arab neighbours grow only one, the influence of that fact will spread more irresistably than a new form of government or art.

Carrying forth the comparison with Hellenism, Wallas observed that the significance for mankind of its entry into Palestine lay not in its direct influence, but in the fact that 'a new type of thought and feeling' which was thus created—Christianity—returned westward to conquer the civilized world. He concluded,

Today the civilised world is again waiting, humbly enough, for some other new type of thought and feeling, some other new channel along which the stream of human hope and pity and reverence may flow... it may not be fanciful to imagine that a word of power may once more come westward from Palestine.

'Maida Vale and Long Island seem only half alive', he reflected, after the 'urgent intensity' he found in Palestine.[110] However, a 'religion of science', as the Positivists of Wallas's youth had discovered, was not enough by itself. Science was a basis upon which a humanistic ethic could build, but a basis only. Perhaps, Wallas speculated, something might arise in the

---

[108] He stayed with Herbert Samuel, who was Honorary President.
[109] 'Palestinian Pioneers', *Nation*, xxxvi (15 Nov. 1924), 257. Wallas, Laski wrote to Holmes, 'has gone cracked on Zionism', which Laski, himself of Jewish background, 'abominate[d]'. (*Holmes-Laski Letters*, 703; 27 Jan. 1925).
[110] Ibid.

Great Society as the 'philosophies' of Zeno and Epicurus did in the Roman Empire:

A book of sayings by some countryman of Confucius or Laotze, who has known Western civilisation and has accepted it without dread and without illusion as an instrument of the good life, may then seem true, not only in Pekin and the cities of the Yangtze valley, but to many thoughtful men and women in New York and London and Moscow and Milan. Artisans and teachers and societies of college students may begin to use some term like 'The Path' for an ethical plan based on a common world-outlook and making a common emotional appeal.[111]

Perhaps, Wallas let himself hope, the efforts of men like himself were bringing that day closer. In the half-conscious accepted morality of his time, there might be taking root the beginnings of a more permanent and more effective 'Wisdom' than that of past philosophies and religions. He thought,

We can already form a rough conception of that form of responsible thought which, in the complexities of modern civilisation, we are now coming to accept as most likely to lead to wise decisions. That conception contains both an intellectual and an emotional element; for few people with experience in affairs would now contend that excellence in a statesman can be attained either by the purely intellectual process of 'enlightened self-interest', or by the purely emotional process of instinctive generosity or instinctive loyalty.[112]

'We are beginning to hope', he wrote in concluding the manuscript that was to be the second half of *Social Judgment*, 'that . . . we may be more successful than our race has hitherto been in so "sublimating" and co-ordinating [our natural impulses] as to make possible a human life in our new environment both richer and better ordered than modern civilisation has yet attained to.' In such a life,

the ideal 'wise man' may be one whose 'character', formed, as Aristotle taught, by successive acts of deliberate choice, guided by his reason and the reason of others and nourished by the 'social' elements in his nature, merges his desire for the 'good' of his fellows and for his own good into a single purpose. And his character and purpose may correspond to the deepest sense of the significance of the universe which men with their imperfect minds and confused passions can reach in the few years of their lives.

[111] *Our Social Heritage*, 290.
[112] Unfinished conclusion for *Social Judgment* (WP).

Wallas in later years

CHAPTER IX

WALLAS IN HIS TIME—AND IN OURS

I

IN THE ferment of political and social thinking during and following the war, Wallas's influence clearly stood out. 'His three books', observed one English writer, 'have made his name indispensable in the literature of politics.'[1] Laski, returned from America, spoke for many when he pointed out the importance of psychology for political science. It was becoming generally recognized that, as Laski put it, 'the dominant need of political philosophy has been the analysis of the complexity of motives by which the actions of men are determined'.[2]

Wallas also succeeded in directing attention to the psychological problems posed by the extension of social scale. 'In this field', a contemporary noted, 'his books, especially his *Great Society*, came to some with the force of a revelation. Like all acute books, they made coherent what many vaguely felt to be true.'[3]

Yet, despite these accomplishments, Wallas began to come under mounting criticism and soon ceased to exert a vital intellectual influence on his time. After having opened up new avenues of thought, he had run out of creative energy and was living off past intellectual capital.

H. G. Wells had already observed a lack of constructive suggestions in *The Great Society*. The concluding three chapters of 'tentative suggestions' were, he had complained, 'as interrogative and as little suggestive as they can well be. It is as if his mind had weakened off from the vigour of its own enterprise.'[4] *Our Social Heritage* was intended to fill this gap, but in this

---

[1] Lewis Rockow, *Contemporary Political Thought in England* (London, 1926), 53.
[2] 'Recent Contributions to Political Science', *Economica*, i (Jan. 1921), 91. For Laski's concern with the same problems Wallas was interested in, see Laski's letter to Wallas, 12 May 1919, and to Holmes, 11 May 1919 (*Holmes-Laski Letters*, 200).
[3] Rockow, op. cit., 54.
[4] 'The Great Community', *Nation*, xv (4 July 1914), 531. Others had perceived this weakness: after reading *The Great Society* at Laski's urging, Holmes pointed this out to Wallas's young admirer. 'I think—unwillingly', Laski replied, 'I have to admit your criticism of Wallas. I felt him far bigger negatively than positively.' (*Holmes-Laski Letters*, 15 (5 Sept. 1916)).

it too failed. 'The one complaint' Wallas's New School audience had, Laski wrote, 'was that you had no panacea'.⁵ It was more than this, however, as Laski himself recognized. He had awaited Wallas's contribution to reconstruction with great interest. 'Some synthesis', it was clear to him, 'is badly needed.'⁶ 'It seems', he wrote to Wallas, 'as though the machines are too big for us unless we can get the insight Tocqueville demanded into the possibilities of new devices.'⁷

For this insight he looked to Wallas in vain. Wallas revealed again, he noted in reviewing *Our Social Heritage*, 'an incomparable gift for detecting flaws in social institutions; more, a gift for tracing those flaws back to causes which, at any rate, partially explain defects'. But, Laski concluded, 'he is not himself a builder.... He applies, one is tempted to say, a quantitative test ... to other people's constructions while he leaves his own philosophy so fluid as to evade a scale of measurement.'⁸

To Justice Holmes, Laski was blunter. 'Really', he confessed, 'outside single and unrelated hints, it's to me a disappointing book, less ample and decisive than the labour he has put into it.'⁹ He reflected a few weeks later,

When I write my book on the state, I do at least want the reader to end up with a considered portrait of the social organisation I postulate. Wallas attacks everyone else and then tells you that he believes in liberty, equality and the free play of reason, which is like telling a man to wash himself in a parched desert.¹⁰

G. D. H. Cole, whose ideas were criticized at length in *Our Social Heritage*, felt much the same as Laski, but did not bother to temper his impatience:

Mr. Wallas, of course [Cole wrote in the *Daily Herald*] stands above all for the application of psychological method to social and political problems; but he is a trifle apt to mistake the mere reiterated assertion that these problems ought to be tackled psychologically, or as he frequently tells us, 'quantitatively', for an actual demonstration in these ways of tackling them. Mr. Wallas is particularly 'down' on what he calls 'professionalism'.... But he nowhere at all clearly defines his own alternative to the dangers admittedly inherent in exclusively Guild organisation.... Mr. Wallas seems to be ageing; and as he ages, he allows his

---

⁵ 21 Mar. 1920 (WP).
⁶ Letter to Wallas, 27 June 1918 (WP).
⁷ 12 May 1919 (WP).
⁸ 'Mr. Wallas as Social Analyst', *Nation*, xxix (9 Apr. 1921), 61.
⁹ *Holmes-Laski Letters*, 321 (13 Mar. 1921).
¹⁰ Ibid., 329 (13 Apr. 1921). Laski's opinion of Wallas fell sharply during his first year back in England. 'My main disappointment', he wrote to Holmes, 'is Graham Wallas.... He is very lovable and charming, but he seems to me totally without the creative instinct.' (*Holmes-Laski Letters*, 376 (18 Oct. 1921)).

prejudices to run away with him and becomes more than ever an observant critic of human follies rather than a constructive social thinker.[11]

Cole's judgement, though harsh, was basically true. Constructive intentions and exhortations were no substitute for actual construction. When it came down to specific suggestions, Wallas proved, as an American friend noted years later, 'rather feeble and inconclusive'.[12] Yet, Wallas himself was unaware of this failing. 'He seriously thinks', Laski complained, 'that political salvation is in that volume [*Social Heritage*] and is quite incapable of considering alternatives.'[13] In *The Art of Thought*, Wallas's weakness on construction seemed even more pronounced. 'Graham's psychological treatise', Beatrice Webb reflected after going through the manuscript, 'is pleasant to read and full of suggestiveness, but it leaves no positive impression. . . .'[14] To Laski it was 'elegant trifling'.[15]

Wallas was found wanting in the post-war period in another less personal way. His work was criticized as either too psychological—ignoring social structure and relations—or as based upon faulty psychology. These two were really one criticism, for his psychological critics, beginning with Wesley Mitchell in 1914, were arguing for a 'more social' social psychology. Wallas's carefully developed middle-of-the-road position, balancing the claims of heredity and environment, now was classed, even after his adoption of a more 'social' position in 1919, as 'individualistic' and 'biologistic'. This was particularly true in America, where the new social outlook was being adopted with enthusiasm. Edward S. Corwin observed to the American Political Science Association in 1929,

Placing the reliance he did on 'instincts', . . . Wallas was led into a two-fold error. In the first place, while dismissing with deserved opprobrium the intellectualist eighteenth century version of the political animal, he under-estimated the plasticity of the human mental constitution; and he consequently, in the

---

[11] 'A Disappointment', *Daily Herald*, 25 May 1921.
[12] H. E. Barnes, in H. E. Barnes (ed.), *An Introduction to the History of Sociology* (Chicago, 1948), 709–10. Many American thinkers, however, were open to the same criticism they made of Wallas. Morton White has pointed out that Dewey, James Harvey Robinson, and others talked continually of being 'constructive', but rarely were. See *Social Thought in America*, 194–6.
[13] *Holmes-Laski Letters*, 376 (18 Oct. 1921).
[14] *Beatrice Webb's Diaries, 1924–32*, 73–4 (27 Sept. 1925). She had found much the same thing wrong with *Our Social Heritage*. Writing to Wallas (probably after having received a gift copy), she praised it warmly—especially its criticism of Guild Socialism—but added that 'from the purely practical standpoint of affecting action, I should like an added section on "Some conclusions for unphilosophic or hasty readers"'. (undated letter, WP).
[15] *Holmes-Laski Letters*, 840 (23 May 1926).

second place, permitted himself to be diverted from the most interesting single problem suggested [by *Human Nature in Politics*], namely, that of the source of the 'political entities' of which he makes so much. These he apparently regards as relatively fixed data, if indeed they are not inherited along with the instincts of which they are categories or antennae, so to speak. We today ... know better.[16]

American political scientists now saw these 'political entities' as socially created, having little connection with any inherited instincts. The social environment, and not some inherited individual 'human nature', was for them the key to behaviour.[17] Wallas had seemed to be moving in this direction in *Our Social Heritage*, but *The Art of Thought* struck many Americans as a 'relapse' into 'individualism'. Even to those Americans, like John Dewey, who were interested in intellectual change, Wallas seemed to be approaching the question backwards. Dewey objected,

The development of natural science is not due to the fact that individual thinkers have learned a better intimately personal art of managing their own thoughts. It is due to the formation of an objective technique of instruments and external procedures together with the accumulation of prior results which direct from without the growth of pertinent problems and fruitful hypotheses. But it is the personal and psychological problem alone with which Mr. Wallas deals. There is no approach to a consideration of the political and economic conditions which stand in social affairs in the way of the development of methods of objective intellectual behavior employing means which almost automatically direct the thoughts of individuals as such.[18]

Wallas's 'individualism', on the other hand, derived from the English traditions of Evangelicalism, with its emphasis on the individual soul, and individual faith and behaviour, and Utilitarianism, with its atomistic calculus. Wallas remained as convinced as his hero, Jeremy Bentham, that the only means of understanding society was to study individual human nature.[19] This tradition gave Wallas, as it had Bentham, a powerful weapon for critical analysis, expertly applied in *Human Nature in Politics*.

[16] 'The Democratic Dogma and the Future of Political Science', *American Political Science Review*, xxiii (Aug. 1929), 583.
[17] Even Laski, who had been an enthusiast for making politics psychological, now reconsidered. In his inaugural address as successor to Wallas in the London University Chair of Political Science, he argued that 'a psychological theory of politics which seeks for an original human nature as the test of institutions fails us for a simple reason. Upon the foundation of inherited impulse, there is that vast superstructure the social heritage, which largely determines its working.' 'On the Study of Politics' (1926), in *The Danger of Being a Gentleman and Other Essays* (London, 1939), 36.
[18] *New Republic*, xlvii (16 June 1926), 118. See also Max Lerner, in *Yale Review*, xvi (July 1927), 828–9.
[19] Letter to M. M. Davis, 3 Sept. 1909 (WP).

As Noel Annan has pointed out, however, it was a frail reed for more positive purposes.[20] To see society as nothing but the sum of the individuals composing it was to miss what was specifically 'social' about society. For this reason the Utilitarian tradition contributed surprisingly little to modern sociology.[21]

Wallas's failure to 'construct' and his outdated social psychology were in part symptoms of a deeper problem, that of his 'Victorianism'. His thinking, already set by 1914, when he was fifty-six, had little appeal to the new generation reaching maturity during the war and after. For all his criticism of the Victorian era, Wallas remained its child. His friend, Gilbert Murray, later noted that there had existed in the late nineteenth century 'a social and intellectual order of immense value which Europe has almost lost and which young people find it difficult to believe in'. 'When I seek for a type of it', he continued, 'one of the figures which comes more than any other to my mind is that of Graham Wallas.'[22] Though he was a critic of established institutions and orthodoxies, his sense of values was as firm as that of any more conventional Victorian. 'While he had no belief in any traditional religious creed', Murray recalled, 'he had no doubt whatever about the importance of seeking truth and acting for the public good.'[23]

In the post-war climate of disillusion and relativism, Wallas's exhortations to unceasing effort and his insistence on 'bring[ing] all the problems of life ... within the sphere of ethics'[24] tended to repel rather than attract. The main point of *The Art of Thought* seemed to Laski, when he read it in manuscript, to be merely an exhortation, 'with abundantly interesting illustration', it was true, 'that you can do better than you think you can, if you only try hard enough'; to this exhortation he responded only with irritation.[25] Wallas shared more with his father and with T. H. Green than he would have admitted, and he shared, too, in the rapid decline of the Evangelical and Idealistic outlooks in the 1920s. Stephen Spender's account of *his* father, with whom Wallas had collaborated in writing *The Case Against Diggleism* in 1894, illustrated this chasm between the generations:

If I had to play football, he impressed on me that this was to harden the tissues of my character. His own accomplishments were to him difficulties surmounted with unflinching resolution at the cost of infinite pains. He spoke often in parables which illustrated the point that life was a perpetual confronting of oneself with

[20] *Curious Strength of Positivism.*
[21] See R. Nisbet, *The Sociological Tradition.*
[22] *Men & Ideas*, 5 (Preface).   [23] *Men & Ideas*, 8.
[24] 'William Johnson Fox', (1924) *Men & Ideas*, 61.
[25] *Holmes-Laski Letters*, 694 (30 Dec. 1924).

vague immensities.... My father's habit of mind created a kind of barrier between him and us which asserted itself even in the most genuine situations.²⁶

Wallas's moralistic 'habit of mind' led him to object to the new tendency deliberately to exclude values from the realm of science. As part of his work in the Senate of London University (which he carried on after his retirement from full-time teaching), he argued against the idea of 'value-free' social science, against excessive specialization, and against the false order of priorities that the prevailing conception of 'research' seemed to him to encourage.²⁷ Wallas was very much in favour of 'the scientific method' and 'research'—he had spent much of his life expounding their importance—but he had never intended them to exclude the 'whole man', with his values and feelings, from intellectual work, nor to bar the most important and urgent problems from consideration.

In one respect he had altered his methodology since *Human Nature in Politics*. The enthusiasm for quantification that had coloured that work had been criticized by his friends, J. A. Hobson and G. Lowes Dickinson, who had argued that the most important political problems were qualitative, and that politics, as an art, was not reducible to statistics.²⁸ Though he had continued to call for a quantitative science of politics, Wallas had pondered these objections and tempered his enthusiasm. Quantitative methods, he came to realize, had their limits in the study of man. 'The facts of human nature which are of greatest importance to the social psychologist', he had warned in *The Great Society*, 'are just those to which laboratory methods are least applicable.'²⁹ This note of caution steadily gained strength over the years, as in America zeal for quantification mounted to what Wallas feared was excess.³⁰

---

²⁶ *World Within World* (London, 1951), 5.
²⁷ Wallas was chairman of the Senate for a few years after the war, and, among other activities, gave evidence before a departmental committee on the reorganization of the University after the Haldane Report, and prepared memoranda for the University on a proposed Sociology degree course and on post-graduate education. He also was a member of a committee set up by the British Institute of Social Service to conduct a survey of social research in the country, and participated in a Carnegie Foundation study of university examinations in Europe and America. His work on the London University Senate, particularly, took up a great deal of time (letter to Wells, 8 Oct. 1926 (Wells)).
²⁸ See Hobson's review in *Sociological Review*, ii (1909), 293–4; Dickinson's, anonymously, in *Nation*, iv (1908–9), 439–40, which expanded on the substance of a letter to Wallas, 26 Nov. 1908 (WP). A number of other reviewers also brought up this point.
²⁹ p. 30.
³⁰ An American student of John Dewey, examining Wallas's thought on the usefulness of 'science' to the methods of the social studies, observed that his early enthusiasm was followed by increasing scepticism and even opposition. Dwight Waldo, 'Graham Wallas: Reason and Emotion in Social Change', *Journal of Social Philosophy*, vii (1942), 149.

The tradition of the practical generalist in social thought, to which he himself belonged, was being undermined by a new conception of social science. Wallas saw that this threatened intellectual fragmentation. Too much emphasis upon being 'objective' and 'rigorous', especially by American students who had taken up the new methods with uncritical ardour, was producing lifeless, timid, over-schematized work.[31] The Ph.D. system of education, he felt, with its uniform and narrow definition of 'research', rewarded diligence and discouraged originality.[32] Within the University, he worked to change this, often swimming against the current. He admitted,

For the technical and descriptive examination of institutions and their history, this large subject [the behaviour of man in society] must of course be divided up and has been divided up, not inconveniently. But for all theoretical and analytic purposes that subdivision should be forgotten. If the student is to be taught to explain human behaviour by human nature or the nature of the universe, he must use that conception for all his specialist studies... the true line of advance in the future would be to consciously link together our specialist social courses by relating them to a common body of thought and knowledge on the human type and the relation of that type to the universe.[33]

An even greater danger than intellectual fragmentation, as Wallas saw it, was posed by the modern determination to be 'realistic' at all costs. This determination led, not to 'realism' as he had known it, but to amoralism. Deeply worried by 'the growing American use... of the word "debunking"', (i.e., clearing away moral pretence) as a term of political approval', he insisted, in the unfinished second part of *Social Judgment*, on the reality of idealistic motives in politics.[34]

These had been in his experience more important than either the 'interests' of the new American school of political scientists and the Marxists, or the unconscious motives of the political Freudians. 'Interests' and irrational motivation were both real, but to Wallas they were, and had always been, unpleasant facts to be faced and overcome. The new 'realists', he felt, not only faced them, but saw nothing else, thus banishing ideals from political life.

Wallas was perfectly consistent with his pre-war pleas for political

---

[31] See 'Effective Social Research', *New Republic*, xii (8 Sept. 1917), 156–7.

[32] See 'Physical and Social Science', (1930) *Men & Ideas*. See also the uncompleted chapter on 'Academic Research' for 'Social Judgment', pt. ii (WP).

[33] Memorandum for London University on a proposed Sociology degree course (WP). To further this aim, Wallas drew up a syllabus for a possible course 'on those psychological facts which are most relevant to social studies'. (WP).

[34] See unfinished manuscript (WP).

realism. Then, the chief intellectual obstacle to political progress, as it appeared to him, had been a naïve idealism devoid of scientific knowledge or method, and he had pursued it to the ground, whether among Oxford dons or his Liberal friends. In the post-war climate of disillusion a 'debunking' science had become the foremost danger to progress by seeming to legitimize the selfish and unreasonable forces at work in politics. In both cases, Wallas fought for a conception of political and social philosophy that united fact and value, science and reform. In human affairs, he was certain, there was no such thing as 'pure' science; for him the social sciences were still—as they had been in his youth—the 'moral sciences'.[35] Having grown up in the midst of the struggle between Darwinism and religion, science was to Wallas part of a philosophy of life, involving moral values and a 'world-view', not merely a method.[36]

If Wallas had not changed, the times had. The new generation, disillusioned by the World War and its aftermath, no longer possessed or even desired the moral certainty of Wallas's contemporaries. They were determined to see things as they were, and not to confuse knowledge with unverifiable values, particularly pre-war values. To these men, Wallas was a moralist, not a scientist.

As a reformer, too, Wallas seemed somewhat old-fashioned in the postwar era. His 'individualism' and his moralism were part of an approach to reform that now was branded 'Victorian'. For Wallas, individual psychology was both the foundation of social science and the fulcrum of social change. The first, most important step in changing society was to change the thoughts, feelings, and motives of its members; after that, the rest would follow by itself.

From his first Fabian lecture to his last efforts on the manuscript of *Social Judgment*, this 'evangelical' conviction never faltered. It set him apart, however, from a generation much more aware of the autonomous power of social institutions, of fundamental conflicts of interest in society, and of how little reason and goodwill mattered in the face of this power and these conflicts. For all his Benthamism, Laski mused, 'at bottom Wallas is a bishop *manqué*'.[37] By the time of the collapse of the Labour

---

[35] See *Men & Ideas*, 201.
[36] When Bertrand Russell was refused permission to travel to America during the war because of his pacificism, Wallas wrote letters to protest both to friends in the Government (Herbert Samuel, particularly) and to the Press. In such a letter to the *Manchester Guardian*, he unwittingly attacked Russell's view (under the impression that it was that of his Government critic) that there was no necessary connection between philosophy and practical life. See WP. See also *Social Judgment*, 125–7.
[37] *Holmes-Laski Letters*, 935 (15 Apr. 1927).

Government in 1931, Wallas seemed a voice from another era. Laski, having abandoned psychology, gave expression to the 'new realism':

each economic regime [he wrote] gives birth to a political order which represents the interests of those who dominate the regime, who possess in it the essential instruments of economic power.[38]

Wallas, in the end, was 'convicted' of the idealist error for which Christopher Caudwell, an ardent Marxist, took H. G. Wells to task in the 1930s:

the error that thought is prior and moves the world and that if only people would see reason (while the capitalist machine remorsely constrains their every movement) they would act rightly.[39]

II

Although too 'Victorian' for his immediate successors, Wallas has gained new relevance for the social sciences in recent years. The 'moral' approach to social study—always strong in Britain—has in the troubled America of the 1960s returned from banishment. The whole question of the possibility of 'value-free' social science, and, even more, of its desirability, has been forcefully reopened in that home of twentieth-century 'scientism'. Wallas's warnings against the harmful consequences of excluding ideals and values have been echoed again and again in the last few years by liberal and radical social scientists seeking to change society.

It is being argued again, most prominently perhaps by the philosopher Noam Chomsky, that the social sciences are inescapably, and properly, 'moral sciences', and that their practitioners have special moral responsibilities. A misguided worship of 'objectivity' has been held responsible for trivialization, political quietism, and even deliberate bias against moral questions and ideals.[40] Consequently, Wallas's analogies of social science with medicine and engineering have reappeared. As a form of medicine, Christian Bay has insisted, 'political science ... should aim at prescribing the organizational innovations and social experimentation

---

[38] *Democracy in Crisis* (Chapel Hill, N. C., 1933) (an expanded version of lectures delivered in America in April 1931), 50.
[39] *Studies in a Dying Culture* (London, 1938), 84.
[40] See, for example, the essays by Roszak, Engler, Bay, and Chomsky in Theodore Roszak (ed.), *The Dissenting Academy* (New York, 1968); Alvin Gouldner, 'Anti-Minotaur: The Myth of a Value-Free Sociology', *Social Problems*, ix. 3 (Winter 1962), 199–213; John Seeley, 'The Making and Taking of Social Problems: Toward an Ethical Stance', *Social Problems*, xiv. 4 (Spring 1967), 382–9; Thomas Ford Hoult, 'Who Shall Prepare Himself to the Battle', *The American Sociologist*, i. 1 (February 1968), 3–7.

that will allow us to cultivate, in Albert Schweitzer's term, a "reverence for life"'.[41] Two other young social scientists have proposed that sociology change its orientation from 'mere objective analyses of society' to 'institution formation', from thinking about society from outside to active involvement in creating a better society.[42] In the struggle against social evils, the Australian Hugh Stretton has similarly suggested, the social scientist 'is a citizen. His duty goes beyond discovering and understanding. It becomes his business to win.'[43]

Today, Wallas's combination of Benthamism and Evangelicalism no longer seems necessarily out of place in the study of society, and cannot be simply dismissed as 'Victorian'. The reaction against Victorianism having run its course, we are now in a position critically to appreciate elements of that era, including its moral commitment. If Wallas, poised between two periods of social thought, fell into errors of each, he also perceived faults in each. Perhaps his position can now be seen, as he came to see it, as a fruitful *via media* between the excesses of idealism and of realism, a valuable corrective to the one-sided zeal of both 'moral' and 'scientific' students of society.

Whether Wallas's particular approach to the social sciences is vindicated or not, it was his indisputable achievement to help open up new fields of social study. His varied and practical life fitted him well to open intellectual doors, by providing much to think about but leaving his mind, as one historian of psychology has put it, 'free from water-tight compartments'.[44] What he wrote about he knew, if not from participation, then from direct observation. Gilbert Murray recalled,

More than anyone I have ever known he was always observing and thinking freshly—always, so to speak, 'taking notice'. Only a minority of mankind spend much effort on thinking; and almost all of those who think hardest keep their thought within narrow limits; the limits of books or laboratories or the practice of a profession. But Wallas studied the world of human beings. In an omnibus, in

---

[41] 'The Cheerful Science of Dismal Politics', in Roszak (ed), *The Dissenting Academy*, 225-6.
[42] Henry Etzkowitz and Gerald M. Schaflander, 'A Manifesto for Sociologists: Institution Formation—A New Sociology', *Social Problems*, xv. 4 (Spring 1968), 399.
[43] Hugh Stretton, *The Political Sciences* (New York, 1969), 431.
[44] L. S. Hearnshaw, op. cit., 116. 'It is wonderful to me', the American social psychologist Edward A. Ross remarked, 'that you keep so fresh in your thinking. A very large amount of this book [*The Great Society*] is the fruit of new thinking and you seem to be as fresh and original in your thought as if you had not read many books touching the topics you treat. I could not help comparing your book with my "Social Psychology", to the decided disadvantages of the latter. In my book I leaned more on my predecessors than you have.' Letter, 15 Sept. 1914 (WP).

a railway carriage, most of all in a Committee of the County Council or the old School Board or London University, when he met both the types he knew and the types he did not know, saw them at work, saw what habits and idiosyncrasies and interests moved them, he was always observing and thinking and from time to time making notes in a pocket-book.[45]

In the study of politics, Wallas was a pioneer. His attempt to change the object of this study from formal institutions and principles to human beings and their actual behaviour was both revolutionary and influential.[46] *Human Nature in Politics* has in recent years been called 'the classic appeal for a realistic approach to the study of politics', and, together with Arthur Bentley's *The Process of Government*, 'the beginning of the modern political behaviour approach', a 'classic . . . eminently relevant today'.[47]

Human Nature in Politics has been important practically as well as theoretically. By bringing to general attention the gap between democratic assumptions and reality Wallas promoted greater realism in political discourse. Today it is largely agreed that, as Robert E. Lane of Yale has put it, 'we must accept realistic standards of performance for the electorate, standards which are in line with the evidence on how people do in fact think and act in the political arena', while seeking (as Wallas sought) improved social institutions and arrangements to maximize these standards.[48]

In *The Great Society* Wallas attempted to develop and apply an instinctivist social psychology that has, by and large, as we have seen, been since

---

[45] *Men & Ideas*, 6 (Preface).
[46] *Human Nature in Politics*, C. H. Driver observed in his study of Edwardian thought 'was the most important book directly relating to political theory which appeared in the reign, and marked the beginning of a new phase of social studies'. F. J. C. Hearnshaw, op. cit., 264. In his argument for a psychological approach to politics, one student of his remarked, he was 'victorious as to the viewpoint, even if somewhat barren as to positive content'. Quoted by Josiah Stamp, who agreed: "The idea that political machinery is a psychological problem, and links with the general problem of behaviour, has fastened its roots deeply upon us all.' *Economica*, op, cit., 400.
[47] David Butler, *The Study of Political Behaviour* (London, 1958), 38, and Heinz Eulau, *et al.*, (eds.), *Political Behaviour* (Glencoe, Illinois, 1956), 7, 8. 'Wallas was a pioneer', Butler wrote, 'in most of the main approaches to the study of political behaviour. He was one of the first to demand that the aid of statistics should be enlisted. . . . He tried as a practical politician . . . to draw academic lessons from his experience, using what has now become the accepted technique of the "participant-observer". Above all, he was one of the first to examine the limits of the purely deductive approach. He pricked a bubble by his denunciation of "the intellectualist fallacy" and his appeal for empirical research', op. cit., 38. Charles Merriam and Harold Lasswell, of the 'Chicago-School', who carried on the behavioural study of politics in the 1920s and 1930s were friends and admirers of Wallas. See letters in WP.
[48] *Political Life* (Glencoe, Illinois, 1959), 356.

discarded in favour of a more 'social' approach. However, the critique he made of the 'crowd psychologists' played an important role in severing the association of social psychology with irrationalism. Present-day social psychologists have given the intellect a much more prominent position than did McDougall or Tarde. Thinking and reasoning, it is now accepted, instigate and guide behaviour as well as providing rationalizations.[49] And though its present form is very different from his conception, 'the science of social psychology', according to a historian of British psychology, 'had with Graham Wallas definitely taken root in this country'.[50]

The Great Society, even more importantly, helped to focus attention upon what has become the chief topic of modern social thought—the transformation in the character of society, brought about by unprecedented technological change, and its 'human' implications. 'The question of whether a great society can be made to work', Walter Lippmann has observed, 'has been one of the great central themes of political thought and research during the past fifty years.'[51] Wallas's work was a stimulus to those urban and industrial sociologists and psychologists, particularly in America, beginning to attack the problem.[52] John Dewey, the foremost American social thinker of his time, took up Wallas's theme in 1927 when he observed that 'the Great Society created by steam and electricity may be a society, but it is no community. The invasion of the community by the new and relatively impersonal and mechanical modes of combined human behavior is the outstanding fact of modern life.'[53] *The* problem of the age, Dewey told his generation, was that of converting the Great Society into a Great Community. We are still asking, as Walter Lippmann did a few years ago, whether 'the great society, which we are born into [can] become a good society, and how can this be brought about?'[54] Now, however, the question has passed from the realm of speculation to the field of politics, and the need for a solution to the dual problems of efficiency and individual satisfaction has become urgent.

As a social reformer, Wallas judged the British institutions of his time by psychological criteria—intellectual efficiency and clarity. Year after year he argued that every national institution, but particularly those

---

[49] See Leonard Berkowitz, 'Social Psychological Theorizing', in Melvin H. Marx (ed.), *Theories in Contemporary Psychology* (New York, 1963), 369–88.
[50] L. S. Hearnshaw, op. cit., 119.
[51] *Newsweek*, lxvi. 21 (22 Nov. 1965), 25.
[52] See Morton and Lucia White, *The Intellectual Versus the City* (Cambridge, Mass., 1962).
[53] *The Public and Its Problems* (New York, 1927), 98.
[54] *Newsweek*, op. cit.

concerned with the creation, application, and diffusion of thought, had to be thoroughly modernized to keep pace with the rapidly increasing complexity of life. In his perception of social trends, Wallas has proved prescient.[55] As the Great Society has developed, and the intellectual demands it has placed upon governments have grown, Parliament has become less important, and the executive and the bureaucracy much more important, while the need for intellectual efficiency and expertise has grown enormously. At the same time, the need for clarification, so that the general populace can understand and participate in government, has grown apace.

Gradually, British institutions have begun to be rationalized and made more responsive to modern needs. Only in the last few years, however, after decades of relative neglect, has the problem of modernization come to the forefront of public attention. Britain in the 1960s has been, as the *Economist* declared a few years ago,

a country in search of a new way of government. It needs more efficient government, in checking the power of the executive which has increased more rapidly than ever in the past twenty years, and in stimulating the ideas of that executive.[56]

In concentrating upon intellectual efficiency and clarity over ideology, Wallas, like John Maynard Keynes and a small number of other Liberal social thinkers of the first few decades of this century, proved more farsighted than his contemporaries who clung to obsolete dogma, of both left and right. Today Wallas appears as one of the unacknowledged prophets of the renewed, modernized Britain sought by all parties.

For all his accomplishments, however, Wallas failed to attain the ends he set for himself. He laid the foundations for a psychology of political and social life, but he did not provide one. He saw the crisis posed by the Great Society, but his constructive efforts were far too limited to constitute any sort of 'solution'. The tinkering that resulted from his attempts at 'social invention' seemed out of scale to his ambitions, while his exhortations were too vague to be helpful. He was not as successful in formulating a general social programme as the Webbs or G. D. H. Cole, and judged by this standard he was found, though suggestive, ultimately 'unconstructive'. 'His discussion', noted R. M. MacIver, 'of the type of social organization which would bring a new harmony of life and environment did not advance much beyond some luminous suggestions as to the need for it.'[57]

[55] See L. S. Hearnshaw, op. cit., 118–19.
[56] 'Rule by Inquiry', ccxvii (30 Oct. 1965), 469.
[57] Quoted by H. E. Barnes, in Barnes (ed.), *Introduction to the History of Sociology*, 709.

Yet to judge him thus would be to misunderstand him. At heart, Wallas was not so much an architect of social reorganization like the Webbs as an educator, 'concerned', as his friend J. A. Hobson put it, 'with impressing right methods of understanding'.[58] He possessed, 'in highest measure', the *Manchester Guardian* noted, 'the power of stimulating communication. . . . Few men ever did more to make the study of politics and political science not merely intelligible—though that as much—but also attractive. He had a unique power of establishing contacts, both human and intellectual.'[59] Wallas's role was 'to teach the teachers, to lead the leaders'.[60] Harold Laski reflected on Wallas's death in 1932: 'All over the world there are first-rate people in the social sciences who owe their original impulse to work to him; and I don't think a man could wish for a finer epitaph.'[61]

Wallas's efforts were directed at getting people to comprehend the nature of their society and the new problems it had created, and pointing out the paths they would have to take to solve these problems. These efforts were successful enough for Laski to call him 'the supreme teacher of social philosophy in the last forty years'.[62] Armed with his map, others would venture forth to build the good society.

Wallas himself remained poised between two worlds—having pushed the Victorian assumptions of his youth into uncharted territory, but never finding rest in these new lands of thought, and ending a critic of his successors. He was a behavioural scientist and a moralist, a 'debunker' and an idealist, a practical reformer and a misty visionary. Above all, Wallas was a pioneer, with the virtues and vices of this role, bringing political and social thought into contact with the new circumstances of the twentieth century.

[58] In a review of *Our Social Heritage*, *Nation* (New York), cxiii (21 Sept. 1921), 323.
[59] 11 Aug. 1932.
[60] His friend and student, Herbert Samuel, 'Master Builder of Ideas', *The Times*, 31 May 1958 (on the centenary of Wallas's birth).
[61] *Holmes-Laski Letters*, 1401 (11 Aug. 1932).
[62] *Political Quarterly*, iii (1932), 464.

BIBLIOGRAPHY OF THE WRITINGS OF GRAHAM WALLAS
(This is the first such listing)

I. UNPUBLISHED (in order of importance)

Graham Wallas Papers. Several dozen box files of correspondence, manuscripts, lecture notes and miscellaneous papers. In the library of the London School of Economics and Political Science.

Letters to Sidney and Beatrice Webb. Passfield Papers, London School of Economics and Political Science.

Letters to Walter Lippmann. Copies in the possession of Miss May Wallas. Originals in the possession of Mr. Lippmann.

Letters to H. G. Wells. H. G. Wells Collection, University of Illinois at Urbana.

Letters to Bernard Shaw. Bernard Shaw Papers, British Museum.

Letters to Edward Pease. Fabian Society Executive Minute Books, 1890–5. In the files of the Fabian Society, London.

Letters to Herbert Samuel. House of Lords Archives.

Letters to Eduard Bernstein. Eduard Bernstein Archive, International Institute for Social History, Amsterdam.

Letters to William James, 1908. Houghton Library, Harvard University.

II. PUBLISHED (starred essays can be found in *Men & Ideas*, ed. May Wallas [London, 1940])

'Personal Duty Under the Present System', *Practical Socialist*, i (July and August, 1886), 118–20, 124–5.

'Aristotle on Wealth and Property', *Today*, x (July and August 1888), 16–20, 49–53.

'The Chartist Movement', *Our Corner*, xii (August and September 1888), 111–18, 129–40.

'Socialists and the School Board', *Today*, x (November 1888), 126–32.

'An Economic Eirenicon', *Today*, xi (March 1889), 80–6.

'Property Under Socialism', in *Fabian Essays in Socialism*, G. B. Shaw (ed.), London, 1889.

'The Right to Labor', *Fabian News*, i (July 1891), 17. Items in *Fabian News* by Wallas are summaries of lectures.

What to Read, Fabian Tract no. 29, first edition November 1891, fourth revised edition October 1901.

'The Conditions of Self-Government', *Fabian News*, ii (April 1892), 5.

'Origins of English Local Government', *Fabian News*, ii (August 1892), 22.
'Working Class Economics', *Fabian News*, ii (December, 1892), 37.
'The Coming School Board Election', *Fabian News*, iv (April 1894).
The Case Against Diggleism, with Harold Spender; printed anonymously London, 1894.
'The Issues of the County Council Elections', *Fabian News*, v (March 1895).
Review of John Rae, *Life of Adam Smith*, *Daily Chronicle*, 28 May 1895.
'Board Schools and Free Meals', *Fabian News*, vi (February 1896).
'A Library of Political Science', *Daily Chronicle*, 7 April 1896.
'The Issues of the School Board Election', *Fabian News*, vii (November 1897).
The Life of Francis Place, London, 1898.
Review of Kent, *The English Radicals*, *Speaker*, 21 October 1899.
'Starving School Children', *Review of the Week*, 2 December 1899.
'The London School Board Election', *Speaker*, 27 October 1900.
Review of Leslie Stephen, *The English Utilitarians*, *Speaker*, 2 March 1901.
'The Local Authority for Secondary Education', *Speaker*, 16 March 1901.
'Religion and Empire', *Inquirer*, 29 June 1901.
*'A Criticism of Froebelian Pedagogy', *Child Life*, July 1901.
'Local and Central Government: Their Relation in Education', *Morning Post*, 17 October 1902.
'The London Education Bill: Its Administrative Futility', *Morning Post*, 9 April 1903.
'The American Analogy', *Independent Review*, i (November 1903), 505–16.
*'Let Youth But Know', *Speaker*, 20 January 1906.
Remember 1880', *Speaker*, 27 January 1906.
'From the Second to the Third Reform Bill', *Independent Review*, iv (February 1906), 228–32.
'Impressions of Paris', *Daily Chronicle*, 13 February 1906.
*'Darwinism and Social Motive', *Inquirer*, 28 April 1906.
*Introduction to new edition of John Ruskin, *The Two Paths*, London, 1907.
*'Oxford and the Nation', *Westminster Gazette*, 28 April 1908.
Review of Sidney and Beatrice Webb, *English Local Government*, vols. II and III, *Economic Journal*, xviii (June 1908), 272–7.
*'The Future of English Education in the Light of the Past', in H. B. Binn, *A Century of Education*, London, 1908.
Human Nature in Politics, London, 1908.
'A Municipal Civil Service', *Nation*, iv (13 February 1909), 745–6.
Letter to *Morning Post*, 20 February 1909.
'A Revolution in Education', *Nation*, v (10 July 1909), 520–1.
'The Future of Cowper-Templeism', *Nation*, v (24 July 1909), 597–8.
'Holiday Thoughts on the Ability to Pay', *Clare Market Review*, October 1909.
'The Money-Power at War', *Nation*, vi (11 December 1909), 453–5.
*'The Beginning of Modern Socialism', *Sociological Review*, iii (1910), 44–50.

'The Science of Preferences', *Nation*, vii (30 April 1910), 166-8.
'The Village Tragedy', *Nation*, x (11 November 1911) 248-50.
'The Psychology of Propaganda', *Fabian News*, March 1912.
'Syndicalism', *Sociological Review*, v (1912), 248-50.
Royal Commission on the Civil Service, *Reports 1912-1914*.
'Social Motive', *Fabian News*, May 1913.
'Parliament and the Report on the Civil Service', published anonymously, *New Statesman*, iii (25 April 1914), 71-3.
The Great Society, London, 1914.
'The Economics of Human Welfare', *Nation*, xv (27 June 1914), 495-6.
*'The Universities and the Nation in America and England', *Contemporary Review*, cv (June 1914), 783-90.
'A United States of Europe', *New Republic*, i (2 January 1915), 24.
'Oxford and English Political Thought', *Nation*, xvii (15 May 1915), 227-8.
*Comment on 'The Peacefulness of Being at War', *New Republic*, iv (11 September 1915), 154-5.
'English Teachers' Organisations', *New Statesman*, v (25 September 1915), 586-7.
'Ante-War Ideals', *Nation*, xviii (2 October 1915), 23.
Review of Christensen, *Politics and Crowd Morality*, *Hibbert Journal*, xiv (October 1915), 224-8.
Review of Veblen, *Imperial Germany*, *Quarterly Journal of Economics*, xxx (November, 1915) 179-87.
'Mobilizing the Administration', *New Republic*, v (6 November 1915), 12-14.
Introduction to R. C. Mills, *The Colonisation of Australia*, London, 1915.
*'Socialism and the Fabian Society', *New Republic*, vii (24 June 1916), 203-4.
'Democracy and the Dangers of Reaction', *The Christian Commonwealth*, 15 November 1916.
Letter to *The Highway*, January 1917.
'The Eastern Question', *New Republic*, ix (27 January 1917), 348-9.
'Effective Social Research', *New Republic*, xii (8 September 1917), 156-7.
'Instinct and the Unconscious', *British Journal of Psychology*, x (November 1919), 24-6.
'The "New Virility" in the United States', *New Statesman*, xiv (31 January 1920), 487-8.
*'The Price of Intolerance', *Atlantic Monthly*, cxxv (January 1920), 116-18.
Our Social Heritage, New Haven, Conn., 1921.
Review of Tawney, *The Acquisitive Society*, *Nation*, xxix (11 June 1921), 401.
Seconding speech to Rationalist Press Association, *Literary Guide and Rationalist Review*, no. 301 (July 1921).
'Social Purpose in Education', *Morning Post*, 1 January 1923.
Introduction to R. M. Dawson, *The Principle of Official Independence*, London, 1922.

'Competition of the Sexes for Employment', *The Vote*, 9 March 1923.
Review of Sidney and Beatrice Webb, *English Local Government: Statutory Authorities*, *Economic Journal*, xxxiii (March 1923), 86–90.
'Jeremy Bentham', *Political Science Quarterly*, (March 1923).
'The Webbs Sum up', *New Republic*, xxxiv, 11 April 1923, pt. ii, 18–20. A review of *The Decay of Capitalist Civilisation*.
Seconding speech to Rationalist Press Association, *Literary Guide and Rationalist Review*, no. 325 (July, 1923).
'Amphibious Strategy', *Nation*, xxxiv (3 November 1923).
Review of Hadley, *Economic Problems of Democracy*, *Economic Journal*, xxxiii (December, 1923) 523–5.
*'William Johnson Fox', Conway Memorial Lecture, delivered at South Place Institute on 20 March 1924, published in *Men & Ideas*, 49–64.
Review of Finer, *Representative Government and a Parliament of Industry*, *Economic Journal*, xxxiv (March 1924), 90–3.
'Palestinian Pioneers', *Nation*, xxxvi (15 November 1924), 256–8.
*'Mental Training and the World Crisis', in *Annual Report of the Association of University Women Teachers*, 1924.
'Zionism', *New Judaea*, 30 January 1925.
*'Lord Sheffield on the London School Board', *Manchester Guardian*, 19 March 1925.
'A Gentile Hope for the Dreamers of All Races', *The New Palestine*, 27 March 1925.
The Art of Thought, London 1926.
Preface to E. D. Simon, *A City Council from Within*, London, 1926.
'The Education of Beatrice Webb', *Nation*, xxxviii (6 March 1926), 779–80.
'Bentham as Political Inventor', *Contemporary Review*, cxxix (March 1926), 308–19.
Presidential Speech to Rationalist Press Association, *Literary Guide and Rationalist Review*, no. 361 (July 1926).
'Occupational Recruiting', *Nation*, xxxix (31 July 1926), 491–3.
'Die Demokratie als Rettung Europas', *Neue Freie Presse* (Vienna), 12 September 1926.
'London University: An Overdue Reform', *Manchester Guardian*, 20 October 1926.
'Authority in Politics', *Nation*, xl (6 November 1926), 171–2.
'"Common Sense" and the General Strike', *Nation*, xl (22 January 1927), 566–7.
'Mr. Churchill on Fascism', *Nation*, xl (29 January 1927), 586 (letter).
'"Beyond the Reach of Objection or Controversy"', *Nation*, xl (19 February 1927), 687–8.
'The Sheffield School Case', *Manchester Guardian*, 1 October 1927.
*'Government', *Public Administration*, vi (1928), 3–15.

Presidential speeches to the Rationalist Press Association, *Literary Guide and Rationalist Review*, no. 374 (August 1927) no. 385 (July 1928), and no. 397 (July 1929).

'Local Officials and the Municipal Reforms: An Urgent Need', *Local Government News*, February 1929.

'An American Moralist', *Nation*, xlv (7 September 1929), 738.

'Address at Hobhouse Memorial Service', *Economica*, ix. 27 (November 1929), 247–50.

Royal Commission on Local Governnment 1929, *Minutes of Evidence*, xiii, 2414.

'Ends and Means in Politics', *Fabian News*, December 1930.

Review of Hobson and Ginsberg, *L. T. Hobhouse*, *New Statesman and Nation*, i (25 April 1931), 326–8.

Social Judgment (pt. i only), May Wallas (ed.), London, 1935.

Men & Ideas, May Wallas (ed.), London, 1940. Eighteen of his most important lectures and articles, written between 1900 and 1931.

INDEX

Addams, J., 117, 118, 151, 169, 174n.
Allport, G., 114
America, American: 69, 76, 82, 84, 97, 98, 141, 203, 205; possibility of peaceful change, 179; criticism of Wallas, **177**, 178, 205–6; naturalism, 162, 167; prestige of Science, 156, 208; recognition of Wallas, 127, 166–74, 214; universities, 165; optimism, 187; failure to develop 'scientific democracy,' 193; capitalism, failure of, 193; 'debunking', 209; Political Science Association, 96, 205; Roman Catholic Church in, 200; 'moral' social science, 211; Wallas in, 43–7, 61–4, 142, 169–75; political and social thought in, 71, 83, 98, 166–9; 'urban renewal' in, 150
Anarchism, 16, 27, 37
Annan, Noel, 67, 207
Anticlericalism, *see* secularism, rationalism
Anti-Corn Law League, 82
Aristocracy, 31, 45, 62
Aristotle, 5, 9, 11–13, 22, 25–7, 44, 54n., 60, 90, 103, 109, 122, 135, 157, 187, 202
Arnold, M., 84, 157, 186
Asquith, H., 191
Attlee, C., 164

Bacon, F., 84, 85, 89
Bagehot, W., 73–5, 87, 120, 185
Barker, E., 100n., 127, 131, 166
Darnes, H. E., 174n., 205
Barnstaple (Devon), 3
Barrès, M., 100
Bay, C., 211
Belloc, H., 101, 149
Benedict, R., 113
Bentham, J., 13, 29, 42, 61, 69, 70, 75, 127, 128, 163, 192–4, 206
Benthamism, 2, 29, 35n, 41, 42, 47, 60–2, 68, 76, 127, 128, 148, 155, 160, 177, 206, 207, 210, 212
Bentley, A., 167, 213
Bergson, H., 83, 131n., 171
Besant, A., 38
Beveridge, W., 179
Blake, W., 162

Bland, H., 48, 49n., 58
Boers, Boer War, 57, 58, 106, 129
Booth, C., 10, 16
Boston, 46, 169
Brandeis, L., 171
Bray, R., 102
Brinley, C. A., 45n.
Britain, *see* England
British Museum, 41
Bruck, M. van den, 100
Bryce, Lord, 66
Bryn Mawr, 44, 46
Buddhism, 159
bureaucracy, *see also* Civil Service, 15, 38, 62, 144, 147, 215
Burke, E., 73
Butler, D., 213, 213n.
Butler, S., 5–8
Buxton, N., 101

Cambridge University, 9, 29, 61, 146–8, 162, 166; Wallas's teaching at, 164, 194
Capitalism, 19, 27, 37, 65, 103, 151, 211
Carlyle, T., 84
Case, T., 8, 9
Caudwell, C., 211
Chartism, 41, 76
Chesterton, C., 58
Chesterton, G. K., 101, 149, 150; *The Napoleon of Notting Hill*, 149
Chicago, 108, 117, 150, 169, 174n.; University of, 173, 213n.
China: anarchy of, 188; philosophy, 159, 202
Chomsky, N., 211
Church of England, 3, 4, 38, 50, 53–5, 137, 138, 165, 199, 200
'civic gospel,' 44
Civil Service, *see also* Royal Commission on the Civil Service 1912–1914; Committee on the Civil Service 1966–1968; 14, 19, 31, 36, 45, 144–8, 164, 194
classics, classicism: influence on Wallas, 5–7, 11–14, 21, 27, 47, 48, 157, 182, 185; English overemphasis upon, 146, 147, 166, 184
Clifford, W. K., 7

INDEX

Cobden, R., 57, 104, 106
Cole, G. D. H., 59n, 149n., 180–3, 204–5, 215
collectivism, see also Socialism, Fabian Society; 26–8, 31, 36, 37, 43, 47, 48, 50, 51–2, 54, 105, 149, 152–4, 159, 192
Colonial Office, 14, 15, 20, 144
Columbia University, 118
Committee on the Civil Service 1966–1968, 147
Commonweal, 26
Communism, 179, 187, 189, 193
Conservative Government, 58; 1895–1900, 53
Conservative Party, 37, 48, 53, 57, 88
Conservatives, Conservatism, 5, 31–4, 37, 38, 48, 73, 75, 95, 98, 107, 124, 125, 129, 130, 134, 149, 166, 177, 179, 184, 186, 191
Continent, see Europe
Co-operation, 27
Corwin, E. S., 96, 205
County Councils, see also London County Council; 53
Croly, H., 169, 171, 173
Cromwell, O., 41
culture, 86n.

Daily Herald, 204
Darwin, Darwinism, 7–9, 13, 27, 72, 73, 83, 85–9, 92, 103, 109–12, 115, 118, 123, 124, 130, 159, 185, 210
Davies, J. C., 113
Davis, M. M., 118, 119, 131
Democracy, 19, 30, 31, 58, 95, 97, 98, 126, 180, 191, 193, 198; criticism of, 31–8, 62, 63–6, 71–5, 77, 78, 81–3, 103, 131, 133, 134, 152, 153, 188; by Wallas, 34, 75, 117, 51, 63, 75, 0, 82–4, 88, 103, 104, 144; defense of, by Wallas, 38, 73, 134, 141–3, 188, 189
Dewey, J., 85n., 110, 167, 205n., 206, 214
Dickinson, G. Lowes, 29, 61, 124–6, 131, 166, 208
Diggle, Rev. J. R., 38n., 50
Disraeli, B., 88
Driver, C. H., 62n., 100, 213n.
Durkheim, E., 72, 98–100, 133n.

Economica, 194
Economist, 215
Education, see London School Board, London County Council, Wallas

Education Act of 1902, 55, 56, 81
Education Bill of 1896, 53
Education Bill of 1908, 138n.
Education, Board of, 54, 146
Edwardian period, 1, 16, 29, 62, 66, 71, 77, 100, 101, 107, 112, 121, 128, 130, 148, 159, 168
efficiency: dangers of, 150; national, 15, 26, 32, 53, 63, 100, 128–30, 143, 153, 159, 160; of thought, 130, 135, 140–3, 148, 152, 180, 190, 195, 196, 214, 215
engineering, social and psychological, see also invention, social and political; 29, 61, 62, 67, 73, 97, 117, 125, 126, 135, 150, 151, 169, 170, 172, 211, 212
England, English: politics and government, 19, 33, 34, 64, 82, 83, 94n, 144–8, 193–5, 215; socialism, 37, 153; liberalism, 126, 169; possibility of peaceful change, 179; resistance to behavioral science, 67, 72, 95, 97, 124–6, 164–6, 168, 172, 206, 207; monarchy, 185; towns, 44, 190; failure to develop 'scientific democracy', 193; psychology, 119, 214; education, 56, 136, 140; elitist tradition, 84; anti-modernism, 100, 101; critics of collectivism, 105; radicalism, 127; inefficiency of, 129, 130
Enlightenment, 71, 110
Etzkowitz, H., 212
eugenics, 88, 129, 177
Eulau, H., 113n., 114n.
Europe, 19, 32–4, 45, 67, 69, 71–3, 83, 88, 98, 100, 106, 156, 158, 161, 177, 187, 193, 200, 201, 207
Evangelicalism, 1, 6, 10, 11, 13, 15, 18, 21, 39, 40, 47, 67, 125–8, 148, 155, 157, 160, 166, 176, 177, 199, 206, 207, 213, 214

Fabian Society, 10, 15–20, 27, 28, 30, 34, 35–9, 41, 45, 47–54, 56–60, 68, 77, 84, 97, 102, 104–8, 111, 129, 144, 149, 153, 169, 172, 173, 180, 186, 188, 191, 192, 210; Conference of 1886, 48; *Fabian Essays in Socialism*, 18, 25, 27, 30, 48; Executive Committee, 48n., 52, 56, 57n., 58; Parliamentary League, 22, 49; Political Committee, 22; *'To Your Tents, Oh Israel!'*, 49, 58; *Fabianism and the Empire*, 56, 106; *Fabianism and the Fiscal Question*, 57
Fascism, 187, 189
Figgis, J. N., 149

INDEX

Flexner, A., 165
Fortnightly Review, 77, 107
France: anticlericalism, 175; civic religion, 157, 159, 199; criticism of democracy, 32–33; criticism of modern society, 98–100; French Revolution, 125, 134; possibility of peaceful change, 179; practical nonexistence of democracy, 111, 188; republicanism, 185
Franchise Acts, 1884, 1885, 19
Frankfurter, F., 171, 174n.
Freud, S., 96, 114, 116, 117, 130, 131n., 171; Freudians, 209
Froebelian Association, 136, 137
Fulton Committee, *see* Committee on the Civil Service 1966–1968
Fulton, Lord, 147n.

Germany: criticism of democracy, 33; criticism of modern society, 99, 100; danger of war with, 158; education, 138, 146; practical nonexistence of democracy in, 188
Gilkes, A. H., 5, 11
Ginsberg, M., 163
Gissing, G., 14
Gladstone, W. E., 31–3, 77
Godkin, E. L., 63, 64, 76, 91, 103
Gooch, G. P., 101, 125, 126, 166
Greeks, Greece, *see also* Classics, Plato, Aristotle, *polis*; 26, 28, 84, 97, 103, 121, 122, 135, 156, 157, 176, 182, 183, 186, 198, 199
Green, T. H., 5–9, 17, 67, 68, 165, 207

Haldane, R., 49
Halévy, E., 58, 197
Hall, G. S., 89
Harrison, F., 17
Harvard University, 167, 168, 170, 174n., 181, 187
Heart of the Empire, The, 101, 102
Hegel, G. W. F., 9, 33
Henderson, H. D., 192, 193
Hewins, W. G., 58
Highgate School, 14
Himmelfarb, G., 2
Hobhouse, L., 65, 66, 131
Hobson, J. A., 66n., 67n., 81, 132, 150, 166, 208, 216
Hofstadter, R., 167, 169
Holcombe, A., 168
Holmes, O. W., Jr., 188, 203n., 204

House of Commons, 37, 144, 193, 215
Hughes, H. S., 71, 72
Humanism, 1
Huxley, T. H., 16
Hynes, S., 1n., 62n., 101, 102

Idealism, 1, 5–9, 17, 18, 20, 67, 68, 165, 166, 207
Imperialism, 56–8, 64, 106, 176
Independent Labour Party, 49, 50, 57, 191
Independent Review, 82
India: British rule in, 141, 142; Fabian Society and, 58; little aptitude for democracy in, 188; village life vs. industrial life in, 109
individualism, 44, 53, 90, 96, 98, 99, 100, 104, 109, 110, 151–4, 169, 178, 191, 205–7, 210
industrialism, industrial revolution, industrial society, 3, 26, 98–107, 163, 168
invention, social and political, 29, 127, 151, 177, 195

James, W., 86–91, 102, 110, 119, 127n., 167, 170, 172
Japan, outlook on life, 156, 157, 159, 199; practical nonexistence of democracy in, 188; transformation of society, 125
jingoism, *see* imperialism

Kant, I., 9
Keynes, J. M., 192, 192n., 193, 215
Kidd, B., 58, 83
Kluckhohn, C., 113

Labour Government, 1929–1931, 193, 210, 211
Labour Party, *see also* Independent Labour Party, 190–3
Lagarde, P. de, 100
Lane, R. E., 213
Langbehn, J., 100
Laski, H., 51, 163, 180–2, 188, 189, 194, 201n., 203, 203n., 204, 204n., 205, 206n., 207, 210, 211, 216
Lasswell, H., 213n.
Layton, W. T., 192, 193
Leach, E., 113n., 115n.
LeBon, G., 33, 72, 73, 133, 133n.; *The Crowd*, 33
Liberal Government, 1892–1895, 49
Liberal Party, 37, 48, 49, 52, 54, 57, 88, 190, 191–3

Liberals, Liberalism, 52, 55, 57, 58, 64, 72, 73, 83, 84, 89, 95, 96, 98, 99–101, 104–7, 125, 126, 131, 137, 166, 190, 193, 211, 215; desertion by many 'old Liberals', 31–4; Wallas's criticisms of, 169, 185, 186, 191, 192, 210
Lippman, W., 6on., 76n., 96, 127, 131n., 158, 170, 170n., 171, 175, 182, 183, 187, 188, 192, 195, 198, 199, 214
Lipset, S. M., 81n.
Lloyd George, D., 186, 192
Locke, J., 192
London, 14, 15, 24, 25, 37, 39, 40, 43, 44, 46n., 52, 53, 62, 76, 81, 97, 101, 103, 120, 121, 139, 141, 150, 155, 190, 202
London County Council, 50, 53, 54, 56, 81n., 120, 127, 144, 192, 212; Technical Education Committee, 52, 55; Education Committee, 81n., 102, 137
London School Board, 24, 30, 38–40, 42, 43, 47, 49–51, 53, 54, 80, 81, 103, 120, 137, 153n., 179, 183, 212; School Management Committee, 52, 80
London School of Economics and Political Science, 30, 34, 81, 112, 145, 146, 162, 164, 173, 179, 181, 193–5
London University, 142, 162, 206n., 209, 212; parliamentary constituency, 190; Senate, 163, 179, 208, 208n.
Lorenz, K., 114, 115n.
Lowe, R., 31
Lowell, A. L., 167, 170

Maine, H., 30, 75
Malinowski, B., 112, 113
Mallock, W. H., 83
Manchester Guardian, 216
Martin, K., 59n., 61, 164, 164n., 190
Marx, K., 18, 19, 198
Marxism, 15, 18, 19, 23, 28, 37, 209, 211
Masterman C. F. G., 149; *Condition of England*, 62, 101, 102
Maurras, C., 100
meritocracy, 31
Merriam, C., 213n.
Metropolitan Radical Federation, 49
Mill, J., 42, 123
Mill, J. S., 84, 186, 192; on democracy, 31, 35; *Political Economy*, 9; *Representative Government*, 35; *System of Logic*, 9
Milner, A., 12
Mitchell, W., 177, 205
Moderate Party (London), 38–40, 50

monarchy, 62, 74, 123, 185
Montesquieu, 64
Moore, D. C., 35n.
moral sciences, *see* social science
Morgan, L., 89
Morris, W., 26, 103, 109, 118, 186
Mosca, G., 72
Murray, G., 190, 207, 212

McBriar, A. M., 23
McDougall, W., 86, 110, 132, 133, 181, 214
Macdonald, M., 145
Macdonald, R., 64–6, 191
Macdonnell Commission, *see* Royal Commission on the Civil Service 1912–1914
Macdonnell, Lord, 145
MacIver, R. M., 215

Nation, 62, 192
National Liberal Club, 78
Nevinson, H. W., 4, 6, 12
New Poor Law of 1834, 71
New Republic, 171–3
New School for Social Research, 173–5, 178, 204
New Statesman, 172, 190
New York, 76, 173, 202
Newbolt, H., 8
Nisbet, R., 96

Olivier, S., 9, 14–20, 144
Ostrogorski, M., 81–84, 93, 97, 124, 125, 127, 131, 142; *Democracy and the Organization of Political Parties*, 81
Oxford University, 21, 68, 139, 140n., 146–8, 162, 164–6, 176, 181, 210; Balliol, 8; Christ Church, 7; Corpus Christi, 5; Wallas's education, 5–11, 17, 67, 83, 141, 144

Painites, 60, 62
Palestine, *see* Zionism
Pareto, V., 72, 73
Parliament, *see* House of Commons
participation, political, 35, 38, 46, 128, 148, 185
Pearson, K., 70
Pease, E., 10, 17; *History of the Fabian Society*, 58
Penty, A. J., 149, 149n.
Pericles, 157n., 186
permeation, 37, 48, 49
Philadelphia, 43

INDEX

Philosophic Radicalism, *see* Benthamism
Place, Francis, *see also* Wallas, *Life of Francis Place*; 41, 42, 47, 62
Plato, 25, 68, 130, 135, 142, 168, 187, 198
polis, 11, 12, 28, 103, 157, 176, 177, 182, 185, 199
political economy, *see* science, economics
Porter, B., 64n.
Positivism: Comtist movement, 1, 15, 17, 18, 20, 201; fusion of fact and value, 66n.; assumption of the possibility of certainty in the study of men, 71, 72
Potter, B., *see* Webb, B.
Progressive Party (London), 24, 38-40, 49-51, 54, 56
Protection, 56, 57
Public Administration, Institute of, 164, 194
public opinion, 39, 40, 45, 63-5, 76, 77, 92, 161

quantification, 70, 71, 73, 95, 96, 167, 168, 181, 204, 208

Radicals, Radicalism, 15, 16, 18, 19, 30, 35, 37, 58, 72, 73, 127, 176, 211
Rashdall, H., 8
Ratcliffe, S. K., 174n.
Rationalist Press Association, 200
Rationalists, Rationalism: anti-religious, 1, 5-14, 165, 200; *see also*, secularism; belief in human rationality, *see* rationality
reform, reformers, 10, 16-18, 29, 32, 47, 57n, 62, 64, 66, 67, 83, 88, 96, 97, 101, 116, 117, 123, 125, 126, 129, 135, 145, 167, 177, 214, 216; psychological, ethical, spiritual, 12, 17, 26, 128, 150, 154, 176, 210; *see also* engineering, social and psychological; and invention, social and political
Reform Act of 1867, 31
relativism, 67, 110, 113, 138, 207
Renan, E., 32, 33
republic, 74; Third Republic (France), 33, 34
Ribot, T., 131
Robinson, J. H., 205
Roman Catholic Church, 199, 200
Romanticism, 37, 75, 76
Rome, 25, 120, 158, 202
Ross, E., 168, 212n.
Round Table, 176, 177
Rousseau, J. J., 118, 123

Royal Commission on the Civil Service, 1912-1914, 145-8, 184
Royal Commission on Endowed Education, proposed, 140
Royal Commission on Local Government, 1928-1929, 194
Royal Commission on the Poor Law, 1906-1909, 71
Ruskin, J., 12, 109, 118
Russell, B., 161, 210n.
Russia: abandonment of parliamentary democracy in, 188; Bolshevism in, 179; defeat by Japan, 156; Wallas's admiration for, 193

Sadler, M., 163n.
Samuel, H., 21, 200, 201n.
Schaflander, G. M., 212
School Boards, *see also* London School Board, 53, 54
Schweitzer, A., 212
science, 6-13, 15, 17, 28, 31, 36, 45-7, 50, 67, 70, 72, 78, 82-5, 110, 112, 116-19, 128, 156n., 165, 167, 195, 198-201, 206, 208, 210, 216; anthropology, 111-13, 177; biology, 70, 83, 110, 111, 114, 159, 165; economics, 18, 42, 70, 76, 84, 100, 105, 133, 134, 164; physics, 70, 73, 110; political science, 46, 60, 61, 67, 68, 70, 72, 73, 76, 81, 89, 95-7, 112, 113, 118, 162, 166, 168, 170, 203, 206, 208, 209, 211, 213; social science, sociology, 47, 67, 70, 72, 97, 98-100, 110, 111, 114, 118, 126, 141, 147, 164-8, 173, 177, 181, 199, 207-12, 214, 216
secularism, 14, 53, 55, 56, 137, 138
Seeley, J., 141
Seligman, C. G., 112
Shaw, B., 15-21, 36-8, 41, 46, 49n., 52, 54, 55n., 57, 77, 80, 80n., 104, 106, 137, 141, 142, 153
Shrewsbury, 4, 5, 11, 47, 67
Sidgwick, A., 52
Sidis, B., 73n.
Simmel, G., 99, 100
Smith, A., 80, 192
Snowden, P., 191
Social Democratic Federation, 15, 48, 49
Socialists, Socialism, *see also* Fabian Society; Social Democratic Federation; Syndicalism; 13, 15, 18, 34, 37-9, 41, 43, 48, 49, 51, 52, 55, 58-60, 64, 90, 97, 102,

228 INDEX

Socialists—*continued*
  103, 106, 107, 111, 124, 149, 152, 153, 157, 175, 176, 188, 191, 199
Socialism, Guild, 105, 149, 149n., 183, 191
Sociological Society, 115
Sociological Review, 115
Soltau, Roger, 32
Sorel, G., 72, 73, 93, 131n., 171
South Place Ethical Society, 67
Spencer, H., 67, 111
Spender, H., 38n., 207
Spender, S., 207
Stabler, E., 24n.
Stamp, J., 146n., 179, 195, 213n.
Stanley, L., 52
Stearns, H., 187
Stephen, J. F., 32
Stephen, L., 69
Stern, F., 100
Stretton, H., 212
Sutherland, G., 7n.
Switzerland, 78, 79
Syndicalism, 131, 152–54

Taine, H., 32, 33
Tarde, G., 133, 214
tariffs, *see* Protection
Thorndike, E. L., 177
Thucydides, 176
Tiger, L., 114n., 115n.
Tocqueville, A. de, 204
Today, 24, 27
Toennies, F., 89
Tory Party, *see* Conservative Party
Toynbee, A., 12, 15, 17, 18
Toynbee Hall, 18, 151
Trade Union Congress, 49
trade unionism, 27, 129, 153n., 183, 191, 193
Trevelyan, G. M., 101
Trilling, L., 114
Trotter, W., 115, 116
Twentieth Century Club, Boston, 46

Ulam, A., 100n.
Unionist Party, *see* Conservative Party
University Extension, 30, 34, 44, 45n., 51, 73
Utilitarianism, *see* Benthamism

Veblen, T., 163
Victorians, Victorianism, 1, 66, 67, 74, 96, 101, 136, 138, 145, 195, 207, 210–12, 216

Voluntary Schools, *see* Church of England

Waldo, D., 208n.
Wallas, Rev. G., 3, 6, 22, 23
Wallas, Graham: Addams, J., and, 117, 118, 151, 169; America, impressions of, 45–7, 172, 173; in America, 43–7, 61, 62, 142, 169–75; anti-intellectualism, criticism of, 83, 84, 130–7, 171, 195, 214; *Art of Thought, The*, 197, 205–7; 'biologism' of, 89, 90, 112, 113, 116, 122–5, 177, 205; *Case Against Diggleism, The*, 38n., 207; criticism of, 203–7, 215; education of, 4–14; belief in education as prime means of social improvement, 22–5, 28, 38–40, 42, 43, 103, 135; English educational system, criticism of, 137–40; environmentalism of, 111, 112, 113, 124, 125, 177; and Freud, 116, 117, 130; Fabian Society, resignation from, 57n.; first Fellow of the Institute of Public Administration, 164; 'Great Society', coins term, 105; *Great Society, The*, 2, 30, 104, 112, 131n., 161, 163, 168, 171, 172, 183, 187, 188, 203, 208, 212n., 213, 214; 'Great *Polis*', ideal of a, 155–60, 182, 199–202; *Human Nature in Politics*, 2, 30, 78, 86, 89, 96, 97, 109, 117, 124–7, 131, 132, 152, 154, 161, 163, 166–71, 176, 180, 181, 188, 196, 200, 206, 208, 213; influence of, 203, 212–16; intellectualism, criticism of, 82, 83; 89–95, 125, 126, 131; Laski, H., and, 180–2, 204, 204n., 205; Lippmann, W., and, 131n., 170, 171, 171n., 182, 183, 187, 188; London government, role in, 24, 38, 42, 47, 49, 56, 58, 60, 61, 137–39; loss of faith in collectivism as a sufficient political creed, 43, 47, 48, 50–2, 103, 105, 157, 159, 186; Malinowski, B., and, 112, 113; Marxism, criticism of, 18–20, 190, 191; moralism of, 1, 2, 4, 11–13, 20, 21, 25, 27, 28, 56, 67, 96, 125, 126, 128, 157, 160, 176, 177, 196, 199–202, 207–12, 216; *Our Social Heritage*, 177, 185, 194, 195, 203–6; personal character of, 4, 20, 21; *Francis Place, Life of*, 30, 80; pluralism, criticism of, 182–5; President of the Rationalist Press Association, as, 200; 'progressive education,' criticism of, 136, 137; Psychological War Research, on Committee for, 179;

INDEX

Wallas, Graham—*continued*
retirement of, 194; Royal Commission on the Civil Service, on the, 145–8, 184; scientism of, 6–13, 46, 47, 61, 67, 68, 70, 71, 84, 95–7, 125, 126, 166, 177, 200, 212, 213; secularism of, 14, 52–6, 137, 138, 175, 193, 199, 200; Shaw, and, 55n., 57, 77, 80, 80n., 106, 137, 141; *Social Judgment*, 187, 192n., 197–9, 202, 209, 210; teacher, as a, 14, 15, 20, 21, 30, 34, 38, 43, 44, 146n., 163, 164, 176, 196, 216; Webbs, and the, *see* B. Webb and S. Webb; Webbs, differences with the, 38, 47, 49, 51–60, 137–40, 143, 172; Wells, H. G., and, 77, 78, 78n., 84, 107, 108, 141–2, 198; Zimmern, A., and, 176, 182, 183; as Zionist, 200, 201
Wallas, K. T., 23n.
Ward, Mrs. H., 59n.
Ward, J., 165, 166
Ward, L., 167
Webb, B., 1, 10, 15, 16, 20, 37, 47, 50–6, 58, 59, 81, 108, 137, 138, 156n., 161, 162, 164n., 169, 172, 176, 183, 190, 192, 193, 205, 205n., 215, 216

Webb, S., 15, 15n., 16–18, 20, 21, 24n., 28, 29, 36–8, 46–56, 58, 59, 68, 80, 105, 127, 129, 130, 137–40, 143, 144, 149, 169, 172, 183, 186, 190, 192, 215, 216
Weber, M., 72
Wells, H. G., 77, 78, 78n., 79, 84, 105, 107, 108, 125, 141, 168, 169, 172, 198, 200, 203, 211; *Anticipations* ..., 77, 78, 107; *Mankind in the Making*, 78, 79, 107; *The New Machiavelli*, 15, 58; *Tono-Bungay*, 130; *A Modern Utopia*, 141, 142
Westminster Gazette, 191
Weyl, W., 171
White, M., 167, 205n.
Winchester, 176
Woolf, L., 59n.
World War I, 67, 121, 140, 148, 161, 162, 210
World War II, 148

Yale University, 174n., 213

Zimmern, A., 59, 138, 157n., 176, 182, 183, 194, 195n.
Zionism, 200, 201